# TEACHER LEADERSHIP FOR SCHOOL-WIDE ENGLISH LEARNING

**MICHELLE BENEGAS**
**AMY STOLPESTAD**

2ND EDITION

tesol press

bookstore.tesol.org

TESOL International Association
1925 Ballenger Avenue, Ste. 550
Alexandria, VA 22314 USA
www.tesol.org

Associate Director of Publications: Tomiko Breland
Copy Editor: Suzy Richardt
Cover Design: Citrine Sky Design
Interior Design: Kathleen Dyson
Head of Education & Events: Sarah Sahr

Copyright © 2025 by TESOL International Association

All rights reserved. Copying or further publication of the contents of this work is not permitted without permission of TESOL International Association, except for limited "fair use" for educational, scholarly, and similar purposes as authorized by U.S. Copyright Law, in which case appropriate notice of the source of the work should be given. Permission to reproduce material from this book must be obtained from www.copyright.com, or contact Copyright Clearance Center, Inc., 222 Rosewood Drive, Danvers, MA 01923, 978-750-8400.

Every effort has been made to copyright holders for permission to reprint borrowed material. We regret any oversights that may have occurred and will rectify them in future printings of this work.

The publications of TESOL Press present a variety of viewpoints. The views expressed or implied in this publication, unless otherwise noted, should not be interpreted as official positions of TESOL International Association.

Recommended citation: Benegas, M., & Stolpestad, A. (2025). *Teacher leadership for school-wide English learning* (2nd ed.). TESOL Press.

ISBN 9781953745446
ISBN 9781953745453 (ebook)
Library of Congress Control Number 2025931183

PURCHASE ORDERS AND BULK PURCHASES
Discounts are available for tax-exempt purchase orders and bulk purchases. Please contact publications@tesol.org for more information.

Second edition, 2025

# DEDICATION

This book is dedicated to Ann Mabbott, Dutch-Indonesian refugee to the United States and professor emeritus of the Second Language Teaching and Learning Program in the School of Education at Hamline University. Thank you for setting an example for how we can mobilize systems that support our newest neighbors. Your career laid the foundation for the ELM Project and this book, now in its second edition. We are forever appreciative of your expertise and your mentorship.

# CONTENTS

**Dedication** .................................................................................................. iii

**Introduction** ................................................................................................ ix

## PART A. FOUNDATIONS IN BUILDING SCHOOL-WIDE SYSTEMS TO SUPPORT LANGUAGE DEVELOPMENT THROUGHOUT THE SCHOOL DAY

**Chapter 1. The Need for a School-Wide English Learning Model** ............................ 3
    Contextual Language Instruction ................................................................... 5
    Approaches to Language Teaching ................................................................. 6
    Comprehensive Program Design: A Direct/Indirect Service Model for
        School-Wide English Learning ................................................................. 8
    Conceptual Frameworks: Distributed Leadership and Teacher Skills, Knowledge,
        and Dispositions ................................................................................... 10

**Chapter 2. Teacher Professionalism, Distributed Leadership, and Peer Coaching** ........ 15
    The Evolution of ELD Teaching as a Profession ................................................ 16
    Distributed Leadership as a Foundation for Peer Coaching Through SWEL ............... 18
    SWEL Coaching Leadership Foundations ...................................................... 19
    New Roles and Expectations for Teacher Leaders .............................................. 24
    Peer Coaching as Teacher Leadership ............................................................ 28

**Chapter 3. Contextual Language Instruction** ............................................. 33
    Academic Language ..................................................................33
    What Does Contextual Language Instruction Look Like in Practice? .........................35
    Noticing and Forecasting: A Guide for Determining Which Language to Teach ..............35
    Learning How to "Build" Learners' Linguistic Toolkits .....................................40
    Writing Language Objectives .........................................................41
    The Cyclical Nature of Text Type–Focused (Genre-Based) Language Instruction .............50
    Foundations in the Language of Identity ...............................................51

# PART B. APPLICATION OF TEACHER PROFESSIONAL DEVELOPMENT OF DISPOSITIONS, KNOWLEDGE, AND SKILLS: PROFESSIONAL DEVELOPMENT PLANS

**Chapter 4. Teacher Dispositions Needed to Effectively and Respectfully Serve Multilingual Learners of English** ......................................................... 61
    Educators Empathize With Circumstances Related to Immigration ........................63
    Educators Are Culturally Sensitive and Sustaining .......................................65
    Educators Believe That Marginalization and Oppression Affect the Educational Experiences of Multilingual Learners of English .........................................68
    Educators Support Their Students' Home Language Development ........................71
    Educators Recognize the Challenges of Learning English and Content Simultaneously .......75
    Educators Are Committed to Ongoing Professional Development .........................78

**Chapter 5. Teacher Knowledge Needed to Effectively and Respectfully Serve Multilingual Learners of English** ......................................................... 85
    Educators Know About Second Language Acquisition and Approaches to Teaching Language Through Content ..................................................86
    Educators Know About Approaches to Supporting Home Language Development ..........91
    Educators Know About the Theories of Cultural Relevance and Sustainability ...............94
    Educators Know Who Immigrants Are and How Immigration Happens ....................98
    Educators Know Systems of Oppression and How They Affect the Educational Experiences of Multilingual Learners of English ....................................... 101
    Educators Know Approaches to Advocacy and the Legal Requirements for Adequately Serving Multilingual Learners of English .................................. 105

**Chapter 6. Teacher Skills Needed to Effectively and Respectfully Serve Multilingual Learners of English** ......................................................... 111
    Educators Can Plan for Language Instruction ......................................... 112
    Educators Can Teach and Assess Language ........................................... 116
    Educators Can Differentiate for Multilingual Learners of English ......................... 126
    Educators Can Support Home Language Development ................................ 131
    Educators Can Enact Culturally Relevant Practices ..................................... 135
    Educators Can Advocate for Immigrant Families ...................................... 139

## PART C. APPLICATION OF PEER COACHING USING A DIRECTED, CYCLICAL APPROACH

### Chapter 7. Setting Up Teachers for Success ... 147
- The SWEL Peer Coaching Cycle ... 149
- The SWEL Lesson Plan Inventory ... 153
- The SWEL Support Tools: Language-Based Teacher Observation Forms ... 155

## PART D. PUTTING SWEL TO WORK IN YOUR SCHOOL: SETTING THE STAGE WITH INTENTIONAL PLANNING

### Chapter 8. Drafting an Annual SWEL Action Plan ... 165
- Needs Analysis ... 165
- Goal Setting ... 169
- SWEL Implementation Steps ... 170
- Supports ... 172
- Concerns and Obstacles ... 173
- Resources ... 174
- To-Do Timeline ... 175
- Administrator Approval ... 176

### Chapter 9. The Cyclical Nature of the SWEL Model ... 177
- Turning a Ship: Changing Systems Takes Time and Collaboration ... 178
- Getting Started: Key Considerations for Implementation ... 180
- Measuring Progress and Adjusting as Needed ... 181
- Moving From Initiative to Systemic Structure: Making SWEL Part of "How Things Are Done" ... 182

### Appendixes ... 185
- Appendix A: SWEL Support Tool 1: Multimodal Instruction Observation Form ... 186
- Appendix B: SWEL Support Tool 2: English Language Development Observation Form ... 189
- Appendix C: SWEL Support Tool 3: Supporting the Language of Identity Observation Form ... 193
- Appendix D: Building Leveled Language Objectives ... 195
- Appendix E: Planning for Word-Level Language Guide ... 202
- Appendix F: Planning for Sentence-Level Language Guide ... 205
- Appendix G: Planning for Discourse-Level Language Guide ... 207
- Appendix H: The SWEL Lesson Plan Inventory ... 209
- Appendix I: SWEL Planning for Professional Development ... 210
- Appendix J: School-Wide English Learning (SWEL) Action Plan ... 213

### Resources Index ... 215

PART C: APPLICATION OF PEER COACHING USING A DIRECTED
CYCLICAL APPROACH

Chapter 7 Stations Up, Teachers Up Stories
The SWD Peer Coaching Cycle in ELA ........................................... 145
For SWD, There is Past Harmony
The Write Support Peer Coaching Cycle in Civics Cheer Plate ............... 155

PART II: PUTTING SWEL TO WORK IN YOUR SCHOOL SETTING THE STAGE
WITH INTENTIONAL PLANNING

# INTRODUCTION

Maggie and Cindy are birds that live at the Iguazu Falls bird sanctuary in Brazil. They are a bonded pair of macaws who were born in captivity and have been adopting rollaway eggs from other macaw couples for the duration of their 14-year relationship. The conservationists explain that despite their attempts to avoid teaching the macaws Portuguese, the birds repeatedly squawk "ARARÁ!" throughout the day. *Arará* means *macaw* in Portuguese. Because they heard it so often in their lives, they assumed it was the sound that macaws should make. As a result, they cannot be released to the wild; they would not be safe because of their lack of proficiency in macaw. (In their natural habitat, macaws can respond with hostility to those who are not fluent in the local dialect.)

For those who are reading this book, you know that language matters. Language is the vehicle through which we express our identity, opinions, needs, and wants to others. Without it, we are as vulnerable as Maggie and Cindy. We see this in the lives and hear this in the stories of the newcomers in our communities. Currently, we are facing the most significant global refugee crisis in history. As of May 2024, the United Nations' Office of the High Commissioner for Refugees (UNHCR) reports that approximately 120 million people worldwide have been forcibly displaced due to persecution, conflict, violence, and human rights violations, with around 43.4 million identified as refugees. One in every 108 people globally is either a refugee, an internally displaced person, or an asylum-seeker (UNHCR, 2024). Unfortunately, we seldom acknowledge the critical role that educators play in the resettlement process or how language is intricately woven into the experiences and identities of immigrants and refugees.

# NEW TO THE SECOND EDITION OF *TEACHER LEADERSHIP FOR SCHOOL-WIDE ENGLISH LEARNING*

The first edition of this book was published and released in March of 2020. For most of us, that month is forever imprinted in our memories. Among many understandable but nonetheless disappointing outcomes of that COVID-19 spring was the cancellation of the 2020 TESOL International Convention, at which our book was scheduled to be released. Suffice it to say, the celebration that Michelle hosted in her backyard for our two families was lovely, but not quite what we had expected.

So much has happened since the first edition was written in the time before COVID-19. Thanks to the miracle of Zoom, we continued to train new SWEL coaches, and they have taught us so much about the transformation that can happen when English language development (ELD) teachers are empowered to be teacher leaders. The second edition of this book includes some key updates that reflect what we have learned over these last 4 years.

You will find new perspectives on how language provides access while supporting student identity. Jeremiah Brown, SWEL coach from Hawaii, created additional resources for the Plargs professional development (PD) plan, and we have updated a few other PD plans to reflect ideas generated in the many trainings we have done with teachers across the country. We also embedded information on theories of how people react to requests to change their actions and behaviors, since changing teaching practices to support multilingual learners of English (MLEs) is part and parcel to the SWEL model. In addition, based on SWEL coach feedback, we have updated and expanded the planning tools for SWEL coaches so that they focus more specifically on targeted observation goals, such as teaching through the four modalities (reading, writing, listening, and speaking), among others. What has not changed since the first edition is that all of the resources and tools we share are meant to be revised and tweaked so that they fit local needs.

## HOW SWEL CAME TO BE

Think about the MLEs in one of your classes. What percentage of each day do they spend with a trained ELD teacher—one who has studied second language acquisition and language teaching? Depending on where you live, answers to this question will vary drastically, given that states vary in their credential requirements for teachers and that some areas are experiencing teacher shortages, which may result in hiring teachers with less formal training. For many, it is a small percentage of time. Professor emerita and cofounder of the English Learners in the Mainstream (ELM) Project at Hamline University Ann Mabbott shares, "It gradually dawned on me that preparing excellent ELD teachers was not enough. All teachers, regardless of their discipline, need to be prepared to meet the linguistic and cultural needs of their immigrant and refugee students." We know that the majority of the time that MLEs spend in school is spent with classroom/content (non-ELD) teachers. For this reason, we can no longer continue to certify ELD teachers who aspire to only work with MLEs as direct service providers. ELD teachers also need to be equipped to be language experts and instructional coaches for their classroom/content teacher colleagues. Failing to respond to this need is failing our MLEs. They deserve enriching curriculum and instruction *throughout* the day, not just for the short period that they work with an ELD teacher. If your child received 25 minutes of comprehensible input during a school day, you would be appalled. When it comes to classroom or content teachers serving MLEs, the most significant equity issues include deficit-based teacher dispositions, limited teacher knowledge, and missing teacher skills.

In 2014, Minnesota teachers and legislators combined forces to draft what would become the most comprehensive piece of MLE legislation in the nation. Authored by Congressman Carlos Mariani and Senator Patricia Torres Ray, the Minnesota Learning English for Academic Proficiency and Success (LEAPS) Act put in statute an increased emphasis on MLE support in schools.

Legislation included provisions in early childhood, elementary, secondary, adult, and teacher education intended to support the school success of Minnesota's MLE population (Minnesota Department of Education, n.d.). As the state with more refugees per capita than any other in the country (Lutheran Social Service, 2019), Minnesota had become a leader for education models, services, and policy in English language education. It is for this reason that many were quick to take action when this legislation was not implemented in the way that its proponents had expected.

Under the Minnesota LEAPS Act, all preservice teachers must learn about research-based practices for MLEs in teacher preparation coursework. Additionally, all practicing teachers must demonstrate engagement in PD in the area of working with MLEs in order to qualify for licensure renewal. Minnesota teachers are generally relicensed every 5 years (Education Minnesota, n.d.). Unfortunately, the implementation of this policy was far from its proponents' intent. At the time that the law was enacted, Minnesota teachers were asked only to write a reflective statement on their experience working with MLEs. Though supporters of the legislation were glad to have the responsibility for serving MLEs legally shared by all teachers, the application of this statute did not represent the spirit in which it was written. The task of writing a reflective statement does not sufficiently demonstrate that teachers have engaged in professional learning around promising practices for MLEs, much less changed their instruction to support MLE academic development.

As former Minnesota ELD teachers and advocates for our state's MLEs, we were crestfallen as the legislation that we had rallied so arduously for resulted in a surface-level task that held little promise for transformed teacher practice. For this reason, when the U.S. Department of Education notified institutions of teacher education that the Office of English Language Acquisition would offer National Professional Development grants to improve the educational experience of MLEs, we decided to apply. At the time and still today, the most common form of teacher PD remains "sit-and-get" (also known as "jet-in jet-out" in the United Kingdom), despite no research demonstrating that this format results in instructional change. In writing our grant proposal, we dreamed up what we thought teacher PD *should* look like: It should be teacher led, immediately relevant, contextualized, and continual. It should not rely on outside experts. One of us (Michelle Benegas) and Ann Mabbott, professor emeritus, were the authors of the grant. We spent 2 months dreaming and toiling over what such a model would look like. With our combined 30 years of experience training classroom/content teachers to work with MLEs, we infused our knowledge and passion into what would become the ELM Project.[1] When the grant was awarded, Amy Stolpestad was hired to serve as the director, working alongside Primary Investigators Michelle Benegas and Ann Mabbott.

Over the course of the 6-year grant, the ELM Project trained 402 ELD teachers to be ELM coaches. These teacher leaders taught in urban, suburban, rural, public, private, and charter schools across the state. Although there are few studies that examine cross-content-area peer instructional coaching, the ELM Project was based on vetted models of instructional coaching (Knight, 2007; Aguilar, 2013), where ELM coaches trained their colleagues to incorporate promising practices in language instruction throughout the school day. ELM coaches agreed to provide one-on-one nonevaluative peer instructional coaching for their classroom/content teacher colleagues and deliver at least 6 hours of targeted PD. In total, ELM coaches conducted 958 observations of their classroom/content teacher colleagues. In the final year of the ELM Project, pre- to postobservation analyses showed that the difference in teacher practice was statistically significant. Although "sit and get" PD does not move the needle when it comes to instructional change, site-based teacher leadership does! Furthermore, having an MLE teacher leadership model in place resulted in fewer language-learning disruptions during the pandemic (Benegas et al., 2021).

---

[1] The ELM Project was developed under a grant from the U.S. Department of Education. However, the ELM Project materials do not necessarily represent the policy of the Department of Education and are not endorsed by the federal government.

## An Unexpected Side Effect: Reprofessionalizing Teachers

We could have never anticipated how the ELM Project would empower teachers. At the end of each academic year, we welcomed coaches to an annual summit where they presented their successes as leaders. With groups of as many as 150 teacher leaders and school administrators at each summit, the atmosphere was electric. Coaches shared how, prior to the ELM Project, their colleagues didn't understand their role, their administrators made decisions without their input, and they felt deprofessionalized.

For some, the ELM Project offered a new set of skills in applied linguistics, coaching, and teacher professional development. For others, it put a name to all of the leadership roles they had already been taking on without recognition or allocated time. "Now that I have this title and time, my colleagues actually understand what I do and they come to me for my expertise!" was a common refrain.

It is hard not to take note of the role of gender in our line of work. In the United States, 75% of teachers are female. For these teacher leaders, the ELM Project allocated time for them to engage in leadership roles and positioned them as experts (rather than assistants) in their schools. This reprofessionalization was an honor to witness.

You may notice a shift from ELM to SWEL (School-wide English learning) in this text. The SWEL model is informed by the ELM Project, a federally funded grant initiative that supported implementation in Minnesota schools from 2016–2021. The SWEL model expands upon what was learned in the implementation of the ELM Project and offers a guide for others who wish to implement a similar teacher leadership model in their schools. With the development of the SWEL model, what could have been a sad occasion (the conclusion of the high-impact ELM Project) turned into an exciting one. Now, under TESOL International Association, the SWEL model represents one of their top PD offerings, and SWEL coaches are being trained both via in-person workshops and through global online cohorts.

The ELM Project laid the foundation and trained the first 402 coaches. Coincidentally, as we gathered data for this book in the summer of 2024, we learned that TESOL has now also trained 402 SWEL coaches (and they are all over the world, as shown in Figure 1). Teacher leadership is resonating. We look forward to the next chapter—and this new edition—of SWEL, in partnership with TESOL.

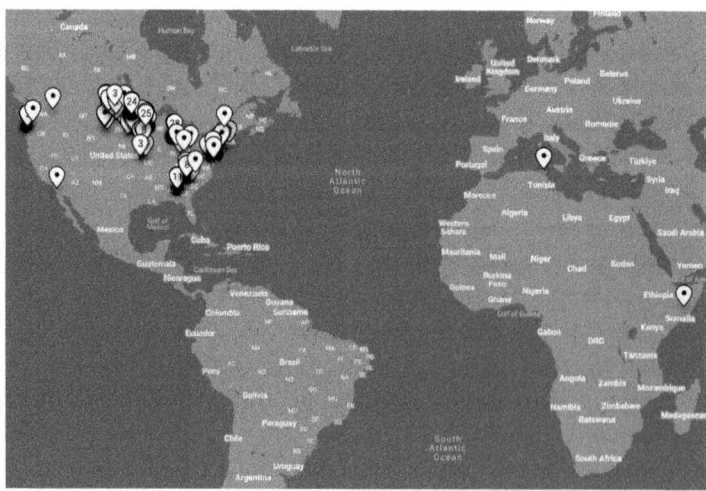

**FIGURE 1.** Where in the world are SWEL coaches? Screenshot from Padlet, September, 2024.

## TERMS

The field of English language teaching is complicated when it comes to terms. Across states, systems, and spaces, we use different terms to refer to our profession, our students, and our colleagues. Though we appreciate the healthy debate over the propriety of these terms, we hope that you can transfer the concepts in this book to your context, even if our naming differs from yours. The terms used in this text are as follows:

**Multilingual learner of English (MLE):** a multilingual student who is learning English

**English language development (ELD) teacher:** a practicing teacher who has received a license or credential to teach ELD and who is employed in a capacity to serve MLEs

**Classroom/content teacher:** a practicing teacher who has received a license or credential to teach any area other than ELD

**Educator:** a practicing teacher, instructor, educational assistant, or school employee who serves MLEs in an educational capacity

**SWEL coach:** a practicing ELD teacher who supports their classroom/content teacher colleagues by providing feedback on instruction, collaborating on planning and curricular development, and/or sharing strategies and resources

**Coachee:** a practicing classroom/content teacher who is supported by a peer coach

*Note: An undergirding premise of the book is that all teachers are teachers of MLEs. For this reason, we do not use terms like* MLE teacher *or* EL teacher. *The specialization of ELD teachers lies not in the population that they serve, but in their knowledge of the discipline of English language development.*

## DISCLAIMER

The SWEL model is designed to transform classroom/content teacher practice. It takes complex theories and linguistic structures and makes them accessible to teachers who do not have a background in linguistics, pedagogical grammar, or second language acquisition theory. Some oversimplification may be noted.

## OVERVIEW OF THE BOOK

This book is designed to facilitate reproducing SWEL at any school that serves MLEs, whether they make up the majority of the student body or are a smaller group within the school. By capitalizing on the expertise that is *already* in the building, schools can transform the educational experience of MLEs throughout the school day. SWEL is the product of the work of many teacher leaders in the field. In Chapter 2, you will see excerpts from Madeline Benson's (2019) master's thesis on the roles and identities of ELD teacher leaders. Madeline is a first-grade teacher who previously worked as an ELD teacher. In Chapter 6, we present Amna Kiran's Multilingual Learner of English Profile—a tool that she developed and continues to use for MLEs in her district. In Chapter 8, we share an adapted version of an action plan developed by ELD teacher Stephanie DeFrance Schmidt and school principal Catherine Rich. This plan was thoughtfully curated to respond to the needs of their school's MLE population. In addition, woven throughout the book, you will see sections called "Voices From the Field." These are quotes from actual ELD teachers and peer coaches who are enacting the SWEL approach in their schools.

The SWEL model is a school-wide system for MLE support throughout the school day. We acknowledge that many of the strategies and approaches presented in this book will benefit a variety of learners, not just MLEs. However, given the long-standing opportunity gap that our MLEs experience, it is critical that we respond to their specific needs with urgency. All students are language learners, and language learners benefit from explicit attention to language. For this reason, the focus of this guide is on ensuring that all educators have preparation to better serve MLEs, with the caveat that these practices benefit all learners.

We have arrived at the materials in this book after years of working in both K–12 schools and teacher preparation programs within the higher education context. Despite our many years in the field, we recognize that our experiences are not universal. Both authors identify as native-English-speaking, cisgender, White women from the Midwestern United States. We acknowledge that the privilege we have may influence our perspectives, and we work continuously to better understand our positionality and how it influences and impacts our work as teachers and advocates of MLEs.

This book is intended for a variety of audiences, including:

- preservice ELD teachers who are preparing for the leadership roles of professional development delivery and peer coaching that may be part of their future positions;
- in-service ELD teachers who would benefit from a guide for professional development delivery as well as tools for peer coaching;
- school administrators (e.g., principals or assistant principals) who are interested in improving the MLE learning experience through a distributed leadership model; and
- district administrators who are interested in designing school systems that position ELD teachers as language experts and teacher trainers as well as direct service providers.

This book is organized in four parts. It can be read sequentially or in an order that best suits the reader's needs. Each chapter closes with discussion questions and take-away tasks. The following provides an overview of the four parts of the book.

## Part A. Foundations in Building School-Wide Systems to Support Language Development Throughout the School Day

This section presents an overview and the conceptual frameworks underpinning the SWEL model. We recommend that all who are interested in the model read Chapter 1, "The Need for a School-Wide English Learning Model." This chapter substantiates the need for teacher leadership and provides a comprehensive program design for continuous attention to language throughout the school day. Chapter 2, "Teacher Professionalism, Distributed Leadership, and Peer Coaching," presents how distributed leadership is well-suited to support ELD teacher leaders. We highly recommend that those in administrative positions focus on this chapter. Chapter 3, "Contextual Language Instruction," explains how teachers can provide learners with the linguistic tools that they need for success while also validating home language varieties in the classroom. This chapter is most critical for anyone who is tasked with teaching content while attending to language or with training colleagues to teach content while attending to language.

## Part B. Application of Teacher Professional Development of Dispositions, Knowledge, and Skills: Professional Development Plans

This part of the book provides ready-to-use PD plans for SWEL coaches to use with their classroom/content teacher colleagues. The plans in these three chapters are recommended for anyone tasked with providing PD for their colleagues about the needs of MLEs. Each plan is designed to be refined for local contexts, and we encourage those who facilitate any of the PD activities included in this book to consider how they might personalize them to ensure their relevance to the MLEs in their school or region.

Chapter 4, "Teacher Dispositions Needed to Effectively and Respectfully Serve Multilingual Learners of English," delineates six critical dispositions. Teacher dispositions are the beliefs or mindset that teachers have toward working with MLEs, and so the activities in Chapter 4 are centered on teacher mindset. Chapter 5, "Teacher Knowledge Needed to Effectively and Respectfully Serve Multilingual Learners of English," presents six key areas of knowledge. Teacher knowledge is defined as mastery of the content area of instruction. The PD plans in Chapter 5 are based on discrete areas of knowledge that will serve educators of MLEs. In these PD plans, readers learn new concepts about the multifaceted experience of the MLE. Chapter 6, "Teacher Skills Needed to Effectively and Respectfully Serve Multilingual Learners of English," provides six skill areas that are critical for all educators of MLEs. Teacher skills are defined as pedagogy. In this chapter, readers hone skills that enhance MLEs' experiences in their classrooms.

## Part C. Application of Peer Coaching Using a Directed, Cyclical Approach

This section offers a how-to for peer instructional coaching. Chapter 7, "Setting up Teachers for Success" presents a variety of resources that coaches can use, such as the coaching cycle, the SWEL Support Tools (language-based teacher observation forms), and the action plan template. This chapter is recommended for anyone who is planning to engage in peer instructional coaching on serving MLEs. It is also useful for administrators to identify how these systems might complement existing systems in districts and schools.

## Part D. Putting SWEL to Work in Your School: Setting the Stage With Intentional Planning

This part of the book will be of interest to anyone planning to implement a continuous and sustainable ELD teacher leadership program in their district or school. Chapter 8, "Drafting an Annual SWEL Action Plan," guides readers through the process of writing a targeted action plan that is informed by the needs of the school community and guided by SMART goals (Doran, 1981). Finally, Chapter 9, "The Cyclical Nature of the SWEL Model," offers key considerations for implementation so that SWEL can serve as a sustainable approach to continuous improvement for MLEs.

# CALLING ALL TEACHER BOOK CLUBS AND PROFESSIONAL LEARNING COMMUNITIES!

This book has been used across the country in teacher book clubs and professional learning communities (PLCs). Feel free to use the discussion questions and take-away tasks at the end of each chapter to guide your discussions. The following is a recommended reading sequence.

| Month | Chapter | Primary Task |
|---|---|---|
| August/ September | Introduction and Chapter 1: The Need for a School-Wide English Learning Model | Welcome administrators to read along and discuss with building leadership how SWEL could be implemented in your school |
| October | Chapter 2: Teacher Professionalism, Distributed Leadership, and Peer Coaching | Small group discussion |
| November | Chapter 3: Contextual Language Instruction | Small group discussion |
| December | Chapter 4: Teacher Dispositions Needed to Effectively and Respectfully Serve Multilingual Learners of English | Individually or in small groups, lead a dispositions-based PD for classroom/content teachers |
| January | Chapter 5: Teacher Knowledge Needed to Effectively and Respectfully Serve Multilingual Learners of English | Individually or in small groups, lead a knowledge-based PD for classroom/content teachers |
| February | Chapter 6: Teacher Skills Needed to Effectively and Respectfully Serve Multilingual Learners of English | Individually or in small groups, lead a skills-based PD for classroom/content teachers |
| March | Chapter 7: Setting Up Teachers for Success | Practice nonevaluative peer instructional coaching using the SWEL tools |
| April | Chapter 8: Drafting an Annual SWEL Action Plan | Alongside school administration, draft an action plan for your school to fully implement SWEL |
| May | Chapter 9: The Cyclical Nature of the SWEL Model | Discuss how SWEL can support continuous improvement for MLEs in your school |

If you enjoy these discussions among your colleagues and would like to become an official SWEL coach, we welcome you to register for SWEL certification and join the global network of SWEL coaches. Reading this book is an important first step, but just the beginning to becoming a certified SWEL Coach. Certified SWEL coaches receive a digital badge upon completion and are also welcome to join the SWEL Teacher Leader Professional Learning Community, which offers continuous PD and support for teacher leaders. Visit www.tesolswel.org to learn more about SWEL coach certification.

# HOW TO USE THIS BOOK

How you use this book depends entirely on your context and position within your school. As mentioned earlier, the book can be read sequentially or in an order that best suits your needs. Regardless of how you approach the SWEL model, *Teacher Leadership for School-Wide English Learning* is a practical guide for implementation and navigating the many resources it provides is easy.

Chapters 1–3 introduce the foundations and principles on which the SWEL model is based. Chapters 4–6 provide a wealth of PD plans centered around the teacher dispositions, knowledge, and skills needed to effectively enact SWEL. Each PD plan is easy to find:

 This "PD Plan" icon indicates the beginning of a PD plan, each complete with objectives, time needed to complete the activity, materials and resources, preparation required, and step-by-step instructions to carry out the plan.

Chapters 7–9 provide detailed and practical steps and resources for making sure the SWEL model is well planned, successfully implemented, and continuously improving—as all professional development should be.

> All online resources can be found on the companion site for this book, www.tesol.org/SWEL-book

Be sure to also take advantage of the Resources Index, which lists the many resources—handouts, articles, websites, and videos, among others—referred to in this book. All of these resources can also be found on the companion site for this book, www.tesol.org/SWEL-book.

---

**Discussion Questions**

1. The introduction presents how a teacher leadership model was used to respond to a need in the state of Minnesota. When it comes to teacher professional development and MLEs, how are the needs similar in your context? How are they different?

2. Teacher leadership, instructional coaching, and professional development aren't new concepts in our field. What are some of the benefits of a planned, cohesive, school-wide approach to improving how we support MLEs?

3. What excites you about SWEL? What causes you to hesitate?

**Takeaway Task**

Gather a brief history of how your school has supported MLEs. Which elements were intentional? Which were haphazard? Which were absent?

---

## References

Aguilar, E. (2013). *The art of coaching: Effective strategies for school transformation*. John Wiley & Sons.

Benegas, M., Morita-Mullaney, T., Cushing-Leubner, J., Stolpestad, A., & Greene, M. C. S. (2021). Systemic infrastructure for multilingual success: ELD teacher responses to emergency remote teaching and learning at the onset of the COVID-19 pandemic. *MinneTESOL Journal, 37*(2).

Benson, M. (2019). *The roles and identities of English as a second language teacher leaders.* [Master's thesis, Hamline University]. Hamline University DigitalCommons@Hamline. https://digitalcommons.hamline.edu/cgi/viewcontent.cgi?article=5468&context=hse_all

Doran, G. T. (1981). There's a S.M.A.R.T. way to write management's goals and objectives. *Management Review, 70*(11), 35–36.

Education Minnesota. (n.d.). *Tiered licensure in Minnesota.* https://mn.gov/pelsb/aspiring-educators/requirements

Knight, J. (2007). *Instructional coaching: A partnership approach to improving instruction.* Corwin Press.

Lutheran Social Service. (2019). *Refugee facts and figures.* https://www.lssmn.org/sites/default/files/2019-12/Refugee%20Facts%20and%20Figures_2020.pdf

Minnesota Department of Education. (n.d.). *LEAPS Act.* https://education.mn.gov/MDE/dse/el/leap/

United Nations High Commissioner for Refugees (UNHCR). (2018). *Global trends: Forced displacement in 2017.* https://www.unhcr.org/5b27be547.pdf

# PART A

**Foundations in Building School-Wide Systems to Support Language Development Throughout the School Day**

# CHAPTER 1

# THE NEED FOR A SCHOOL-WIDE ENGLISH LEARNING MODEL

*Before my colleague and I became involved in school-wide English learning (SWEL), we had great difficulty getting a time slot for delivering professional development to our coworkers. Being a part of the SWEL community gave us regular opportunities to select, create, and present relevant staff development as well as to make positive one-on-one connections classroom/content teachers. Through that process, we became regular go-to people for our school, a new identity that we fully embrace!*

—SWEL coach

The following is a story from Michelle Benegas, coauthor of this book:

> *It was November, the time had recently changed, and I noticed that it was dark outside as I put a frozen lasagna in the oven for dinner. I had no energy for anything more complicated. My kids sat transfixed in front of the TV, tired after a long day of school. It was 6 pm and I was exhausted and ready to go to bed. If you live in a cold climate, you can likely relate to this easing into human hibernation that happens in late fall. As my husband was taking off his coat, the doorbell rang. I cocked my head. Apologetically, he said, "It's the insurance salesman. Sorry. I forgot to tell you that he was coming tonight."*
>
> *The salesman handed me multicolored folders and spread papers across our dining room table, making himself comfortable for a long stay. "Would you like GAP insurance? A floater policy? If this 1914 house burned to the ground they would want*

> to replace it with a sheetrock box, you don't want a sheetrock box, do you ma'am?" I struggled to stay engaged in the conversation. I understood a fraction of the words that he was using. I wanted to ask him to leave, but I knew that I couldn't because we needed insurance. It was in our best interest to get a comprehensive and economical plan. "Blah Blah liability, blah blah act of god, blah blah slight increase in premium . . ." Lasagna smells wafted through the air. I wondered what my kids were watching on TV. As my frustration increased, my understanding of his words decreased. We ate cold lasagna at 8 pm and everyone went straight to bed. I haven't talked to an insurance salesperson since.

This is an everyday example of an exchange between someone who holds information that is vital to the other person and someone for whom the information is not entirely comprehensible. We are all able to tell stories like these. In these situations, we are often humbled, embarrassed, and frustrated. If we are secure enough in what we do know, we may find humor in our language blunders. This is not the case for many of our students.

We know that language has significant societal implications—and not just for multilingual learners of English (MLEs). For these reasons, attending to language development in the classroom may be the most important equity initiative that a school can take up. Halliday and Hasan (1989) explain,

> Language is a political institution: those who are wise in its ways, capable of using it to shape and serve important personal and social goals, will be the ones who are "empowered" (to use a fashionable word): able, that is, not merely to participate effectively in the world, but able also to act upon it, in the sense that they can strive for significant social change. (p. x)

We are sized up by the language that we use in all social environments. Our language gives us access to relationships, employment, housing, and healthcare. If we think of language as a critical tool for survival and social mobility, it is hard to argue *against* a need for explicit attention to language in every classroom.

"All teachers are language teachers" has become a cliché in the English language teaching field. For English language development (ELD) teachers, it is a stark reminder that our responsibility is more than direct service for MLEs. For classroom/content teachers, the phrase can be read either as a hopeful plea and call to action or as a dismal reality check for those who have not considered that aspect of their role. Whether or not teachers identify as language teachers, they *are* language teachers by default, because language is the vehicle through which they deliver instruction and evaluate student mastery of the content. So, the question for all teachers is not, "Do you want to be a language teacher?" It is "What kind of language teacher do you want to be?"

Let's let go of the idea that ELD is for some, not all. Explicit language instruction is for *all students*, and it has a particularly critical implication for nonfluent speakers of English, speakers of the many varieties of English, and struggling readers (Buly & Valencia, 2002; Edmonds et al., 2009; Nation & Snowling, 2004). If we have the expectation that our students talk and write like scientists, historians, and mathematicians, it is our responsibility to teach them to do so rather than assume that they will understand, or somehow infer from mere exposure, how to use those structures and content-specific words.

# CONTEXTUAL LANGUAGE INSTRUCTION

Contextual language instruction (CLI) builds upon traditional perspectives on academic language instruction (Dutro & Moran, 2003; Zwiers, 2008) while incorporating modern approaches, such as translanguaging (García, 2009) and language architecture (Flores & Rosa, 2015). It reconciles two often polarized commitments in language education:

1. Teachers acknowledge that English is a form of social capital and it is their responsibility to provide students with this tool for social mobility.
2. Teachers acknowledge the importance of validating and valuing home languages and dialects and welcoming them into academic spaces (Benegas & Benjamin, 2024).

Rather than viewing these commitments as contradictory, CLI encourages educators to embrace both. Rejecting language hierarchies, this approach focuses on sustaining and expanding linguistic instruction. Educators create linguistically sustaining environments by welcoming students' home languages and dialects into the classroom, and educators create linguistically expanding environments when they explicitly teach students the linguistic features needed to succeed across academic disciplines. CLI offers students a broader linguistic repertoire, enhancing access, choice, and validation across contexts.

We've learned a difficult lesson over the last few decades. Additive approaches to multilingualism haven't fulfilled their promises (García, 2009). The additive bilingual model encourages parents to use their home language with their children while teachers focus on ELD at school. This approach was touted to support both academic English and home language development, advancing multilingualism and multiculturalism. However, without classroom support for home languages, these additive approaches often resulted in subtractive outcomes. Children experienced a deficit view of their home languages and varieties. Many lost their home language entirely—leading to communication barriers in families, identity-related mental health issues, and loss of cultural knowledge. We are doing a disservice to all if we perpetuate English-only classrooms, thinking that advising parents to use their language at home is enough to sustain home language. To achieve this, we need to first dismantle policies that segregate home and school languages.

"But how can I do this? I don't speak that many languages!" is a typical response to this challenge. Surely, the ELD teacher's role is *not* to teach the Vietnamese, Spanish, or Yoruba languages, unless they happen to have those skills. Rather, the ELD teacher is an expert in English language development and their role is to expand students' linguistic repertoires. When it comes to the language of identity, the ELD teacher's role is to publicly value and validate students' home languages and varieties as worthy of being used in the classroom. They should offer opportunities for students to speak, hear, read, and write in their home language or variety (to the extent it is possible). Technology has made this feat far more achievable than it ever was before.

Let's remember that human brains are hard-wired for multilingualism. More than half of the world's population is multilingual (Luk, 2017). Sixty-seven percent of people living in Europe speak more than one language, compared to 55% in Canada, 25% in India, and 20% in the United States (Luk, 2017; Office of the Registrar General & Census Commissioner, India, 2001). Not only is multilingualism a normal human function, but it is also linked to enhanced executive function, preventing cognitive decline and delaying or reducing the risk of dementia (Hack et al., 2019). Long story short, language is not *either/or*, it is *both/and*. More language is better than less language. Multilingualism is an equity issue.

### Four Types of Multilingual Learners of English

Because ELD services are linked to school funding and school funding is linked to policy, it is important that policymakers recognize that differing student backgrounds result in differing needs when it comes to language instruction. For this reason, it is important that we look carefully at four different types of MLEs served in our schools.

**Highly Literate Newcomers:** Students who have received the same amount and quality of formal education as their peers, but need to learn English.

**Students With Limited or Interrupted Formal Education:** Sometimes referred to as "SLIFE," these are students who immigrate at an older age and who have interruptions in their education. These students are often, but not always, refugees. Students with limited or interrupted formal education meet at least three of the following five requirements. They

1. come from a home where the language usually spoken is other than English, or they usually speak a language other than English.
2. entered school after Grade 6.
3. have at least 2 fewer years of schooling than their peers.
4. function at least 2 years below expected grade level in reading and mathematics.
5. may be preliterate in their native language.

(Minnesota Department of Education & Midwest Comprehensive Center, 2016)

**Recently Arrived Multilingual Learners of English:** MLEs who have been enrolled in U.S. schools for fewer than 12 months (Minnesota Department of Education, 2017).

**Experienced Multilinguals:** Also known as "long-term English learners (LTELs)" (Huynh & Skelton, 2023), these students have been in the country for more than 6 years, but their academic progress remains hindered by their level of English proficiency. Many experienced multilinguals are children of immigrants but are not immigrants themselves, and they are most often found in the middle and secondary grades.

The preceding identifiers are intended for schools and teachers to consider how they are meeting the needs of each group that they serve. These labels are not intended to be used directly with or when referring to students, nor are they mutually exclusive. Rather, they serve as a mechanism to support school-wide planning for MLE success. In conducting a school needs analysis and drafting an action plan (see Chapter 8), you must know the varied types of MLEs that your school serves.

## APPROACHES TO LANGUAGE TEACHING

When you hear the term *grammar school*, what images do you conjure? If you are from the United States, you likely imagine a school from a bygone era, in which students trod to a one-room schoolhouse toting books tied with string. We know that early U.S. schooling placed high value on grammar, but time allocated specifically for English grammar is seldom seen in our classrooms today. There have been many iterations of language teaching since the days of grammar school. One thing is for sure—we are still unable to agree on the best way to teach language. The following is a brief overview of predominant models of English language instruction used in the United States:

- **Grammar-Translation Method:** This method is rooted in Latin instructional approaches dating back to the 16th century. Central to this method are explicit grammar instruction, memorization of grammatical rules, and translations from one language to another. It remained a predominant approach to language instruction through the late 1800s and early 1900s. Despite having no theoretical basis, it is still used in classrooms today.

- **Audiolingual Method:** At the onset of World War II, early proponents of this method noticed the defense advantages to having multilingual citizens. Rooted in behaviorism, the belief was that language could best be learned through memorization and repetition. Many people still remember tape players, headphones, and repeated speech drills in language labs. This method proved successful in training learners to memorize dialogues, but it fell short in preparing learners to interact in authentic situations.

- **The Natural Approach:** In an effort to enhance the natural process of learning language, Krashen and Terrell (1983) developed the natural approach. This approach puts attention on communication, rather than grammar, with the intent of language acquisition, rather than language learning.[1] It suggests that language be scaffolded and that students learn best in a low-stress environment. However, critics of the natural approach say that although its attention to access is appropriate, it lacks focus when it comes to application, and it fails to address language structure (the grammatical systems in language). The natural approach remained popular throughout the 1980s and 1990s in the United States.

- **The Communicative Approach:** This approach is based on the theory of communicative language teaching, which has an explicit focus on meaningful communication. Beginning in the 1980s and still popular in a variety of educational settings, the communicative approach promotes use of authentic texts and focuses on meaning rather than form. In a communicative classroom, the teacher is the facilitator of conversation and serves as a language model for students. Critics note that because the model prioritizes function (the purpose of the language that we use to communicate) over structure, critical gaps in formal language can persist.

- **Content-Based Instruction (CBI):** Founded on communicative language theory principles, CBI is the predominant continuum of approaches in ELD instruction today. It allows for the focus on form found in the grammar-translation method as well as the focus on meaning found in the audiolingual method, the natural approach, and communicative language teaching. In CBI, teachers anticipate what language students will need in order to engage in and make sense of the already planned content (Brinton et al., 1989). In CBI, content drives language.

- **Functionalism:** With many similarities to CBI, a functionalist approach is focused on the functions of language that are immediately needed, such as in daily tasks and content-area lessons. With learners focused on function, rather than form, they can engage in authentic conversation with peers and stay on track with content learning.

- **Contextual Language Instruction (CLI):** CLI combines what is known from functionalism (informing ELD instruction) with what is known from raciolinguistics and translanguaging (supporting the language of identity). Also known as LILA (language of identity, language of access; Benegas & Benjamin, 2024), CLI supports expanding students' linguistic repertoire while sustaining their home language skills. This book uses the CLI approach.

---

1 Krashen argues that language acquisition and language learning are discrete skills that cannot transfer from one environment to another. He considers language acquisition to happen unconsciously, as a result of exposure to language, and learning to happen purposefully, with a focus on form.

Figure 1 shows how the pendulum has shifted from form-focused approaches, to communication-focused approaches, to where we are today—function-focused approaches to language instruction.

| **Form Focused** | **Function Focused** | **Communication Focused** |
|---|---|---|
| Grammar Translation Method | Content-Based Instruction | Natural Approach |
| Audiolingual Method | Functionalism | Communicative Approach |
| | ★ Contextual Language Instruction | |

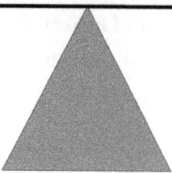

**FIGURE 1.** U.S. methods and approaches to English language education.

A functional approach to language instruction is based on the idea that language should be taught in context. In the field of ELD, this may mean that ELD teachers work alongside classroom/content teachers to infuse explicit language instruction into the curriculum; however, coteaching and coplanning models do not exist everywhere. Regardless, teaching the language that the context requires is widely accepted as the most effective way to help students develop language. Because ELD teachers cannot always be involved in the planning and delivery of content-area lessons, there is a need for all teachers to know how to teach language through content.

Though there is a general consensus about a function-focused approach to language instruction for MLEs, there are a variety of program models used in schools. Known by many names, they are often referred to as "push-in" and "pull-out" models. These names refer to where an MLE is in relation to students who are proficient in English. The ELD teacher plays a critical role when the learner is both *in* and *apart from* the general education setting.

## COMPREHENSIVE PROGRAM DESIGN: A DIRECT/INDIRECT SERVICE MODEL FOR SCHOOL-WIDE ENGLISH LEARNING

ELD teachers are masters of their craft. It's easy to see why MLEs often feel so at home with the ELD teacher. ELD teachers understand the complexity of language and the role of culture in learning. We applaud these master educators for the gains that they are able to make with their students. However, the fraction of time that MLEs spend with an ELD teacher is small compared to the time that they spend in a general education classroom. SWEL is evidence of another evolution in the field of ELD, as much more can be done to tend to the forest if teachers can briefly step away from tending their own trees.

As our field has evolved over time, so has the role of the ELD teacher. It is no longer sufficient for an ELD teacher to serve *only* as a direct service provider to MLEs. They are now asked to serve as coteachers, resource teachers, PD facilitators, site-based experts, and teacher coaches. MLEs deserve a more comprehensive approach to learning language and content simultaneously. Students need to learn and use language in context.

The SWEL model for designing system-wide services for MLEs considers that schools support MLEs in three ways. Consider Figure 2.

| **Indirect Service** | **Integrated Service** | **Direct Service** |
|---|---|---|
| **What:** Explicit, targeted language support | **What:** Explicit, targeted language support | **What:** Explicit, targeted language support |
| **Who:** Classroom/content teacher | **Who:** ELD teacher + classroom/content teacher | **Who:** ELD teacher |
| **Where:** Non-ELD classroom | **Where:** Non-ELD classrooms or ELD classrooms using grade-level content | **Where:** ELD classroom |
| **How:** Teacher training via coaching and/or professional development | **How:** Coplanning, coteaching, sheltered instruction | **How:** Pull-out, newcomer programs |

**FIGURE 2.** Direct/indirect service model for school-wide English learning (SWEL).

For a school to adequately serve MLEs, all of the elements shown in Figure 2 need to be integrated into the school day. It's important for teachers and administrators to examine how they are attending to each of these three areas. We also need to consider what teachers feel prepared to do and where students spend the majority of their time. Commonly, ELD teachers report feeling most prepared to offer direct service, somewhat prepared to offer integrated service, and minimally prepared to provide indirect service. Unfortunately, the inverse is true when it comes to the amount of time that MLEs spend in each setting. They often spend the smallest amount of their school day in direct service, second to integrated service, with the majority of their time in a general education setting that could be supported through indirect service but is not. It is critical that ELD teachers feel prepared to move beyond serving MLEs through direct service models (i.e., pull-out) and integrated service models (i.e., coplanning, coteaching, and sheltered instruction) alone. Both of these models are sound approaches to MLE instruction; however, they should be implemented in tandem with an indirect service teacher leadership model in which ELD teachers are prepared to facilitate peer coaching, deliver targeted PD, and serve as site-based experts.

New to TESOL International Association's *Standards for Initial TESOL Pre-K–12 Teacher Preparation Programs* (2019) is the requirement that ELD teachers be prepared to serve as school-based instructional leaders. Under this standard, ELD teacher candidates in TESOL-accredited institutions will learn about adult learning theory and approaches to teacher PD. The field of English language teaching is moving from a direct service–only model to a direct/indirect service model. To be clear, a direct/indirect service model includes both providing direct instruction to MLEs and providing support to colleagues so that MLEs are appropriately supported in their language development within the general education context. The model does not favor indirect over direct instruction, but rather recognizes that ELD teachers can do both with a reimagining of how an ELD teacher spends their day and with the right structures, such as scheduled time for peer coaching, in place. This book serves as a guide for preservice and in-service teachers who will assume the role and identity of an ELD teacher leader. We invite you to join us for the SWEL Certification Workshop Series to become a certified SWEL Coach. Please visit www.tesolswel.org for more information.

# CONCEPTUAL FRAMEWORKS: DISTRIBUTED LEADERSHIP AND TEACHER SKILLS, KNOWLEDGE, AND DISPOSITIONS

Consider the following sports analogy as it relates to the way that PD is usually conducted in the field of education, where outside experts are hired with the intent of improving teacher practice.

> Imagine going to the finest basketball camp in the world and being explained the perfect technique for the jump shot. You will receive instruction from an expert coach on how to complete every element of the jump shot; however, you will not be in a gym. Not only will you be outside of a gym, but you will have no ball to practice with and there will not be a hoop in sight. The hope is that you take the techniques you learned in isolation, and then on your own time, incorporate them into your regular practice. Tough sell! (Ferlazzo, 2018)

For many teachers, the basketball camp metaphor hits close to home. Beyond university-based teacher education, teacher PD often lacks the context and practicality needed for it to transform practice. Intensive one-size-fits-all workshops remain the most common platform for continuing education in the field of English language teaching. Though it is cost-effective, many educators report that this model fails to move the needle in their practice (Baum & Krulwich, 2016; Ferlazzo, 2018). Known as "sit-and-get" in the United States and "jet-in-jet-out" in the United Kingdom, decontextualized teacher PD is not supported by the research to change instructional practices.

The SWEL approach responds to the shortcomings of the sit-and-get PD model in the following ways:

1. by ensuring that the PD facilitator is a member of the school community,
2. by offering continuity of support over time,
3. by providing opportunities for active learning of new strategies,
4. by delivering right-on-time constructive feedback needed to improve practice, and
5. by demonstrating research-based effectiveness.

Through harnessing the capacity of teachers' existing expertise, schools can experience transformative building-wide instructional growth without spending more money than is already being spent on outside consultants. The SWEL model is personalized, relevant, engaging, intentional, continual, and cost-effective. The conceptual frameworks that inform the SWEL model are (1) distributed leadership and (2) teacher skills, knowledge and dispositions. The following sections explain these frameworks.

## Distributed Leadership: Shared Responsibility for Professional Learning

The first conceptual framework that underpins the SWEL model is distributed leadership. As described by Spillane (2005), distributed leadership focuses on an interactive leadership practice that involves not just leaders, but also followers and the context. In this model, leadership is the responsibility of many rather than a few, which is why it is sometimes referred to as shared or democratic leadership (Spillane, 2005). In such organizations, there are multiple leaders who may or may not have formal leadership titles and roles. The SWEL model is well supported by such a practice, although it can exist without a conscious embrace of distributed leadership, as many existing partners in this work have proven.

In many ways, leadership is and has always been an inherent part of teaching in a K–12 classroom. This is demonstrated by the fact that teachers are responsible for planning at both the macro and micro levels, keeping in mind the overall scope and sequence of a given unit of study while also considering where students are headed next. Teachers also need to pivot when those plans require readjustment, a skill that effective leaders rely on when things do not go as planned. Further, strong relationships play a critical role in the students' and the school's success, which means that teachers need to demonstrate leadership skills, such as team building and drawing on the individual strengths of students. As a result, it stands to reason that many teachers who run successful classrooms also have the potential to become strong administrative and instructional leaders.

In 2014, the Teach to Lead Initiative was announced by then U.S. Secretary of Education Arne Duncan at the National Board for Professional Teaching Standards Teaching and Learning Conference (Duncan, 2014). Teach to Lead is a teacher leadership initiative undertaken in partnership by the U.S. Department of Education, the National Education Association, and the National Board for Professional Teaching Standards. It was designed to advance efforts to develop more teachers into leaders, recognizing that there are ways to do this without requiring teachers to give up classroom teaching altogether. Duncan emphasized that providing opportunities for teacher leadership would give voice to the instructional experts who are too often left out of the conversation. The secretary of education was not alone in his efforts to cultivate teacher leaders; in 2014 the National Education Association partnered with the National Board for Professional Teaching Standards and the Center for Teaching Quality to create the Teacher Leadership Initiative (National Education Association, 2018) and as of 2019, 35 states had policies to advance teacher leadership opportunities (National Council on Teacher Quality, 2019).

It should go without saying that for a teacher to take on leadership responsibilities, structural changes to support that work are essential if the work is to be effective. Clearly, teachers need to know what is expected of them as teacher leaders, which requires a job description and frequent interaction with school administrators. Teacher leaders also need time to do their work, which can mean some changes in scheduling procedures. Perhaps most important, teachers need agency to make decisions based on their professional expertise. All of these supports, among others, point to the rationale for intentionally implementing the practice of distributed leadership.

Distributed, or shared, leadership is a model that allocates responsibility for various organizational goals and duties based on the staff's areas of expertise. In the past, school principals served as administrators—taking care of the budget, personnel, and scheduling, for example—as well as instructional mentors. They served as the building expert on instructional practices, often evaluating teacher effectiveness in the process. Today, there are far more administrative duties to cover, district initiatives to launch and monitor, and specialty areas in teaching for which principals have little to no training. A practice of distributed leadership is a means by which to share these responsibilities in a team made up of the principal, teachers, and others in the school community. In some schools, parents and students are also included in the leadership team.

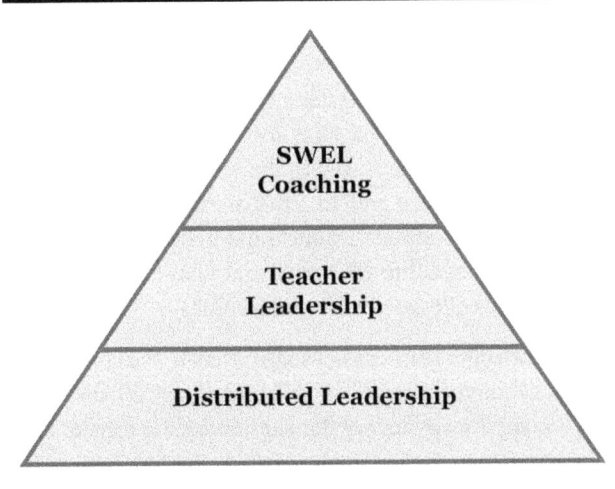

**FIGURE 3.** Leadership foundations for school-wide English learning (SWEL) coaching.

Distributed leadership is uniquely supportive of the SWEL coaching model (see Figure 3). It asks that principals work closely with their ELD teaching staff so that those teachers have the ability to share their knowledge about language learning with the entire school staff and that they have the structural supports to do so effectively. Depending on the school, this support can take a variety of forms.

Some SWEL coaches have an extra prep hour during the school day, which is spent working on SWEL teacher leadership responsibilities. In other schools, it may be one day of the week when the SWEL coach does not work directly with students but instead serves as a peer coach, modeling instructional strategies, coplanning, and meeting with classroom/content teachers to support their work with MLEs. Regardless of the support method in place for SWEL coaches, the model is most effective when the driving leadership practice in the school is based on distributed leadership, which ensures that

- all voices are heard,
- asking probing questions in order to learn and improve is the norm,
- decision-making is a group process, and
- clear and focused goals drive the work (Burgess & Bates, 2009).

## Fostering Dispositions, Imparting Knowledge, and Developing Skills

The second conceptual framework that underpins the SWEL model is that of teacher dispositions, knowledge, and skills. King and Newmann (2000) posit that "to be effective, professional development should address three dimensions of school capacity—educators' knowledge, skills, and dispositions" (p. 578). The SWEL model focuses on these three areas for classroom/content teacher learning and defines them as follows:

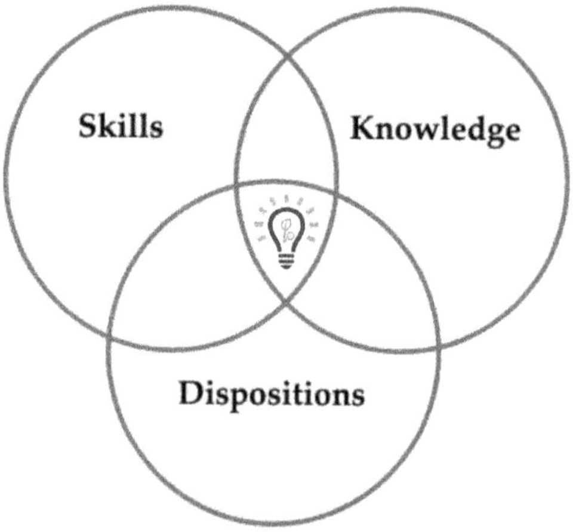

**Dispositions:** Teacher dispositions refer to the values, commitments, and professional ethics that influence teacher behaviors and affect student learning, motivation, and development as well as the educator's own professional growth. They are the professional attitudes, values, and beliefs demonstrated through verbal and nonverbal behaviors as educators interact with students, families, colleagues, and communities.

**FIGURE 4.** School-wide English learning (SWEL): A model for teacher learning.

**Knowledge:** Teacher knowledge refers to the comprehensive set of understandings and competencies that educators possess which are necessary for effective teaching and fostering student learning. It encompasses a range of domains, including content and pedagogical knowledge.

**Skills:** Teacher skills refer to the abilities that educators must possess to effectively facilitate learning and manage a classroom. These skills encompass a broad range of areas, including instructional techniques, classroom management, communication, and professional development.

All three components are equally essential for teacher preparedness to best serve MLEs (see Figure 4). The dispositions, knowledge, and skills framework is evident in the PD plans in Chapters 4, 5, and 6, as well as the coaching foundations in Chapter 7.

Because opportunities for teacher learning can often be lopsided (overly focusing on dispositions but not attending to skills, for example), this book prepares SWEL coaches to design a school-wide implementation model that attends to all three areas of teacher learning. TESOL International Association also offers online and in-person preparation to be a SWEL coach. Learn more at www.tesolswel.org.

**Discussion Questions**

1. Which types of MLEs (p. 6) are present in your school? Why is it important to consider differing MLE backgrounds when planning for SWEL?
2. Consider the two commitments in language education presented on page 5. How does your school demonstrate each of these commitments?
3. Consider the direct/indirect service model for SWEL. In which of the three areas is your school in need of the most development?

**Takeaway Task**

Find a non-ELD colleague and discuss the following questions as they relate to MLE instruction:

- Of the three areas for teacher learning (dispositions, knowledge, and skills), which do you think we need to work on most as a school? Explain.
- Which do they need to work on most as teacher? Explain.

## References

Baum, K., & Krulwich, D. (2016, August 15). *No professionals say, 'I became great at my work by attending workshops.' Why do we treat teaching differently?* Chalkbeat. https://www.chalkbeat.org/posts/us/2016/08/15/no-professionals-say-i-became-great-at-my-work-by-attending-workshops-why-do-we-treat-teaching-differently/

Benegas, M., & Benjamin, N. (2024). *Language of identity, language of access (LILA): Liberatory learning in multilingual classrooms.* Corwin.

Brinton, D. M., Snow, M. A., & Wesche, M. B. (1989). *Content-based second language instruction.* Heinle & Heinle.

Buly, M. R., & Valencia, S. W. (2002). Below the bar: Profiles of students who fail state reading assessments. *Educational Evaluation and Policy Analysis, 24*(3), 219–239.

Burgess, J., & Bates, D. (2009). *Other duties as assigned: Tips, tools, and techniques for expert teacher leadership.* ASCD.

Duncan, A. (2014, March 14). *Teach to lead: Advancing teacher leadership.* U.S. Department of Education. https://www.ed.gov/teaching-and-administration/teaching-resources/professional-development/teach-to-lead

Dutro, S., & Moran, C. (2003). Rethinking English language instruction: An architectural approach. In G. G. Garcia (Ed.), *English learners: Reaching the highest level of English literacy* (pp. 227–258). International Reading Association.

Edmonds, M. S., Vaughn, S., Wexler, J., Reutebuch, C., Cable, A., Tackett, K. K., & Schnakenberg, J. W. (2009). A synthesis of reading interventions and effects on reading outcomes for older struggling readers. *Review of Educational Research, 79*(1), 262–300.

Ferlazzo, L. (2018, June 12). *Response: Too many professional development 'horror stories.'* EducationWeek. http://blogs.edweek.org/teachers/classroom_qa_with_larry_ferlazzo/2018/06/response_too_many_professional_development_horror_stories.html?cmp=SOC-EDIT-FB

Flores, N., & Rosa, J. (2015, December). Undoing appropriateness: Raciolinguistic ideologies and language diversity in education. *Harvard Educational Review, 85*(2), 149–171.

García, O. (2009). Education, multilingualism and translanguaging in the 21st century. In A. Mohanty, M. Panda, R. Phillipson, & T. Skutnabb-Kangas (Eds.), *Multilingual Education for Social Justice: Globalising the Local* (pp. 128–145). Orient Blackswan.

Hack, E. E., Dubin, J. A., Fernandes, M. A., Costa, S. M., & Tyas, S. L. (2019). Multilingualism and dementia risk: Longitudinal analysis of the nun study. *Journal of Alzheimer's Disease, 71*(1), 201–212. https://doi.org/10.3233/JAD-181302

Halliday, M. A. K., & Hasan, R. (1989). *Language, context and text: Aspects of language in a social-semiotic perspective* (2nd ed.). Oxford University Press.

Huynh, T. & Skelton, B. (2023). *Long-term success for experienced multilinguals.* Corwin.

King, M. B., & Newmann, F. M. (2000). Will teacher learning advance school goals? *Phi Delta Kappan, 81*(8), 576–580.

Krashen, S. D., & Terrell, T. D. (1983). *The natural approach: Language acquisition in the classroom.* Prentice Hall Europe.

Luk, G. (2017). Bilingualism. In Hopkins, B., Geangu, E., & Linkenauger, S. (Eds.), *The Cambridge encyclopedia of child development* (2nd ed., pp. 385–391). Cambridge University Press. https:/doi.org/10.1017/9781316216491.062

Minnesota Department of Education. (2017). *English learner education: Recently arrived English learners.* https://education.mn.gov/MDE/dse/el/

Minnesota Department of Education & Midwest Comprehensive Center. (2016). *SLIFE.* https://education.mn.gov/MDE/dse/el/slif/

Nation, K., & Snowling, M. J. (2004). Beyond phonological skills: Broader language skills contribute to the development of reading. *Journal of Research in Reading, 27*(4), 342–356.

National Council on Teacher Quality. (2019, October). *NCTQ Databurst: Teacher Leadership Opportunities.* https://www.nctq.org/publications/NCTQ-Databurst:-Teacher-Leadership-Opportunities

National Education Association. (2018). *The teacher leadership competencies.* https://www.nea.org/resource-library/nea-teacher-leadership-competencies-foundational-competencies

Office of the Registrar General & Census Commissioner, India. (2001). Table C-18: Population by bilingualism, trilingualism, age and sex. https://censusindia.gov.in/nada/index.php/catalog/22952

Spillane, J. P. (2005). Distributed leadership. *The Educational Forum, 69*(2), 143–150.

TESOL International Association. (2019). *Standards for initial TESOL pre-K–12 teacher preparation programs.* https://www.tesol.org/media/v33fewo0/2018-tesol-teacher-prep-standards-final.pdf

Zwiers, J. (2008). *Building academic language: Essential practices for content classrooms, grades 5–12.* Jossey-Bass.

# CHAPTER 2

# TEACHER PROFESSIONALISM, DISTRIBUTED LEADERSHIP, AND PEER COACHING

*Bee was excited to begin their 3rd year of teaching multilingual learners of English (MLEs) at River Middle School. The first 2 years had been challenging but fulfilling, and they were beginning to feel at home in the school and in the role. Two weeks before staff returned to the building in August, Bee received an email from the school's principal asking them to deliver an hour of professional development to the entire staff on how to work more effectively with MLEs. Given a recent retirement and other staffing changes, Bee was the most senior teacher on the English language development (ELD) team in the building. Bee was open to this new opportunity to share what they had spent so much time studying in their teacher preparation program, but they had no idea where to begin or what to cover with only 60 minutes to present.*

Many of you reading this book can relate to Bee's situation. In fact, we have seen myriad social media postings from ELD teachers asking for ideas and support in instances where they are charged with delivering professional development (PD) to their colleagues. We use the example shown in Figure 1 in our SWEL (school-wide English learning) Teacher Leadership trainings.

**FIGURE 1.** Sample social media post showing the need for resources for teacher leaders.

In this real-life example, the person being asked to provide the PD is a 1st-year teacher. Clearly, it is no longer exceptional for ELD teachers to be site-based deliverers of PD for their colleagues. As discussed in the first edition of this book, these additional job responsibilities conflict with what ELD teachers may have imagined when they decided to go into the field, given that people who choose a teaching profession in the K–12 environment generally expect to be working with children rather than adults. Since the first edition was published in 2020, however, the field has seen an increase in staffing shortages, larger MLE student–teacher ratios, and the use of ELD teachers as substitutes when classroom/content teachers are absent. The post-COVID-19 educational environment has only increased the urgency of scaling MLE teacher knowledge across all classrooms and educational spaces.

Many ELD teachers are excited to take on the responsibility of working with the adults in their school as a mechanism for indirectly supporting MLEs. However, it remains extremely rare that a K–12 ELD teacher preparation program's curriculum includes knowledge of adult learning principles and techniques for PD design and delivery. That leaves many in-service ELD teachers trying to figure out how to do this in the moment—starting from scratch, rather than building on a base of understanding. The SWEL peer coaching model is designed to address this gap in training for ELD teachers.

## THE EVOLUTION OF ELD TEACHING AS A PROFESSION

How would you react if

- your dentist said, "I'm no expert in teeth, but it seems to me that you should get a root canal."
- your accountant said, "I'm no expert in the tax code, but I think that you're okay to skip deductions this year."
- your surgeon said, "I'm no expert in medicine, but I don't think that you need a biopsy."
- your auto mechanic said, "I'm no expert in cars, but you might consider getting a new transmission."

These scenarios are hard to imagine because they are highly unlikely to take place. However, in the field of education, professionals often doubt their own expertise. Though educators may see this as a sign of humility among colleagues, it is problematic from the perspective of other stakeholders.

Take, for example, policymakers. If teachers do not position themselves as experts in the field, their input will not be considered when it comes to federal and state lawmaking, as well as district and school policymaking. When policies are made without teacher input, students suffer because it is teachers who have firsthand knowledge of the day-to-day experiences of students, which makes their input invaluable. Another example, and one that is most critical, is that of our students. When you consult with a dentist, accountant, surgeon, or mechanic, you do so because your health, livelihood, or mobility is compromised. The stakes are high. The same is true for MLEs and their families. Many have made great sacrifices to get to where they are, and they know that English proficiency is essential to academic and personal success. Expertise, of course, is relative, and even the most expert among us still has plenty to learn. However, if the ELD teacher does not position themself as a leader in language teaching, no one will. It is time that our profession breaks free from failing to own our expertise in the name of egalitarianism. Our students cannot afford it.

Relative to teaching in general, ELD is a recent addition to the teaching profession and its definition has continued to vary across the United States since the field emerged after the landmark 1974 Lau v. Nichols case, which ruled that not providing language instruction to nonnative English speakers in public schools was a violation of the 1964 Civil Rights Act. In some states, such as Minnesota, a K–12 ELD license is required to teach in public school districts. Other states, such as Texas, do not have a standalone ELD teaching license and instead offer an ELD endorsement that serves as an add-on to another licensure area.

Despite variations across the country, many issues that ELD teachers face are similar regardless of geography:

**The evolving understanding of the role that ELD teachers play in a school:** The field has never been static when it comes to a definition of an ELD teacher's job, perhaps in many ways because the knowledge base on how second languages are learned and the best methods for instruction are still debated by linguists and other scholars in the field. Further evolution in the field is pushed by research that demonstrates that not all MLEs are the same and that home language literacy, in particular, plays an enormous role in the acquisition of English.

**Changing demographics:** According to the National Center for Education Statistics, MLEs made up 10.6 percent or 5.3 million students in U.S. public schools in 2021 (NCES, 2024). Keeping up with these rapid changes while also trying to surmise the best method of language instruction poses real-time challenges across all regions of the country.

**Program delivery and limited resources:** Finally, the dilemma over program delivery overlaid by limited resources for serving students stands as a challenge for many school districts. Though there is a legal obligation to provide language instruction to MLEs, there is a great deal of flexibility in the ways in which these laws can be enacted through programming for students. This allows local entities to make instructional decisions based on the needs of their setting, but it also results in tremendous variety and inconsistency in how MLEs are served.

Today, more and more institutions are recognizing that the experience Bee had in the vignette at the beginning of this chapter is far from uncommon. Even though it was published a decade ago, a professional paper published by TESOL International Association in 2014 entitled *Changes in the Expertise of ELD Professionals: Knowledge and Action in an Era of New Standards* (Valdés, Kibler, & Walqui) addressed the need for ELD preservice teachers to be trained in MLE advocacy through the sharing of their expertise with colleagues. This, in turn, has pushed the profession to meet the needs of MLEs in ways that support the students across the school day, not just during their brief direct instruction period provided by a licensed or certified ELD teacher. Valdés et al. (2014) addressed providing PD for content teachers and explicitly named this as a reconceptualization of language instruction. The message is underscored by the 2019 TESOL Pre-K–12 teacher preparation standards, which say that preservice teacher licensure candidates need to "demonstrate knowledge of effective collaboration strategies in order to plan ways to serve as a resource for ELL [English language learner] instruction, support educators and school staff, and advocate for ELLs" (p. 11).

Time has demonstrated the need to discover new ways to leverage ELD teacher expertise to support and advocate for students across the school day. As teacher preparation programs work to redesign their curricula to better reflect new professional obligations related to collaborating, providing PD, and serving as a resident consultant or mentor within a given school, in-service teachers are also rethinking the ways in which they serve MLEs. The SWEL peer coaching model is one way in which in-service ELD teachers can reconfigure their roles within the school and help to ensure that all teachers have the capacity to provide instruction that serves the language learning needs of MLEs.

The goal of SWEL coaching depends on the learning context, and the model is designed to flexibly meet the needs of the local setting. In general, SWEL coaches help to ensure that classroom/content teachers know how to differentiate for language learning. ELD teachers who become SWEL coaches already have expertise in differentiation and the four language modalities (reading, writing, listening, and speaking), so the SWEL peer coaching model is designed to address effective methods for teaching adults, or *andragogy*, and what to do when your principal asks you to teach your colleagues everything they need to know about how to teach vocabulary during a 30-minute staff meeting.

---

### VOICES FROM THE FIELD

It's just really elevated ELD teachers in each building in our district. This is happening at the same time in our district as a district-level committee has been drafting an ELD vision. I think SWEL coaching has definitely contributed to elevating the needs of MLEs across our district. The superintendent is now looking at the ELD teacher and saying, "How can we tap this person's expertise?"

I think that has definitely happened at my building and at some of the other elementary schools that I've heard from the other SWEL coaches. Personally, it's felt like I had this half of my role where I'm an ELD teacher and half where I'm an instructional coach. So it felt like this beautiful integration where I can go to work and have one mission . . . It felt very integrative and good. *(SWEL coach)*

---

## DISTRIBUTED LEADERSHIP AS A FOUNDATION FOR PEER COACHING THROUGH SWEL

Reconceptualizing the role of ELD teachers inevitably means reconceptualizing traditional school leadership structures and methods for completing the myriad tasks that are associated with leading a school. A reconceived model works to build a collaborative culture of colearning that utilizes the talents of all professionals in the school. Filtered through the lens of Spillane's (2005) definition of distributed leadership practice, where all stakeholders in a school play a role in leadership, not only do ELD teachers need to reimagine their roles, but all members of a school's leadership, staff, and community must reconsider the ways in which they do their work. If ELD teachers are going to be instrumental to instructional coaching and development of their teacher colleagues at the school level (which is a job that has traditionally been filled by administrators, such as principals and assistant principals), then the overarching leadership practice of the school will likely need to evolve to accommodate these changes.

In the first chapter, we introduced the SWEL Coaching Leadership Foundations (Figure 3, Chapter 1), which is built on the definition of distributed leadership described by Spillane (2005). Distributed leadership—sometimes referred to as shared or democratic leadership—is a practice that can help to provide a supportive framework for the work of peer coaching and PD facilitation that an ELD teacher provides to colleagues. In essence, distributed leadership allows for all members of a team or organization to take up leadership work based on their various areas of expertise. It stands to reason, with so few administrators who also have degrees related to second language acquisition or instruction, that leadership be shared with the ELD teachers in order to support the instruction of MLEs.

Of course, distributed leadership may not be the only type of leadership that a principal or school leader enacts, because it can be used situationally. The practice also does not happen magically—it needs to be established with intention. Paramount to distributed leadership practice is a common understanding of the purpose for sharing leadership roles among a school's staff, particularly when it comes to teacher learning of practices to support MLE success.

## SWEL COACHING LEADERSHIP FOUNDATIONS
### The Risks and Rewards of Distributed Leadership

There are some risks, along with rewards, to establishing a practice of distributed leadership for professional learning, including slower decision-making processes because of the inherent need to build consensus. This means that more voices contribute to decision-making in a school building, and though it takes time to bring these voices together and find agreeable solutions, it can also lead to greater buy-in from the entire school staff. This, in turn, has tremendous potential to build a culture of trust and collaboration, where shared professional learning is the norm rather than the exception. As it relates to implementing the SWEL model, including the voices of not just the ELD teachers and administrators, but also the classroom/content teachers and MLEs' families, will help to ensure that all parties with a stake in the work will have a chance to participate in the implementation.

Distributed leadership systems also ask teachers to step forward and acknowledge their expertise, which is essential to sharing that knowledge with colleagues. Historically, teachers have operated in a strongly egalitarian system, where stepping forward to share unique or specialized knowledge may be seen as stepping out of line. This can result in resistance from colleagues or even social ostracization of the teacher who is serving as the expert, if their colleagues deem them one of "them" instead of one of "us." This is why setting up the system of distributed leadership must be done with a great deal of intent and attention to building a culture that supports coleading and embraces teacher expertise. If this is to happen effectively, school leaders, particularly principals, are linchpins (Menken & Solorza, 2015). Along with district-level administration, principals can support SWEL coaches by helping to

- ensure that the entire staff understands the role they play in serving MLEs,
- carve out time in a way that allows SWEL coaches to manage both their direct and indirect services to students, and
- support PD facilitation related to second language acquisition.

That said, ELD teachers also have agency when it comes to initiating change in their schools, which is discussed in the next section.

Though the work to cultivate a practice of distributed leadership—at least as it applies to addressing PD to support teaching MLEs—may seem Herculean to some, the effort is worthwhile in myriad ways. First, distributing leadership helps to spread responsibility across a number of capable stakeholders, making the school leader's work more manageable and efficient. Second, distributing some of the leadership duties to teachers helps to create a cohesive culture of collaboration and shared professional learning. Many ELD teachers have been asked to coteach with classroom/content teacher colleagues, for example, and a system that distributes leadership can help to ensure that the ELD teacher plays an essential role in the instructional design and delivery rather than simply serving as a tutor or observer in the back of the content-area classroom. In fact, ELD teachers often experience marginalization and isolation, and distributed leadership practices provide a systematic approach to solving this issue (Brooks et al., 2010). Lastly, these practices also help to create an environment where silos between content areas are broken down so that ideas for effective instruction in one context, such as inquiry-based teaching methods in a science classroom, can be experimented with in other contexts.

> **VOICES FROM THE FIELD**
>
> SWEL coaching has completely changed the way I see myself and the way my colleagues perceive my role. Before coaching, I often felt "othered" as an ELD teacher. There were many teachers I worked with that did not understand what EL teaching was, and it was challenging eliciting [sic] people to collaborate or coteach with me. After years of SWEL coaching, I am now invited to tables of leadership. My colleagues ask for my advice or counsel during professional learning community (PLC) meetings, and most are open to the idea of coteaching if they haven't specifically asked to do it. I am a confident presenter and enjoy sharing ideas and best practices in front of large groups of people. I feel that SWEL coaching has elevated my career in many ways and hope to one day find myself in a greater leadership role, with my background in SWEL as my foundation. *(SWEL Coach)*

## The Role of Teacher Agency in Teacher Leadership

Though administrators are instrumental in establishing a practice of distributed leadership that supports ELD teacher leaders working as peer coaches, teachers also have some sway in the roles they play, including ELD teachers. In fact, distributed leadership practices can be initiated by teachers who work closely in grade-level and department teams, even if the overarching leadership model in the school is more traditional. We are frequently impressed by the creative ways in which the SWEL coaches we work with have been able to establish themselves as instructional leaders without a deliberate or systematic shift toward a more distributed practice on the school or district level.

One such ELD teacher who, like so many others, builds her teaching schedule at the beginning of the school year, argued successfully for an additional prep hour 1 day a week. During this time, she works one-on-one with her classroom/content teacher colleagues to plan for MLEs by modeling lessons, observing, and conducting peer coaching conversations. Though the principal in her building was not resistant to this work, it did not occur to her that this would be a worthwhile way for an ELD teacher to spend a portion of the school day. In this case, and many others like it, the ELD teacher harnessed her agency to advocate for herself and her students. We acknowledge that not all ELD teachers work in environments that allow for this degree of professional agency. A teacher leadership model like SWEL may not be successful in more rigid environments, and this does not reflect a shortcoming of the teacher.

## Peer Coaching: A Nonevaluative Method of Teacher Professional Development

Most teachers have been observed. Beginning in a teacher preparation program, teachers are expected to have supervisors and/or mentors observe their teaching as a means of both support and evaluation of effectiveness. In fact, it is not unlikely that teachers associate observations with evaluation, as it has been a key component of deciding whether a teacher is successful in their efforts to help students progress academically and deserving of tenure where that is an option.

It is important to clarify that the SWEL model is a relatively new way of thinking about coaching and mentoring, particularly because it is a means of sharing professional knowledge through dialogue and modeling in order to support MLEs, rather than a means of measuring a teacher's effectiveness. The SWEL model acknowledges that a majority of teachers did not have coursework on second language acquisition or working with MLEs in their teacher preparation programs (OELA, 2023). In their 2020 study, Duggan et al. "found that the overwhelming majority of states do not currently have a policy in place that requires general education teachers to complete any amount of MLE–related professional development in order to renew their general education certification" (p. 6). The SWEL coach, using the SWEL Support Tools (Appendixes A–C) as a driver of reciprocal peer-coaching conversations, shares in the learning with their colleagues. The reciprocity comes in the form of shared knowledge, as the classroom/content teacher being coached also shares their content-area expertise with the SWEL coach. Ultimately, the SWEL model of coaching is very different from what many teachers know to be part of the observation cycle of their work. This means that, with the support of school leadership, it must be clear to the entire staff that the SWEL model is both nonevaluative and a means of shared professional learning.

The SWEL model of coaching is based on a set of key principles that acknowledge unique qualities of nonevaluative peer coaching. We draw on the work of instructional coaching scholars such Knight (2007) and Aguilar (2013), as well as Garmston and Wellman's (2009) norms of collaboration, while simultaneously acknowledging that most SWEL coaches do not have the same responsibilities that a full-time instructional coach does. As such, the principles on which the SWEL model of coaching is built are the following:

1. Parity
2. Shared learning
3. Presuming positive intentions
4. Asking questions
5. Goal-driven decision-making

Each of these principles should be explicitly stated and agreed upon between the SWEL coach and coachee. This will ensure clarity of roles and common expectations of the collaborative coaching work.

### *SWEL Coaching Principle 1: Parity*

In order to set the stage for positive and collaborative interactions, it should be established from the outset that the SWEL coaching model is one that is based on a professional peer relationship rather than one that results in awards or consequences. Parity is at the heart of the model, addressing the problem of ELD teacher marginalization (Brooks, Adams, & Morita-Mullaney, 2010; Benson, 2019) by having teachers take up a new way to share their expertise. Both the SWEL coach and the coachee benefit from explicit recognition that one person is not more knowledgeable than the other. Rather, the relationship provides an opportunity to share different areas of expertise.

### SWEL Coaching Principle 2: Shared Learning

The SWEL model is specifically focused on positioning ELD teachers to be coaches to their classroom/content teacher colleagues. Therefore, it is inevitable, and essential, that SWEL coaches come away from this work with new ways of teaching because of the experiences they have observing other professionals and engaging in thoughtful discussion around teaching practices. For this reason, shared learning is a foundational principle in the SWEL model and one that acknowledges that every teacher is simultaneously an expert and learner.

### SWEL Coaching Principle 3: Presuming Positive Intentions

Drawn from the work of Garmston and Wellman (2009), the SWEL model is based on a common willingness to presume that everything said and heard is coming from a place of good intention. In other words, teachers enacting the SWEL model give each other the benefit of the doubt. Both the SWEL coach and the coachee benefit greatly from consciously adopting this mindset. It is not uncommon to feel defensive when discussing growth areas for a lesson or unit plan that required a tremendous amount of work to plan, prepare for, and execute; however, changes in teaching practice to benefit students require such conversations. By normalizing the idea that intentions are generally positive and about the work rather than the person, teachers can make the most of these discussions to evolve teaching practices that most effectively reach students.

### SWEL Coaching Principle 4: Asking Questions

In the SWEL model, goal setting is derived from the conversations between teachers. The ability of the SWEL coach to ask probing questions is essential to creating a strong, measurable goal that is meaningful to the teacher being coached. In turn, the coachee can utilize question asking to draw from the language teaching expertise of the SWEL coach. This reciprocity of question asking is essential to the shared learning that occurs between SWEL coach and coachee.

### SWEL Coaching Principle 5: Goal-Driven Decision-Making

Part and parcel to the principle of asking questions is the fact that SWEL coaching should be driven by concrete, measurable goals set in collaboration with the coachee. It is likely that the SWEL coach will have many ideas for ways in which the coachee could make the content, classroom, and instructional materials more accessible to MLEs, but the ultimate choice should lie with the coachee. Giving choice and agency to the coachee will help to ensure that the goal is meaningful and, more importantly, accomplished.

Now that we have established the leadership and coaching principles on which the SWEL model is based, it is also critical that we attend to the ways in which the model itself addresses language learning in the general education classroom.

## The 6 Principles for Exemplary Teaching of English Learners®: SWEL Coaches

SWEL aligns with TESOL's 6 Principles for Exemplary Teaching of English Learners. See how SWEL coaches can support classroom/content teachers to effectively and respectfully teach MLEs:

*Principle 1: Know your learners.*
- SWEL coaches support classroom/content teachers in getting to know their MLEs through using student profiles that focus on language development across modalities, funds of knowledge, home language skills, and social-emotional development.

> "The concept of funds of knowledge…is based on a simple premise: people are competent, they have knowledge, and their life experiences have given them that knowledge." (González et al., 2024, p. 1)

*Principle 2: Create conditions for language learning.*
- SWEL coaches support classroom/content teachers in their efforts to create a classroom environment that recognizes and utilizes multilingualism.
- SWEL coaches support classroom/content teachers in designing lessons that provide MLEs frequent opportunities for oral interaction that is connected to the content students are reading, listening to, and writing about.
- SWEL coaches support classroom/content teachers to provide visible representations of language whenever possible.

*Principle 3: Design high-quality lessons for language development.*
- SWEL coaches support classroom/content teachers in writing language objectives that attend to word-level language features, such as phonology (how words sound), morphology (word parts), and semantics (what words mean/vocabulary).
- SWEL coaches support classroom/content teachers in writing language objectives that attend to sentence-level language features of syntax.
- SWEL coaches support classroom/content teachers in writing language objectives that attend to discourse-level language features of text type (genre) and pragmatics (genre in action).
- SWEL coaches provide guidance and serve as a professional resource on scaffolding and differentiating content materials for MLEs.

*Principle 4: Adapt lesson delivery as needed.*
- SWEL coaches support classroom/content teachers in adapting lessons for MLEs based on noticing areas of ELD need.
- SWEL coaches support classroom/content teachers in adapting lessons for MLEs based on forecasting areas in need of explicit language instruction in text, task, and tests (any assessment).

*Principle 5: Monitor and assess student language development.*
- SWEL coaches work with classroom/content teachers to design lessons that are based on MLEs' language development.
- SWEL coaches support classroom/content teachers in developing linguistically appropriate assessments of content knowledge.

*Principle 6: Engage and collaborate within a community of practice.*

- SWEL coaches work alongside classroom/content teachers in an ongoing, iterative relationship that is mutually beneficial to both professionals.
- SWEL coaches contribute their expertise in teacher communities of practice across content areas and grade levels.
- SWEL coaches deliver professional development to colleagues that responds to the needs of the MLEs in the school community.

## NEW ROLES AND EXPECTATIONS FOR TEACHER LEADERS
### Finding the Time: Making Room for SWEL Coaching in a Busy Schedule

The evolving role of ELD teachers also means reenvisioning the ways in which ELD teachers spend their time within a given school day. It is not surprising that enacting distributed leadership as a teacher leader through providing PD and instructional support to colleagues requires dedicated time to fulfill these responsibilities. In fact, many of our colleagues respond initially by asking how they are ever going to find the time to be a teacher leader. We use Wenner and Campbell's (2017) definition of teacher leadership, which is: "teachers who maintain PreK–12 classroom-based teaching responsibilities while also taking on leadership responsibilities outside of the classroom" (p. 140). Clearly, these added responsibilities also need to be accounted for in the teacher's schedule in order to provide the time and space required to carry out the duties successfully. In other words, implementing the SWEL model does not necessarily mean finding more time, but rather reconfiguring how existing time is being used.

Having dedicated time for teacher leadership may require that the principal or team of people who create the master schedule for the school year make it clear to everyone in the building how that time is going to be used. This goes back to the egalitarian culture that can exist among teachers. If the way that time is meant to be spent by the teacher is not widely understood, then there may be resistance to the efforts made by a teacher who is perceived to spend less time with students and more time with administrators. Also, time to fulfill the duties of a teacher leader, such as PD delivery, will help to ensure that the benefits of having an on-site expert can ultimately be measured by the ways in which teachers support MLEs in the content-area classrooms.

Sample schedules from current SWEL coaches are shown in Table 1 (elementary school), Table 2 (middle school), and Table 3 (high school). Bear in mind that there are many ways to configure a SWEL coach's schedule, so these are just a few of many potential options. Of course, creating this kind of schedule will require input from the principal or administrative team and the ELD teacher.

It is worth repeating that the sample schedules represented in Tables 1, 2, and 3 are just a few of many possible variations. The idea here is that teachers who work as teacher leaders through peer coaching and PD delivery are given dedicated chunks of time in the school day to fulfill these responsibilities while also maintaining responsibilities as the teacher of record during the remaining portion of the school day. How this dedicated time might be spent is discussed in the following section, but suffice it to say that making sure there is specific time carved out in the school day to do this work is essential. It is also critical that everyone in the school understands the roles and responsibilities of the ELD teacher leader and that the principal is willing to create a leadership system that allows for both support and autonomy of the ELD teacher's work.

**TABLE 1.** Elementary SWEL Coach: Sample Schedule

| Time | Monday | Tuesday | Wednesday | Thursday | Friday |
|---|---|---|---|---|---|
| 8:00 am–8:45 am | Peer coaching | Peer coaching | Peer coaching | Peer coaching | Peer coaching |
| 8:45 am–10:15 am | 3rd grade ELD | 3rd grade ELD | 3rd grade ELD | 3rd grade ELD | 3rd grade ELD |
| 10:15 am–10:45 pm | Rotating pull-out groups: 3rd grade ELD | Rotating pull-out groups: 2nd grade ELD | Rotating pull-out groups: 3rd grade ELD | Rotating pull-out groups: 2nd grade ELD | Peer coaching prep and conversations |
| 10:45 am–12:00 pm | 2nd grade ELD | 2nd grade ELD | 2nd grade ELD | 2nd grade ELD | 2nd grade ELD |
| 12:00 pm–12:50 pm | Lunch and prep with 2nd grade team | Lunch and prep | Lunch and prep with 3rd grade team | Lunch and prep | Lunch and prep with 4th grade team |
| 12:50 pm–1:30 pm | 4th grade ELD | 4th grade ELD | 4th grade ELD | 4th grade ELD | 4th grade ELD |
| 1:30 pm–2:00 pm | Newcomer group: 2nd, 3rd, and 4th grades | Newcomer group: 2nd, 3rd, and 4th grades | Newcomer group: 2nd, 3rd, and 4th grades | Newcomer group: 2nd, 3rd, and 4th grades | Newcomer group: 2nd, 3rd, and 4th grades |
| 2:00 pm–2:45 pm | Peer coaching | Peer coaching | Peer coaching | Peer coaching | Peer coaching |
| 2:45 pm–3:00 pm | 3rd grade ELD | 2nd grade ELD | 4th grade ELD | 3rd grade ELD | 2nd grade ELD |

ELD = English language development

Table 2 shows a middle school SWEL coach's schedule, where this particular teacher works just under full time. SWEL coaching is reserved for "green days" and is scheduled in two periods back to back so that coaching can take place flexibly and with more than one classroom/content teacher.

**TABLE 2.** Middle School SWEL Coach: Sample Schedule (.9 FTE [Full-Time Equivalency])

| Period | Green Day | Blue Day |
|---|---|---|
| 1 | Not contracted | Not contracted |
| 2 | SWEL coaching | Prep |
| 3 | SWEL coaching | 8th grade Spanish |
| 4 | 8th grade Spanish | 8th grade Spanish |
| 5 | 8th grade Spanish | 8th grade Spanish |
| 6 | Flex period | Flex period |
| 7 | 8th grade Spanish | 8th grade Spanish |

The high school schedule in Table 3 shows a school where all five of the ELD teachers are trained SWEL coaches. With a few years of coteaching across the content areas already in place, this school enrolled too many MLEs to ensure that they were all placed in the cotaught classroom. Using the SWEL model, they found a way to support the entire department rather than just a single teacher or classroom through what they chose to call "cluster classrooms," which is a period when SWEL coaches use the time to coach other teachers in that content area who are on prep and go into the classroom to coteach and model strategies. It is a flexible block of time when the SWEL coach works with teachers covering the same content, such as chemistry, to ensure cross-department use of language teaching strategies.

As you study this schedule, keep in mind that you do not have to be in a school where the entire ELD team are trained as SWEL coaches. Instead, look at a single SWEL coach's schedule from Table 3 and consider how it might fit or be adjusted for your context.

**TABLE 3.** High School Schedule: Block Schedule with Multiple Trained SWEL Coaches

|  | Period 1 | Period 2 | Period 3 | Period 4 | Period 5 | Period 6 | Period 7 |
|---|---|---|---|---|---|---|---|
| SWEL Coach 1 | English 1 (MLE Class) | Prep/ Biology (Cluster Class) | SWEL Coaching Geometry (Cluster Class) | Biology (Co-Teaching) | Geometry (Co-Teaching) | English 1 (newcomer class) | Prep/ MLE Duty |
| SWEL Coach 2 | Prep/ MLE Duty | US History (Co-Teaching) | US Literature (Co-Teaching) | Chemistry (Co-Teaching) | SWEL Coaching Algebra 2 (Cluster Class) | Prep | SWEL Coaching Chemistry (Cluster Class) |
| SWEL Coach 3 | English 3 reading/EM Grades 9–10 (ML Class) | Geography (Sheltered Co-Teaching) | SWEL Coaching 9th Grade Social Studies (Cluster Class) | Prep/MLE Duty/10th Grade Cluster Class | MLE Coordination | English 10 (Co-Teaching) | Prep/ Economics (Cluster Class) |
| SWEL Coach 4 | English 2 (MLE Class) | Prep / English 9 (Cluster Class) | ELA choice creative writing (Sheltered Co-Teaching) | Earth Science 9 (Sheltered Co-Teaching) | Prep/MLE Duty | English 9 (Sheltered Co-Teaching) | SWEL coaching/ Earth Science (Cluster Class) |
| SWEL Coach 5 | English 3 language Grades 9–12 (ML Class) | SWEL World History (Cluster Class) | Prep/ MLEDuty | Prep/ Intermediate Algebra (Cluster Class) | Intermediate Algebra (Co-Teaching) | Creative Writing (Co-Teaching) Speech (Co-Teaching) | |

Cluster Class: A period when SWEL coaches use the time to coach other teachers in that content area who are on prep and go into the classroom to model strategies and co-teach.

EM: Experienced Multilingual Learner

## ELD Teacher Identity: From Glorified Tutor to Site-Based Expert

If you are an ELD teacher reading this book, you have likely experienced deprofessionalization in some capacity. Perhaps you were relegated to the role of building substitute, asked to make copies for a colleague, or treated like a glorified tutor. Findings from Froemming's (2015) research on perceptions of ELD teachers' roles within school communities indicate that classroom/content teachers seldom understand the role and expertise of ELD teachers. As a result, they are often regarded as support staff, rather than language experts. Not only is this tremendously frustrating for professionals in the field, it also results in a significant equity issue for MLEs, as they are not consistently provided robust language support in school.

As much as SWEL is a model for improved services for MLEs, it is also a teacher empowerment plan. As SWEL coaches experience teacher leadership opportunities, they become more confident supporting and coaching their colleagues. They identify as language experts, PD facilitators, curricular collaborators, and peer instructional coaches. One coach shared,

> I struggled with that identity a lot when I first came into the field because I felt like as an ELD teacher people did not understand the role or there was [sic] so many misconceptions about the role. Like *Oh, you're a reading teacher.* No. *You're a homework helper.* No, not that either. *Oh you're here to do whatever I need you to do.* Not that either. I teach language! (Benson, 2019, p. 80)

Benson's (2019) findings suggest that "exposure to the practices that support language learning provides classroom/content teachers and administrators a lens into the daily roles and expectations of ELD teachers" (p. 85). The increased visibility of the role and expertise of ELD teachers through ELD teacher leadership has benefits across the school community and results in an increased sense of professionalism among ELD teachers.

---

### VOICES FROM THE FIELD

I got to be more of a leader in our school. For my own direction in my professional journey, I would like to get into more teacher coaching and teacher development. It really made me happy to get that embedded in my current job. So that was a great opportunity. *(SWEL coach)*

---

## Turning the Ship: The Evolving Role of ELD Teachers

The SWEL teacher leadership model has been implemented across the country. Of note is the impact that the initiative has continually had on ELD teacher role and identity. Coaches affirm that working with classroom/content teachers in a collaborative way has given their colleagues new insight into what they do. They shared that this reimagined professional relationship increased their opportunities to collaborate and offer support to classroom/content teachers. One noted, "I feel more empowered as a teacher to provide informal support to teachers outside of my [SWEL] partnerships" (Benson, 2019, p. 69). Another teacher noted that even though some colleagues did not participate in coaching, they were impacted by a "ripple effect." After hearing about the transformational PD and coaching that their colleagues received, they more frequently sought out the ELD teacher for support and asked to be coached in the following year.

> ### VOICES FROM THE FIELD
>
> I feel like at our school, we became more of a resource for the teachers that don't normally meet with ELD teachers, which I thought was really important to happen because what happened in our school was ELD teachers were assigned to work with the ELA [English language arts] teachers. So we pushed in during ELA and we were seen a lot as teachers' support for guided reading. By opening up and meeting with the middle school science teacher, the middle school social studies teacher, or meeting with the math teacher. . . . I even worked with the reading interventionist . . . and I felt like there were other teachers coming to us and asking "What can we do for our students?" . . .
>
> Ninety-six percent of our population is already MLEs, so it was really important that they were reaching out and using us as resources. I would say of everything that was probably the biggest accomplishment or biggest positive change that happened, because that's what we wanted to be and that's not what we were seen as before. *(SWEL coach)*

Increased collaboration among classroom/content teachers and their ELD colleagues manifests in strategy sharing, soliciting feedback on instructional approaches, as well as celebrating the successes of an MLE. This is in line with the findings of Knight (2007) and Tolbert (2015), who attest that among the benefits of peer coaching is the resulting increased collaboration among teachers. Though ELD teachers often hesitate to take time previously allocated to direct instruction of students and redirect it to peer coaching, they found that the end product (continuous attention to language development throughout the school day) was more impactful on MLE achievement than pulling them out of class for direct instruction via small group work.

> ### VOICES FROM THE FIELD
>
> Before I was teaching in this position, I was teaching in a different state and I felt like I constantly got professional development and I was constantly growing. Then when I got to the building where I am teaching, I was learning but I was in a little silo. I know it sounds terrible. I missed that [connection] and then I felt like getting together with other SWEL coaches and talking about other schools, and I did that [through TESOL's SWEL Professional Learning Community] and I felt like I was growing more professionally. It feels nice to have a professional community again where I feel like I am growing. *(SWEL coach)*

## PEER COACHING AS TEACHER LEADERSHIP

Teacher leadership and instructional coaching are defined differently, depending on the context. For some schools, *teacher leadership* is an unfamiliar term, and *coaching* is already used but with a different and/or setting-specific definition; this can make it difficult to use the term *coach* without confusion with the existing coaching program. In terms of teacher leadership, which can take many shapes, there is no single, agreed-upon definition. In essence, "teacher leadership is an idea that emphasizes that teachers hold an important and central position within the schools" (York-Barr & Duke, 2004). A system of distributed leadership allows a school to leverage the central position that teachers hold (Spillane, 2005; Brooks, Adams, & Morita-Mullaney, 2010).

As previously stated, we base our work on Wenner and Campbell's 2017 definition of teacher leadership and consider SWEL coaches as teacher leaders who work collaboratively with their colleagues to support instructional practices that serve to improve educational outcomes for MLEs. In the case of SWEL coaches, the area of expertise is in second language acquisition and pedagogy, and the leadership role they play is to share that knowledge with other teachers during part of the school day through PD delivery and one-on-one or small group peer coaching. For many of the ELD teachers we have trained, the PD delivery actually takes place in after-school staff or professional learning community (PLC) meetings, during the opening weeks of school, and on the days when students are not in the building. We have found that the majority of ELD teachers deliver PD to their whole staff, even if they are only providing one-on-one peer coaching to a handful of their colleagues. Table 4 lists some of the additional ways in which current SWEL coaches serve as ELD teacher leaders based on systems that are already established (e.g., designated PD days or PLCs) and new systems that are put in place to support SWEL coaching.

**TABLE 4.** Ways in which SWEL Coaches Serve as Teacher Leaders

| | |
|---|---|
| Previously Established Systems | Lead a PLC for classroom/content teachers who elect to participate in SWEL coaching |
| | Provide small or whole group PD sessions during regularly scheduled staff development time (e.g., "sunrise sessions" before school once a month) |
| | Provide coplanning SWEL support during regular grade or department level team meetings |
| | Change one block of additional time in a schedule (e.g., additional tutorial time for Level 2 students one or more days per week) to be consulting time when classroom/content teachers and school staff sign up to get planning, modeling, and teaching support for MLEs. |
| | Intentionally use assigned coteaching blocks to enact SWEL peer coaching and PD. |
| Newly Developed Systems | "Buy" 0.1 or 0.2 FTE (full-time equivalency) time in a SWEL coach's schedule to create a block for dedicated consulting with one or more classroom/content teachers. |
| | Coplanning blocks for teachers in schools that have not used this program structure. |
| | Small group PD facilitation at the district level for multiple schools. |
| | Cofacilitating PD with other SWEL coaches from the building or district. |
| | Regular district-level SWEL coach meetings and book studies. |

The term *coach* can be complicated because of the number of schools that hire full-time instructional coaches, often with a focus on core content areas like math and literacy. Such instructional coaches often play a role in the evaluation of teachers and teacher quality, so it is also important to state that SWEL coaches are in no way evaluative in their work. Instead, SWEL coaches engage in professional dialogue (Knight, 2007) to address skill, knowledge, and dispositional gaps that were not addressed in preservice teacher programs or that require attention in order to better meet the needs of students. In some districts where the term *coach* has taken on another meaning, they have opted to use other terms, such as *consultant*, *mentor*, or *colleague*.

Knight (2007) frames dialogic coaching as coaching in which there is a strong partnership between the two participants, rather than an expert-apprentice relationship. Clearly, classroom/content teachers have much to share with ELD teachers, so parity should exist between the two in a way that might not exist were one is strictly the expert and the other a complete novice. Engaging in conversation is the means by which each teacher shares their knowledge and gains insights from the other. This conversation is intended to be ongoing and responsive to the students being taught, so it might look very different from teacher to teacher or classroom to classroom, even within the same school. Ultimately, the goal is colearning among colleagues to ensure that MLEs are successful as they gain both content and English language skills simultaneously.

---

**Discussion Questions**

1. How has your role evolved to include some of the responsibilities described in this chapter that go above and beyond direct instruction of MLEs?

2. After looking at the sample SWEL coach schedules (Tables 1, 2, and 3), how do you imagine your schedule could be set up to reflect your role as a SWEL coach? What would need to be adjusted and who could support these changes?

3. What systems already exist in your school that might provide opportunities to embed SWEL coaching?

**Takeaway Task**

Draft two or three potential SWEL coaching schedules for yourself and create a list of possible coaching activities you would offer during your SWEL coaching time.

---

## References

Aguilar, E. (2013). *The art of coaching*. Jossey-Bass.

Benson, M. (2019). *The roles and identities of English as a second language teacher leaders* [Master's thesis, Hamline University]. Hamline University DigitalCommons@Hamline. https://digitalcommons.hamline.edu/cgi/viewcontent.cgi?article=5468&context=hse_all

Brooks, K., Adams, S., & Morita-Mullaney, T. (2010). Creating inclusive communities for ELL students: Transforming school principals' perspectives. *Theory into Practice, 49*(2), 145–151. https:/doi.org/10.1080/00405841003641501

Civil Rights Act of 1964, Pub.L. 88–352, 78 Stat. 241 (1964).

Froemming, A. C. (2015). *Perceptions of ESL teachers' roles within school communities* [Master's thesis, Hamline University]. Hamline University DigitalCommons@Hamline. https://digitalcommons.hamline.edu/cgi/viewcontent.cgi?article=1185&context=hse_all

Garmston, R., & Wellman, B. (2009). *The adaptive school: A sourcebook for developing collaborative groups* (2nd ed.). Christopher-Gordon.

González, N., Moll, L. C., & Amanti, C. (Eds.). (2005). *Funds of knowledge: Theorizing practices in households, communities, and classrooms*. Routledge. https://doi.org/10.4324/9781410613462

Knight, J. (2007). *Instructional coaching: A partnership approach to improving instruction*. Corwin.

Lau v. Nichols. 414 U.S. 563 (1974).

Menken, K., & Solorza, C. (2015). Principals as linchpins in bilingual education: The need for prepared school leaders. *International Journal of Bilingual Education and Bilingualism, 18*(6), 676–697. https:/doi.org/10.1080/13670050.2014.937390

National Center for Education Statistics (NCES). (2024, May). *Condition of education: English learners in public schools*. U.S. Department of Education, Institute of Education Sciences. https://nces.ed.gov/programs/coe/indicator/cgf

Office of English Language Acquisition (OELA). (2023, June). *Educators of English learners: Availability, projected need, and teacher preparation* [Infographic]. https://ncela.ed.gov/sites/default/files/2023-06/ELsTeachers-Infographic-20230616-508.pdf

Spillane, J. (2005). Distributed leadership. *The Educational Forum, 69*, 143–150.

TESOL International Association. (2019). *Standards for initial TESOL pre-K–12 teacher preparation programs*. https://www.tesol.org/media/v33fewo0/2018-tesol-teacher-prep-standards-final.pdf

Tolbert, M. K. (2015). *An interview study of instructional coaches' and teachers' experiences with an elementary instructional coaching program* [Doctoral dissertation, Dallas Baptist University]. ProQuest Dissertations and Theses Global. (UMI No. 10101024).

Valdés, G., Kibler, A., & Walqui, A. (2014, March). *Changes in the expertise of ELD professionals: Knowledge and action in an era of new standards*. TESOL International Association. https://www.tesol.org/media/y5mj4cdr/changes-in-standards-professional-paper-26-march-2014.pdf

Wenner, J. A., & Campbell, T. (2017). The theoretical and empirical basis of teacher leadership. *Review of Educational Research, 87*(1), 134–171.

Williams, R. (2023, April 24). *English learners: Analyzing what works for whom and under what conditions*. Inside IES Research, U.S. Department of Education. https://ies.ed.gov/blogs/research/post/english-learners-analyzing-what-works-for-whom-and-under-what-conditions

York-Barr, J., & Duke, K. (2004). What do we know about teacher leadership? Findings from two decades of scholarship. *Review of Educational Research, 74*(3), 255–316. https:/doi.org/10.3102/00346543074003255

# CHAPTER 3

# CONTEXTUAL LANGUAGE INSTRUCTION

*Do the best you can until you know better. Then when you know better, do better.*

—attributed to Maya Angelou

Perhaps the area that has most changed since the first edition of this book was published in 2020 is the approach to language instruction. Since the publication of *Teacher Leadership for School-Wide English Learning*, we've given great thought to our possible role in perpetuating the marginalization of language-minoritized youth. We've landed on an approach for teachers who are committed to linguistically sustaining pedagogies and who seek to empower students with linguistic capital for social mobility. Contextual language instruction (CLI) reinforces home languages and varieties in academic spaces while also providing targeted language instruction on the word-, sentence-, and discourse-level features that are needed to access content across the curriculum.

## ACADEMIC LANGUAGE

Just 3 months after the first edition of this book was published in the spring of 2020, George Floyd was killed a few miles from where both authors lived. Shortly thereafter, in July 2020, the Conference on College Composition and Communication released demands to address anti-Black racism in education. Among them was the following: "We DEMAND that teachers and researchers acknowledge that socially constructed terms such as academic language and standard English are false and entrenched in notions of white supremacy and whiteness that contribute to anti-Black linguistic racism" (Baker-Bell et al., n.d.).[1]

For a field committed to multiculturalism and empowerment, this demand cannot be ignored. Those benefiting from White privilege, such as the authors of this book, must scrutinize their

---

[1] Since the list of demands was originally published in 2020, Baker-Bell et al. have changed the language of the first demand to "We demand that teachers stop using academic language and standard English as the accepted communicative norm, which reflects White mainstream English" (Baker-Bell et al., n.d.).

practices to combat linguistic oppression. The concept of academic language rose to prominence as a result of Cummins's (1979) framework of basic interpersonal communication skills (BICS) and cognitive academic language proficiency (CALP). However, educators have struggled to come to a consensus on a definition for the term. When asked, most respond that academic language is "the language of school," which is not a definition, but rather a synonym for the word academic. Consider the following quotes from prominent scholars in the field as they describe their understandings of the term *academic language*.

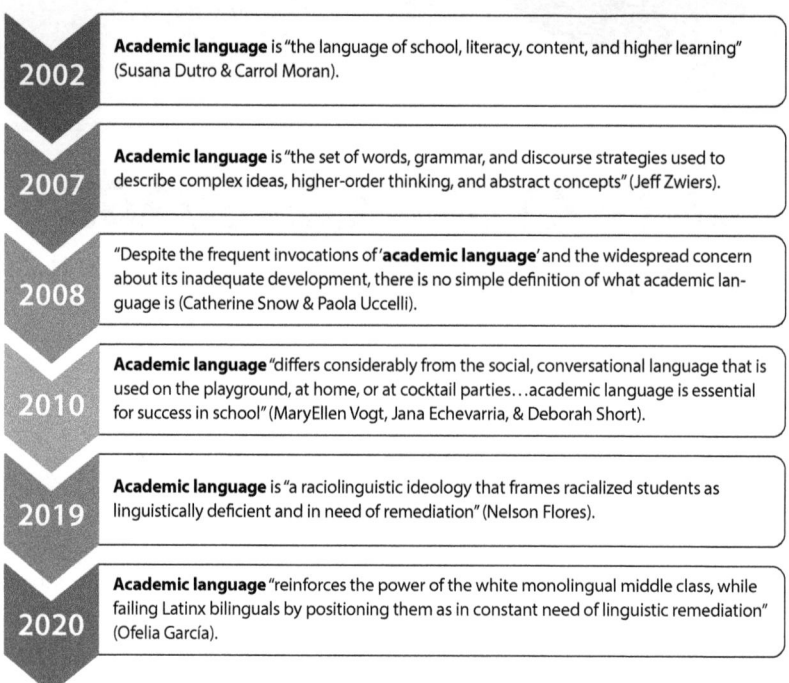

**FIGURE 1.** Timeline of quotes from prominent linguists on academic language. From *Language of identity, language of access (LILA): Liberatory learning in multilingual classrooms,* by M. Benegas & N. Benjamin, 2024, Corwin. Reprinted with permission.

The evolution of understanding of this term is evident in the timeline shown in Figure 1. It has functioned and been understood as both a neutral and an exclusionary term.

Justice-oriented educators challenge the dichotomies of home/school and basic/cognitive when considering students' capacities for learning and engagement. Certainly, language in the home is not exclusively *basic*, and language at school is not exclusively *cognitive*. Time will tell if the term "academic language" will continue to evolve and remain in the nomenclature of education, or if it will be retired and replaced with another term.

A robust conversation continues in the field about whether we should abandon the term academic language entirely (Benegas & Benjamin, 2024). We remain engaged in these discussions and committed to keeping a critical eye on the experiences of racialized people in contact with the concept of academic language. For now, for the sake of continuity between first and second editions of this book, and because it remains part of the teaching lexicon, we will interchangeably use the terms *language* and *academic language*, defining it as "the language needed to engage in classroom discourse and demonstrate understanding of discipline-specific content."

# WHAT DOES CONTEXTUAL LANGUAGE INSTRUCTION LOOK LIKE IN PRACTICE?

The following sections present the fundamentals of expanding students' linguistic repertoires and sustaining home language skills. These sections synthesize complex topics in applied linguistics. They are presented separately; however, skilled educators attend to both in their instruction.

## Expanding Students' Linguistic Repertoires

Discipline-specific language varies significantly. Contrary to the common saying, kids are not "like sponges." They have complex brains and they exert effort to learn language. Learners thrive when educators offer explicit instruction in English language development (ELD), rather than expect them to simply absorb it through exposure. Explicit language instruction is critical to equitable education across the content areas.

Consequently, educators must be adept at language pedagogy. Despite the presence of language learners in most general education classrooms, only about 30% of classroom/content teachers have received any training in language pedagogy (Ballantyne et al., 2007). A common question among educators is "Which language should I teach?" Language educators know that this does not come naturally. Supporting teachers with planning for explicit language instruction is a critical role for the school-wide English learning (SWEL) coach.

Central to all good instruction is good planning. There are a variety of factors involved in designing lessons that develop fluency in content-specific language. The following is a step-by-step approach to helping classroom/content teachers plan lessons that will level the linguistic playing field for all learners. This approach is appropriate for ELD as well as classroom/content teachers. In the context of SWEL coaching, it is recommended that the coachee first identify an upcoming lesson sequence or unit.

> Planning for, instructing, and assessing language is difficult. Most SWEL coaches report challenges in this area. Expect there to be a learning curve with your colleagues. Start with what is familiar and provide encouragement along the way. The work of preparing all teachers to consider language development in curriculum and instruction is a long-range endeavor. It will not happen overnight.

# NOTICING AND FORECASTING: A GUIDE FOR DETERMINING WHICH LANGUAGE TO TEACH

Prior to thinking about language objectives, teachers need to consider *which* language to teach. Think about this like a doctor's appointment. Your doctor will look over your vitals and identify any areas of concern as well as discuss preventive and/or planful measures that you can take considering life stages that are to come. With guidance from a SWEL coach, teachers can do the same and develop the skills to look beyond the content words that are listed in bold or in word banks. They can notice areas for growth and forecast areas that can benefit from added attention early on. Noticing and forecasting is a framework to walk classroom/content teachers through the areas of greatest linguistic need with a particular group of students in a particular content area.

## Noticing Language Needs

Teachers are mixed-methods researchers who collect quantitative (assessment scores) and qualitative (observations, conversations) data and make data-informed instructional decisions every day.

Noticing is a structured way to think about how to collect qualitative data in order to teach students in linguistically appropriate ways.

Noticing is a reflective exercise. Teachers should ask themselves, "What do I notice about my students' language that needs attention? What language have they mastered? Where are there areas for growth?" Most often, teachers notice gaps in students' productive language because they can hear or read the error or oversimplification. Table 1 shows examples of noticing language needs.

**TABLE 1.** Examples of Noticing Student Language Needs

| Level of Language | Examples of Noticing |
|---|---|
| Word-Level Semantics | Students overuse general use words like *very*, *thing*, and *stuff*. |
| | Students misuse vocabulary words (e.g., "When I pulley the rope, the bucket goes up"). |
| Word-Level Phonology | Student writes "110" when the teacher says "one-tenth." |
| | Student pronounces the *t* in words like *revolution* and *explanation* with hard /s/ sounds rather than /sh/ sounds. |
| Word-Level Morphology | Student tells you that he "unapproves" of a decision. |
| | Student writes that the chapter was "insultive." |
| Sentence-Level Syntax | Student tells another student that "they going to lunch." |
| | Student consistently begins sentences with a subject and verb. |
| Discourse-Level Text Type | Student writes an autobiography using third person and does not create paragraphs with topic sentences. |
| | Student develops a presentation, and the slides include long paragraphs of descriptive text. |

Following a discussion about student language that the classroom/content teacher notices, the coach can guide the teacher toward writing, integrating, and assessing language objectives that are tailored to their students' needs.

## Forecasting Language Needs: Text, Task, and Test

Unlike noticing, forecasting is a forward-thinking exercise. Teachers should ask themselves, "What language do students need to successfully engage with the content?" When a medical doctor wants to better understand what is happening inside a patient's body, they may call for a scan. There are different types of scans that illuminate different systems in the body in an effort to identify specific areas that need attention. Forecasting is a lot like a medical scan. In the following sections, we discuss the three types of language scans that educators can conduct to plan for ELD. They can forecast text, task, and test at the word, sentence, and discourse levels.

### *Forecasting Text*[2]

Throughout this book, the word *text* will refer to any body of language, written or spoken, that is being used as a focal point for instruction. Linguists refer to forecasting text as *text analysis*. When planning for a lesson, it is critical that teachers consider the text that students will engage with and any areas in which they may need additional language support. Teachers can look at selections of

---

[2] All text excerpts in this section are from Minnesota Comprehensive Assessments—Series II, Reading Item Sampler, Grade 4, Minnesota Department of Education (n.d.).

text or consider oral language production that would meet the lesson objective and scan them for new or difficult language.

**Word-Level Text Scanning.** A word-level scan may help the teacher identify vocabulary words that they will need to teach early in the lesson. The following is an example of a selection of text that has been scanned at the word level. The teacher identified and bolded words that may be new to students.

> Even though they fly, bats do not have **feathers**. Instead, they have **fur** like many other **mammals**. Bats do not have actual wings, either. Most bats come out only at night, although some may fly at **sunset**.

In the example, the teacher has identified words that stand out as content specific and those which may not be part of students' daily lexicon. These words will be considered for language objectives prior to and while engaging with this text.

**Sentence-Level Text Scanning.** During a sentence-level scan, the teacher should look for any structural areas that they anticipate will be difficult for multilingual learners of English (MLEs). The following is an example of the same selection of text that has been scanned at the sentence level. The teacher identified and bolded structural areas that may be new to students.

> **Even though** they fly, bats do not have feathers. **Instead**, they have fur like many other mammals. Bats do not have actual wings, **either**. Most bats come out only at night, **although** some may fly at sunset.

In this example, the teacher identified a variety of areas of syntax that need to be understood to engage with this text. In this case, it would be helpful for the SWEL coach to help their colleague, the coachee, to prioritize which language to teach first. Unlike vocabulary, all of the bold terms cannot be taught together. Rather, individual structures should be explicitly taught independently with separate language objectives. For example, the teacher could write a language objective about how to contrast two or more things using conjunctions like *instead*, *although*, and *even though*. During another lesson, the teacher could write a language objective about how to negate (make something negative) using *not* and *either*. Each content-area lesson should focus on *no more* than one grammar point.

**Discourse-Level Text Scanning.** During a discourse-level scan, the teacher is looking to identify language norms of a particular text type. They are *not* searching for individual words; rather, they are identifying distinguishing aspects.

> Bats are important creatures that many people misunderstand. First, some people think they are birds, but they are not. Even though they fly, bats do not have feathers. Instead, they have fur like many other mammals. Bats do not have actual wings, either.
>
> Second, bats are nocturnal. Most bats come out only at night, although some may fly at sunset. Because they are awake at night, they sleep during the day.
>
> Finally, some people believe that bats are dirty and scary. Actually, they are very clean and groom themselves frequently. They are also very helpful to people because they eat mosquitos. They do not suck people's blood!

The preceding example shows a longer piece of text with some notable markers of its text type. The teacher may notice that this text begins with a thesis and that the thesis is supported by the organized paragraphs below it. Also, transition words are used and facts are backed up with contextual explanations. These are all characteristics of a descriptive text. A discourse-level language objective would focus on students recognizing the language norms of a descriptive text and modeling those language norms in their own production of a descriptive text.

## *Forecasting Task*

When teachers prepare an activity as a part of a lesson, it is important that they consider the language that will be needed for students to engage in the activity. They must question any assumptions that they have about their students' language to ensure that the activity is accessible to all. Central to forecasting task is identifying the language function that students will be expected to carry out. Table 2 shows examples of how a teacher might forecast a task (function words in bold).

**TABLE 2.** Examples of Forecasting Task

| Content Objective/Learning Target | Language Needed to Engage in Activity |
|---|---|
| After reading Chapter 11 from *Where the Red Fern Grows*, students will **retell** what happened after Little Ann fell through the ice into the river. | Word Level<br>• *Yelped, collapsed, gave way, frigid, sibling, shock*<br>Sentence Level<br>• Sequential language: *First, second, third, next, after*<br>• Irregular past tense verbs like *fell, cried, broke*<br>Discourse Level<br>• Multiple paragraph narrative structure |
| Students will **predict** what will happen to different sized pieces of clay when they are placed in a beaker of water. | Word Level<br>• *Disintegrate, beaker, porous, waterproof, insert*<br>• Prefixes (morphemes) such as *pre–*, and suffixes (morphemes) such as *–ion*<br>Sentence Level<br>• Clauses: *I think that, I predict that*<br>• If-then statements<br>• Future tense: *will* and *going to*<br>Discourse Level<br>• Science lab narrative |
| Students will **explain** value in mathematical sentences, such as "15 > 4," "9 < 12," and "10 = 10." | Word Level<br>• *Value, equivalent, compare, contrast*<br>• *–er* and *–est* suffixes (morphemes)<br>Sentence Level<br>• Comparative language: *greater than, less than, equal to*<br>• Synonyms: *greater than, bigger than, more than, less than, smaller than, fewer than, equal to, same as*<br>Discourse Level<br>• Math talks |

The activities in Table 2 have clear function words (in bold). For those functions that are also linguistic in nature, such as *explain* and *retell*, the same function can be used in the language objective. SWEL coaches should be sure to clarify the difference between a *cognitive* function and a *language* function. A language function requires that language be used to carry out the task. A cognitive function does not. For example, function words like *solve, find, categorize,* and *demonstrate* may be carried out using only cognition. If no language is needed to carry out the function, it cannot be used for a language objective.

*Forecasting Test*

In addition to considering the language of a text and task, teachers must also consider language when they develop assessments (formative and summative). Forecasting test can be the most difficult of the three types of forecasting because it involves a comprehensive look at the language taught, and the stakes are high for students. However, if both the content and language objectives are aligned with instructional standards and assessments in a given lesson or unit plan, this will be a more straightforward exercise.

**Avoiding Unintentional Language Assessment.** The first question that teachers should ask themselves is, "Are students familiar with the language used in this assessment?" If the answer is no, they should closely examine the assessment to remove or rework any items that prevent students from demonstrating content knowledge as a result of language constraints. This may involve reconsidering any evaluative items that teachers know students are unfamiliar with or language they have not explicitly taught. Consider the following sample assessments:

1. *Health (9th Grade)*: Has technology improved or worsened the childhood experience? Justify your claim with evidence.

2. *Social Studies (5th Grade)*: How would you have felt had you experienced something similar to Anne Frank?

3. *English Language Arts (6th Grade)*: After reading the article, write a 2-page script for a short play about global warming.

The first question implies word-level knowledge of the terms *justify*, *claim*, and *evidence*. If these terms have not been explicitly taught, the student may be unable to satisfactorily answer the question, even with content-area knowledge. In this case, the teacher can either a) preteach the necessary vocabulary or b) reword the end of the question so that it has more simple language. (E.g., "Explain your opinion with examples.") The second question implies sentence-level knowledge of the perfect conditional, which may be an unnecessarily complicated verb tense for the question. If this tense was not taught, the structure of the question should be simplified so that all students are able to demonstrate mastery of the content. (E.g., "How do you think Anne Frank felt?") Doing so will not lessen the quality of the assessment and will likely yield a more accurate measure of student knowledge. Finally, the third item cannot be completed without knowledge of the structure of a script. If a student is unfamiliar with this text type, they will be unable to complete the task. This, of course, indicates that teachers need to survey student background knowledge and preteach where there are gaps in understanding. Alternatively, the teacher can choose a more familiar text type for the assignment (E.g., "Write a two-page essay about global warming.")

**Designing Assessments for Targeted Language Instruction.** The second question that teachers should ask themselves is, "Am I assessing the language that I taught?" If the answer is no, they should consider adding items that assess *language* knowledge alongside *content* knowledge. Word-level assessments tend to be quite common, as teachers often test students on vocabulary words. Discourse-level assessments are also quite common, as many units scaffold up to a culminating summative assessment. Sentence-level assessments are not nearly as common, however. If a particular area of grammar is taught, it should also be assessed within the context of the lesson. This can be as simple as adding a rubric item that focuses on the structures that were taught so that students know that they will be accountable to language, as well as content.

Forecasting test is an important place for SWEL coaches to come into play. We want all students to have equitable opportunities to engage with content and succeed. Teachers can show coaches assessments that they are planning to use and together they can cross-check any language that the assessment evaluates with the language that has been taught.

The following example shows that it is not only K–12 teachers that are responsible for noticing and forecasting. See how a university nursing department sought to make their program more equitable by soliciting the expertise of a site-based language expert.

> *In the undergraduate nursing program, it became clear that we needed to solve our multiple-choice testing problem. Our MLE nursing students were struggling to pass multiple-choice exams and to pass the nursing licensure exam. Most of the MLEs were high performers in clinical and lab and could verbally explain their knowledge of nursing but could not demonstrate their knowledge on our multiple-choice exams. We enlisted an applied linguist at our university who oversaw our ELD program. We sent her a few exams and then she met with us and explained how she rewrote the exam questions. She taught the nursing faculty how to write test items that focused on clarity and linguistic simplicity, which reduced the reading load of test items while maintaining the questions' content and integrity.*
>
> —Susan Ellen Campbell, Professor Emeritus, Saint Catherine University

## LEARNING HOW TO "BUILD" LEARNERS' LINGUISTIC TOOLKITS

### VOICES FROM THE FIELD

We saw a need in our school—many teachers know what a language objective is, but they don't know why it's important, so there is not a lot of "buy in." We sought to bring that important aspect of language objectives to life and really dig deep into the core of language objectives, how to pull out academic language, and make sure it aligned in the classroom. *(SWEL Coach)*

The first task in coaching a classroom/content teacher colleague is to ask how they currently attend to language development in their instruction. Often, they will respond with how they attend to vocabulary instruction by pointing to word walls, word banks, and the bold words in textbooks. Perhaps they have items in the classroom labeled in English or the students' home languages. Teachers who are already providing these visuals have taken a critical step toward recognizing their role in student language learning. This is a great platform to honor the work that they are doing with language *and* guide them toward expanding their thinking about what specific linguistic features students will need in order to succeed in class.

Figure 2 shows the three levels of language (word, sentence, and discourse) and their alignment to the five elements of language (phonology, morphology, semantics, syntax, and

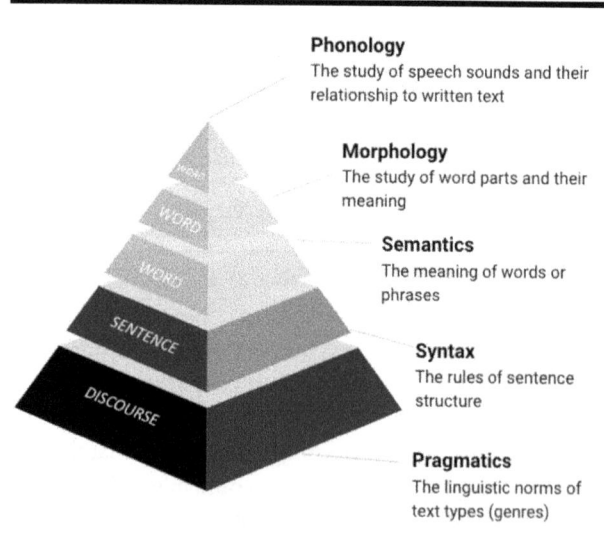

**FIGURE 2.** The Language Pyramid: Mapping the Elements of Language to Language Levels

pragmatics). Building on Dutro and Moran's (2003) framework of bricks and mortar and Zwiers's (2008) work on academic language, the SWEL model breaks the levels of language (word, sentence, discourse) down into bricks, mortar, and buildings. This chart (Table 3) is particularly helpful when working with classroom/content teachers as it illustrates the complexity of the levels of language in a way that resonates across classrooms and content areas.

**TABLE 3.** Levels of Language

|  | Word | Sentence | Discourse |
| --- | --- | --- | --- |
| **Metaphor** | Bricks | Mortar | Building |
| **Definition** | Bricks are **vocabulary specific to the content, phonemes,** or **word parts**. | Mortar refers to **general utility language** required for constructing sentences and paragraphs. | Buildings are a combination of bricks and mortar to form a **text type** (also known as a **genre**). |
| **Elements of Language** | **Phonology** (sounds of letter combinations), **morphology** (word parts), or **semantics** (word/phrase meaning; vocabulary) | **Syntax** (how words fit together; also known as grammar, structure, or form) | **Pragmatics** (language norms of a text type) |
| **Examples** | *Science*: volcano, tsunami, earthquake<br><br>*Math*: addition, subtraction, multiplication<br><br>*Social Studies*: amendment, constitution<br><br>*Language Arts*: omniscient, alliteration | *Connecting Words*: for example, however, although, whereas<br><br>*Phrases with prepositions*: think about, improve on, in addition to<br><br>*Comparatives*: Greater than, less than, equal to, as big as | *Science*: lab reports<br><br>*Math*: structure of a math problem, structure of a math proof, oral report of how a problem is solved<br><br>*Social Studies*: formal debate, history report, news article<br><br>*Language Arts*: letter, narrative, screenplay, autobiography |

Based on Dutro & Moran, 2003; Zwiers, 2008.

A critical role of a SWEL coach is to teach classroom/content teachers how to scaffold levels of language *across* lessons and units of study. When breaking language down into these levels, the SWEL coach can ask teachers to consider "What happens if we only teach bricks?" They may discuss how memorized lists of words can often fail to transfer to conversations or writing. When asked, "What happens if we only teach mortar?," some recall experiences in world language classes when they memorized verb conjugations but were never able to apply those conjugations to actual discourse. Lastly, when asked "What happens if we only teach buildings?," teachers may reflect on a common occurrence in English language arts, in which students learn about different text types, like a five-paragraph essay, but do not have the word- or sentence-level skills to successfully recreate them. This book provides a roadmap for preparing classroom/content teachers to write, integrate, and assess language objectives at the brick, mortar, and building (word, sentence, and discourse) levels.

## WRITING LANGUAGE OBJECTIVES

It must first be stated that coaching classroom/content teachers to write language objectives should come after significant background in planning for language instruction through noticing and forecasting as well as an understanding of the levels of language. Writing strong language objectives is difficult and will require patience and a slow pace. We recommend that you start with what is familiar (in many cases this is vocabulary) and move on from there.

Language objectives are used to guide the language instruction required for students to master the content objective (also called the learning target) and, ultimately, the standard that guides the lesson or unit plan. A language objective is content based, and it stems from noticing and forecasting. It should be tailored to a specific language level.

## Functions: The Foundation for the Leveled Language Objective

Writing content and language objectives that are function-driven ensures that 1) students are required to use higher order thinking skills, and 2) lesson activities and assessments reflect the language that is required to master the content material. It is critical that SWEL coaches engage with classroom/content teachers in a way that *supports* their content instruction, rather than competes with it. In other words, it is important for SWEL coaches to convey the symbiotic nature of content and language instruction.

For many teachers, this means beginning with discussions about what students need to *do* with the language that they are required to use. Are they going to compare two concepts, things, or events? Do they need to justify an opinion or position in a debate? Most teachers are familiar with Bloom's Taxonomy (1956), so this is a solid starting place for moving into discussions on language functions and the importance of identifying how the language that teachers want students to produce is utilized in a given lesson or unit plan.

When identifying a function, the teacher must first consider if it is a language function or a cognitive function. Some words, like *solve*, *find*, and *understand* can be used as cognitive functions without a linguistic aspect. It is also important that the teacher not confuse function words with modalities (reading, speaking, listening, writing). Modalities should be incorporated into every lesson and are too broad to be used as functions. Here are some examples of language functions:

### Language Function Examples

| explain | infer | compare |
| justify | summarize | describe |
| retell | predict | synthesize |

The same function word may appear in both the content objective and the language objective. See Appendix D, Building Leveled Language Objectives, for a more comprehensive list of language functions. (Appendix D is available for download on the companion website for this book, www.tesol.org/SWEL-book; also see Activity 2 under "Educators Can Plan for Language Instruction" in Chapter 6.)

## Assessing Language Needs for Content-Area Instruction

Prior to deciding on a focal level of language for a language objective, it is important to conduct an inventory of the language demands in a particular lesson. See the following form, Language Demands Inventory (also available for download on the companion site for this book, www.tesol.org/SWEL-book).

**LANGUAGE DEMANDS INVENTORY**

1. **Identify Your Content Objective(s):**

2. **Language Function(s):** What are you asking students to do with language? (e.g., analyze, compare/contrast, explain, interpret, argue, persuade, categorize, describe, predict, question, retell, summarize, justify with evidence)

3. **Content Vocabulary:** What key vocabulary (word level; "the bricks") do you need to introduce/review with students? Which word parts could be pretaught? Which sounds are difficult for students to pronounce?

4. **Syntax:** What syntax (sentence level; "the mortar") is present in the materials that you are going to teach?

5. **Discourse:** What text type (discourse level; "the building") will students need to produce?

This inventory can be used to decide which levels and areas of language are in need of explicit attention.

## Language Supports

At this early stage, teachers should consider possible language supports that could assist learners to meet the language objective. Language supports are defined as "scaffolds, representations, and instructional strategies that teachers intentionally provide to help learners understand and use the language they need to learn within disciplines" (Indiana University, n.d.). Following is a list of sample sensory, graphic, and language supports (WIDA Consortium, 2012, p. 11).

### *Sensory Supports*

- Real-life objects (realia)
- Manipulatives
- Pictures and photographs
- Illustrations, diagrams, and drawings
- Magazines and newspapers
- Physical activities
- Videos and films
- Broadcasts
- Models and figures

*Graphic Supports*

- Charts
- Graphic organizers
- Tables
- Graphs
- Timelines
- Number lines

*Interactive Supports*

- Pairs or partners
- Triads or small groups
- Whole group activities
- Cooperative group structures
- Websites or software programs
- Home language
- Mentors

Note that not all supports are language supports. For example, a multiplication chart or mathematical formulas could offer content-area support to learners but they do not offer language support. When considering how to support language learning in a lesson, consider tools that develop language use and understanding.

---

### VOICES FROM THE FIELD

One thing that was pretty apparent through multiple professional development sessions and coaching interactions is how much the teachers in my building equated what English learning is and what MLEs need with vocabulary . . . You kind of saw a gradual shift away from just "they need to learn these words" . . . Moving from just the word level to the sentence level and the discourse level has been a pretty big deal. *(SWEL coach)*

---

## Word-Level Language Objectives

Most word-level language objectives focus on semantics (word meaning), but others focus on morphology (word parts) and phonology (word sounds). Use the Planning for Word-Level Language Guide (available as Appendix E on the companion site for this book, www.tesol.org/SWEL-book) to coach your colleague through the process of writing a language objective at the word level.

### PLANNING FOR WORD-LEVEL LANGUAGE GUIDE

| Step 1: Name the Content Objective/Learning Target |
|---|
|  |

## Step 2: Decide Which Language to Teach

**Noticing:** What do I notice about my students' language that needs attention? Choose one area:

*Phonology*:

*Morphology*:

*Semantics*:

**Forecasting:** What word-level language do students need to have to successfully engage with the content?

*Text*:

*Task*:

*Test*:

## Step 3: Choose a Function

The function drives the language objective. A function is how language is used to carry out cognitive processes (such as those described in Bloom's Taxonomy, 1956). This language needs to be explicitly taught. (E.g., *describe, explain, retell*)

## Step 4: Identify Language Supports

Identify a tool that will assist in developing language use and understanding.

## Step 5: Decide on the Level of Language

**Word Level (Bricks):** Check the area that you will focus on at the word level and provide content-based examples of that area.

Phonology (word sounds)  ☐ ex:_____

Semantics (word meaning)  ☐ ex:_____

Morphology (word parts)  ☐ ex:_____

> **Step 6: Write a Language Objective**
>
> **Word-Level Sentence Frame:** Fill in all sections based on the preceding information.
>
> I can _____ [function] using _____ [vocabulary, or phonological/morphological topic], such as _____ [examples of language structure], with the support of _____ [support(s)].

> **Sample Word-Level Language Objectives**
>
> Semantics: I can explain how bats are different from other mammals using vocabulary such as *herbivore, frugivore,* and *insectivore* with the support of sentence frames.
>
> Phonology: I can explain how bats are different from other mammals using correct stress for words, like *herbivore, frugivore,* and *insectivore*, with the support of an audio recording.
>
> Morphology: I can explain how bats are different from other mammals using the suffix *–ivore* for words like *herbivore, frugivore,* and *insectivore* with the support of flashcards.

## Sentence-Level Language Objectives

Sentence-level language objectives focus on syntax (also called grammar, structure, or form). After planning for language instruction, use the Planning for Sentence-Level Language Guide (available as Appendix F on the companion site for this book, www.tesol.org/SWEL-book) to coach your colleague through the process of writing a language objective at the sentence level.

### PLANNING FOR SENTENCE-LEVEL LANGUAGE GUIDE

> **Step 1: Name the Content Objective/Learning Target**

> **Step 2: Decide Which Language to Teach**
>
> **Noticing:** What do I notice about my students' language structure (syntax) that needs attention?
>
> **Forecasting:** What sentence-level language do students need to have to successfully engage with the content?
>
> *Text*:
>
> *Task*:
>
> *Test*:

**Step 3: Choose a Function**

The function drives the language objective. A function is how language is used to carry out cognitive processes (such as those described in Bloom's Taxonomy, 1956). This language needs to be explicitly taught.

**Step 4: Identify Language Supports**

Identify a tool that will assist in developing language use and understanding.

**Step 5: Decide on the Level of Language**

**Sentence Level (Mortar):** Provide the area of syntax that you will focus on in this lesson. Include examples of this type of language from the context.

**Syntax:**

**Examples:**

**Step 6: Write a Language Objective**

**Word-Level Sentence Frame:** Fill in all sections based on the preceding information.

I can _____ [function] using _____ [language structure/syntax], such as _____ [examples of language structure], with the support of _____ [support(s)].

---

**Sample Sentence-Level Language Objectives**

I can <u>summarize</u> how bats contribute to pollination using <u>ordinal numbers</u>, such as <u>*first, second,* and *third*</u>, with the support of <u>a word wall</u>.

I can <u>compare</u> per capita consumption of India and Canada using <u>comparative language</u>, such as <u>*greater than, less than,* and *as _____ as*</u>, with the support of sample sentences.

I can <u>compare</u> the experiences of immigrants and refugees using <u>past tense verbs with the –ed ending</u>, such as <u>*lived, traveled,* and *walked*</u>, with the support of <u>a regular past tense verb list and a T-Chart</u>.

*Contextual Language Instruction*

## Discourse-Level Language Objectives

Discourse-level language objectives focus on text type and pragmatics. After planning for language instruction, use the Planning for Discourse-Level Language Guide (available as Appendix G on the companion site for this book, www.tesol.org/SWEL-book) to coach your colleague through the process of writing a language objective at the discourse level.

### PLANNING FOR DISCOURSE-LEVEL LANGUAGE GUIDE

**Step 1: Name the Content Objective**

---

**Step 2: Decide Which Language to Teach**

**Noticing:** What do I notice about my students' language that needs attention, given this text type?

**Forecasting:** What discourse-level language do students need to have to successfully engage with the content?

*Text*:

*Task*:

*Test*:

---

**Step 3: Choose a Function**

The function drives the language objective. A function is how language is used to carry out cognitive processes (such as those described in Bloom's Taxonomy, 1956). This language needs to be explicitly taught.

---

**Step 4: Identify Supports**

Identify a tool that will assist in developing language use and understanding.

**Step 5: Decide on the Level of Language**

**Discourse Level (Building):** Provide the text type that you will focus on in this lesson (e.g., lab report, persuasive essay, opinion editorial, debate, interview).

Discourse:

---

**Step 6: Write a Language Objective**

**Discourse-Level Sentence Frame:** Fill in all sections based on the preceding information.

I can _____ [function] in _____ [text type] structure, with the support of _____ [support(s)].

---

**Sample Discourse-Level Language Objectives**

I can <u>describe</u> density in a <u>science lab report</u> with the support of my <u>Cornell Notes</u>.

I can <u>describe</u> how bats disperse seeds in <u>an organized oral presentation</u> with the support of <u>a cycle diagram</u>.

I can <u>compare</u> per capita consumption patterns with classmates in <u>a group discussion</u> with the support of <u>a bank of sentence starters</u>.

Writing language objectives is challenging for most teachers. It requires looking at content through a new lens. It is normal for this process to take some time. Once teachers become versed in writing language objectives, they will find that the process is iterative. New language objectives will be needed for new course content and new student populations. The following section explains further the cyclical nature of planning for content-based language instruction.

---

## VOICES FROM THE FIELD

We believe these [language objectives] are areas classroom teachers at our school struggle with. We recognize that language objectives are not the end-all-be-all of providing access for MLEs, but it is a start and really gets teachers thinking about how to best support their students' language development. *(SWEL coach)*

# THE CYCLICAL NATURE OF TEXT TYPE-FOCUSED (GENRE-BASED) LANGUAGE INSTRUCTION

A challenge working as a SWEL coach is identifying where teachers should start with language instruction. In practice, integration of language instruction is part of a cyclical process. It is difficult to identify a discrete starting place. Figure 3 illustrates the ongoing and multidimensional nature of the SWEL teaching and learning cycle.

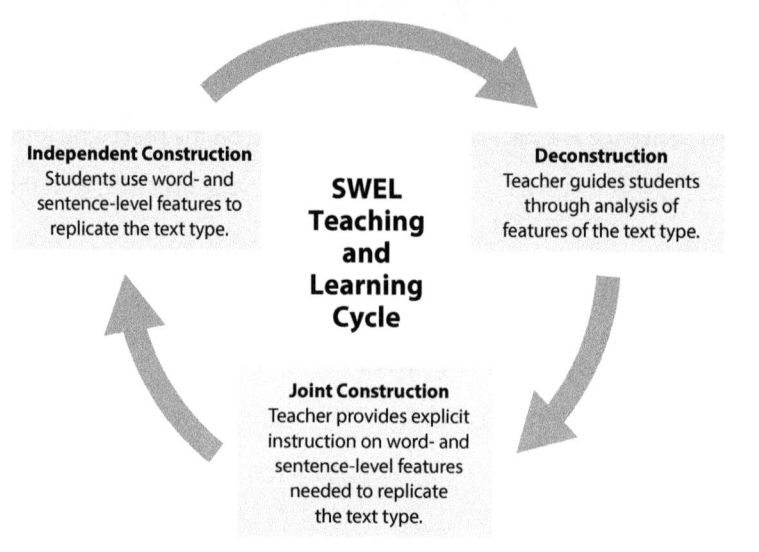

**FIGURE 3.** SWEL teaching and learning cycle. (Based on the teaching and learning cycle from North South Wales Department of School Education, 1992)

The SWEL teaching and learning cycle demonstrates the nature of content-based language instruction that is focused on text type. It allows for practice with word- and sentence-level features in a given text type. Though it is critical that the teacher begin by explicitly presenting the text type and end with independent student construction of the text type, what happens in the middle is flexible. Word- and sentence-level features can be taught in the order that makes the most sense, given the context and the student population.

### VOICES FROM THE FIELD

One of the big things that we've focused on is how to integrate sentence frames into different content areas and how to use that to have intentional student-to-student talk . . . [My colleagues] expressed some excitement about their success with that and the student learning that took place. They would bring these supports into a lesson and they would notice more student participation. But the students were also responding to them in a more positive way, like saying, "that was a good lesson," so feeling that reinforcement in their own perception and in the feedback they're receiving really opened them up to try other things. *(SWEL coach)*

# FOUNDATIONS IN THE LANGUAGE OF IDENTITY

The language of identity refers to the language or language varieties used during a student's formative years and/or in a student's home. The role of the teacher (both ELD and content/classroom) is quite different when it comes to the language of identity. While it is their job to *teach* content-specific language, it is also their job to *support* the language of identity (i.e., students' home languages). You don't need to be an ELD teacher for long before you get this question: "How many languages do you speak?" There is an assumption that we have some working knowledge of all of the languages in our classrooms, which is generally false. While we tend to love languages and we try to learn them as we are able, multilingualism is not a requisite skill for the job.

So, what does it look like to support home language? Let's imagine that we are creating a model for what scholarly multilingual spaces look like. When we encourage parents to use home language at home, let's also show them how their home languages are valued and validated in the classroom. After all, when we sit in English-only classrooms and tell parents to read to their kids in their home language, we can clearly see why the message falls flat. We need to walk the walk and not just talk the talk.

## Translanguaging and Multilingual Identity

Translanguaging refers to the language practices of multilingual students (Garcia, 2013). Unlike code-switching, where multilingual speakers are thought to switch between distinct language codes, translanguaging involves drawing from a single linguistic repertoire. Translanguaging is simply how multilingual/multidialectal brains work. The opposite of translanguaging is linguistic suppression (asking someone to disregard the linguistic tools at their disposal).

Translanguaging not only refers to the complex language practices of multilinguals, but it also encompasses pedagogical approaches that utilize these practices (García et al., 2017). It encourages a shift in how language is perceived and promotes classroom actions based on the actual linguistic practices of multilingual people. Educators are encouraged to adopt this research-based perspective that views the multilingual learner's language repertoire as an asset rather than a deficit (García et al., 2017). Yosso (2006) refers to this as community cultural wealth, which they define as "an array of knowledge, skills, abilities and contacts possessed and utilized by Communities of Color to survive and resist macro and micro-forms of oppression."

With this mindset, educators can implement a translanguaging pedagogy that includes strategies to

- help students engage with complex content,
- develop linguistic practices in school settings,
- integrate multilingualism and diverse identities into the classroom, and
- support students' socioemotional growth and multilingual identities.

Translanguaging practices focus on how students use language for meaning-making, and the "translanguaging corriente (current)" influences the content being communicated (García et al., 2017).

The language(s) we speak, the words we choose, and the accent we have are how others come to understand (correctly or incorrectly) who we are. For this reason, there is risk involved with suppressing home language use. If young people believe that the language they hear at home isn't appropriate for the classroom, they may develop negative associations with that aspect of their identity. Over time, this can lead young people to shift the way they perceive themselves toward the identity that holds the most power and prestige, losing sight of their own heritage and often losing their familial/home language (L1) entirely. The opposite end of this is equally troubling. A learner may perceive that they can never "crack the code" of the language of power, so they opt out entirely. These young people mostly disengage with school due to feelings that they don't belong. Translanguaging is a linguistic ideology that has the potential to shape young identities toward simultaneously embracing where they are from and where they are going.

When considering how to support translanguaging in the classroom, educators must take into account their stances on multilingual identity development, intentional translanguaging pedagogies, and the inherent critical nature of language in society. The remainder of this chapter offers suggestions for how educators can support students to read, write, hear, and speak their language of identity in the classroom. Consider your learners and your desired outcomes when choosing which strategies will work best in your classroom.

## Translanguaging Pedagogies That Support L1 Writing

Translanguaging pedagogies that support L1 writing include various strategies and practices that leverage students' entire linguistic repertoire to enhance their writing skills. Here are some examples:

1. **Bilingual Brainstorming**: Encourage students to brainstorm ideas for writing assignments using all of their linguistic resources. They can jot down notes, create mind maps, or discuss ideas with peers in their preferred language(s).

2. **Multilingual Drafting**: Allow students to write initial drafts using a mix of languages. They can express their ideas more fluently and later translate or refine, ensuring that the content remains rich and comprehensive.

3. **Language Bridges**: Use side-by-side translations where students write a paragraph in their home language and then translate it into English. This helps them understand nuances and transfer skills between languages. It also assumes L1 literacy, so it may not be appropriate for all learners.

4. **Cultural Connections**: Encourage students to draw on their cultural backgrounds and experiences in their writing. They can include cultural references, idioms, and examples from their own lives, which makes their writing more authentic and engaging.

5. **Peer Collaboration**: Promote collaborative writing activities where students work in pairs or small groups, using their combined linguistic resources to produce a piece of writing. This can include peer review sessions where they give and receive feedback in multiple languages.

6. **Multimodal Resources**: Integrate visual aids, audio recordings, and digital tools that support writing in multiple languages. For instance, students can use bilingual dictionaries, translation apps, or multilingual word processors to assist with their writing.

7. **Scaffolding Techniques**: Provide writing frames, sentence starters, and graphic organizers in multiple languages to help students structure their writing. These tools can guide students in organizing their thoughts.

8. **Code Meshing**: A cousin to code-switching, code meshing encourages students to mix languages within a single piece of writing. This practice reflects their authentic language use and can make their writing more relatable and expressive.

9. **Translanguaging Journals**: Have students maintain journals where they can freely write using all of their linguistic resources. This ongoing practice helps them build confidence in their writing abilities.

10. **Bilingual Writing Prompts**: Provide writing prompts in both English and students' home languages. This approach ensures that students fully understand the prompt and can respond more thoughtfully and creatively.

By implementing these translanguaging pedagogies, educators can create a more inclusive and supportive writing environment that acknowledges and values the linguistic diversity of their students.

## Translanguaging Pedagogies that Support L1 Listening

Translanguaging pedagogies that support L1 listening are designed to improve students' listening comprehension and overall learning experience in all of their languages. Here are some examples:

1. **Bilingual Audio-Visual Resources**: Provide videos, podcasts, and audiobooks in both English and students' home languages. Students can listen first to the content in their L1 to build understanding before engaging with the English version.

2. **Multilingual Transcripts**: Offer transcripts of listening materials in both English and students' home languages. Students can follow along in their L1 to support comprehension as they listen in English.

3. **Bilingual Listening Guides**: Create listening guides or worksheets with key vocabulary and questions in both English and students' home languages. This provides scaffolding and helps students focus on essential information.

4. **Interactive Listening Activities**: Design activities where students listen to content in English and then discuss or summarize it in their home languages. This encourages deeper processing and understanding.

5. **Multilingual Peer Support**: Pair students with peers who share the same home language for listening activities. They can support each other in understanding and discussing the content.

6. **Bilingual Storytelling**: Use storytelling techniques that incorporate both English and students' home languages. For example, tell a story in English and provide explanations or elaborations in the home language(s) common in your classroom.

7. **Visual Aids with L1 Annotations**: Use visual aids, such as images, charts, and diagrams, with annotations in students' home languages. These aids can help students understand and retain information they hear in English.

8. **L1 Note-Taking**: Encourage students to take notes in their home languages while listening to content in English. This allows them to capture key points and details more effectively.

9. **L1 Listening Comprehension Questions**: Provide listening comprehension questions in students' home languages. This helps them focus on understanding the content rather than struggling with the language of the questions.

10. **Reflective Listening Practices**: Have students reflect on what they have heard in their home languages. This could be done through written reflections, group discussions, or journaling, helping them process and internalize the information.

Implementing these translanguaging pedagogies can enhance students' listening comprehension by making use of their entire linguistic repertoire, creating a more inclusive and effective learning environment.

## Translanguaging Pedagogies that Support L1 Speaking

Translanguaging pedagogies that support L1 speaking utilize students' home languages to enhance their speaking skills and overall communication abilities. Here are some effective strategies:

1. **Bilingual Discussion Groups**: Organize discussion groups where students can use both English and their home languages. This allows them to express complex ideas comfortably and then practice translating those ideas into English.

2. **Dual Language Presentations**: Encourage students to give presentations using both English and their home languages. They can start in their L1 to build confidence and then switch to English for parts of the presentation.

3. **Multilingual Role-Playing**: Create role-playing activities where students use both English and their home languages. This helps them practice real-life scenarios in a supportive and familiar linguistic context.

4. **Bilingual Storytelling**: Implement storytelling activities where students share stories in their home languages before translating them into English. This can help them focus on fluency and narrative skills in both languages.

5. **Translingual Conversations**: Encourage students to engage in conversations where they can switch between their home language and English. This mirrors natural bilingual communication and helps them practice fluid transitions.

6. **Peer Teaching in L1**: Allow students to teach a concept or skill to their peers using their home languages. They can then switch to English to teach the same concept, reinforcing their understanding and speaking abilities.

7. **Cultural Sharing Sessions**: Create opportunities for students to share cultural experiences, traditions, or customs in their home languages. This not only validates their cultural identity but also encourages them to articulate these experiences in English.

8. **Bilingual Debates**: Organize debates where students can argue points in both English and their home languages. This helps them develop persuasive speaking skills and practice expressing complex arguments bilingually.

9. **Language Buddies**: Pair students with language buddies who speak the same home language. They can practice speaking tasks together in their L1 before switching to English, providing mutual support and building confidence.

10. **L1 Support in Public Speaking**: When preparing for public speaking tasks, allow students to outline and rehearse their speeches in their home languages first. They can then practice delivering the speech in English with greater confidence and clarity.

By incorporating these translanguaging pedagogies, educators can create a supportive environment that leverages students' home languages to enhance their speaking abilities.

## Translanguaging Pedagogies that Support L1 Reading

Translanguaging pedagogies that support L1 reading involve strategies that use students' home languages to enhance their reading skills and comprehension. Here are some examples:

1. **L1 Prereading Activities**: Conduct prereading discussions and activities in students' home languages. This can include discussing key vocabulary, themes, and background information to activate prior knowledge and prepare students for the text.

2. **Multilingual Glossaries**: Create glossaries that include key terms in both English and students' home languages. Students can refer to these glossaries while reading to aid comprehension.

3. **Parallel Reading**: Encourage students to read a passage in their home language and then read the same passage in English. This helps them make connections between the two languages and enhances understanding.

4. **L1 Summarization**: After reading a text in English, have students summarize the main points or write reflections in their home languages. This reinforces comprehension and allows them to express their understanding more fully.

5. **Bilingual Annotations**: Allow students to annotate texts using both their home languages and English. They can make notes, highlight important information, and ask questions in their L1, which helps them engage more deeply with the text.

6. **Translanguaging Reading Groups**: Organize reading groups where students can discuss texts in both their home languages and English. This collaborative approach helps students support each other and enhances comprehension.

7. **Cultural Connections**: Select texts that reflect students' cultural backgrounds and experiences. Encourage students to draw connections between the text and their own lives, discussing these connections in their home languages.

8. **Dual-Language Storybooks**: Use storybooks written in both English and students' home languages. Younger students, in particular, can benefit from seeing and hearing stories in both languages.

9. **L1 Reading Comprehension Questions**: Provide reading comprehension questions in students' home languages. This ensures they fully understand the text and can think critically about it without language barriers.

10. **Bilingual Reading Logs**: Have students keep reading logs where they record their thoughts, summaries, and reflections in both their home languages and English. This encourages ongoing practice and engagement with both languages.

By integrating these translanguaging pedagogies, educators can support students' L1 reading skills while also enhancing their ability to read and comprehend texts in the target language.

There is a good reason why teaching is considered a craft. We may be presented with tools, such as those shared in this chapter, but ultimately we need to make our own instructional choices about how to attend to language in our classrooms. There is no one-size-fits-all in education. Take inventory of your learners. What linguistic assets do they bring? Where do they need more development? Once you are skilled at knowing and responding to your learners' linguistic strengths and needs, you are ready to coach your colleagues to do the same.

**Discussion Questions**

1. Reflect on the demand from the Conference on College Composition and Communication (p. 33) addressing anti-Black racism in education. Share your thoughts.
2. Which elements of noticing and forecasting do you already do? How could this frame be helpful to non-ELD teachers?
3. Of the five elements of language (phonology, morphology, semantics, syntax, and pragmatics), which do you feel most comfortable teaching? Which do you feel the least comfortable teaching? Why?
4. Why do you think language objectives are so difficult?

**Takeaway Task**

Working with a SWEL coach implies some vulnerability. It can help coachees to know that coaches are also not always confident in their skills. Consider the element of language that you feel least comfortable teaching and set a goal to teach that element. Afterward, discuss with your colleagues how it felt to push yourself out of your comfort zone.

## References

Baker-Bell, A., Williams-Farrier, B. J., Jackson, D., Johnson, L., Kynard, C., & McMurtry, T. (n.d.). *Demand 1*. Black Linguistic Justice. http://www.blacklanguagesyllabus.com/demand-1.html

Ballantyne, K. G., Sanderman, A. R., & McLaughlin, N. (2007). *Dual language learners in the early years: Getting ready to succeed in school*. National Clearinghouse for English Language Acquisition.

Benegas, M., & Benjamin, N. (2024). *Language of identity, language of access (LILA): Liberatory learning in multilingual classrooms*. Corwin.

Bloom, B. S. (1956). *Taxonomy of educational objectives, Handbook I: The cognitive domain*. David McKay.

Dutro, S., & Moran, C. (2003). Rethinking English language instruction: An architectural approach. In G. G. Garcia (Ed.), *English learners: Reaching the highest level of English literacy* (pp. 227–258). International Reading Association.

García, O. (2013). Theorizing translanguaging for educators. In C. Celic & K. Seltzer, *Translanguaging: A CUNY-NYSIEB guide for educators*. CUNY-NYSIEB. https://www.cuny-nysieb.org/wp-content/uploads/2016/04/Translanguaging-Guide-March-2013.pdf

García, O., Johnson, S. I., & Seltzer, K. (2017). *The translanguaging classroom: Leveraging student bilingualism for learning*. Caslon.

Indiana University. (n.d.). *Understanding academic language in edTPA: Supporting learning and language development*. https://education.indiana.edu/students/undergraduates/clinical-experiences/_docs/Academic%20Language.pdf

Minnesota Department of Education. (n.d.). *Minnesota comprehensive assessments—Series II, reading item sampler, grade 4*.

New South Wales Department of School Education (1992). *The action pack: Activities for teaching factual writing*. https://nla.gov.au/nla.cat-vn2660985

WIDA Consortium. (2012). *2012 amplification of the English language development standards: Kindergarten–Grade 12.* Board of Regents of the University of Wisconsin System. https://wida.wisc.edu/sites/default/files/resource/2012-ELD-Standards.pdf

Yosso, T. J. (2006). *Critical race counterstories along the Chicana/Chicano educational pipeline.* Routledge.

Zwiers, J. (2008). *Building academic language: Essential practices for content classrooms, grades 5–12.* Jossey-Bass.

# PART B

**Application of Teacher Professional Development of Dispositions, Knowledge, and Skills: Professional Development Plans**

# CHAPTER 4

# TEACHER DISPOSITIONS NEEDED TO EFFECTIVELY AND RESPECTFULLY SERVE MULTILINGUAL LEARNERS OF ENGLISH

*Sharon was one of the founders of Great Plains School, a K–8 school in the upper Midwest of the United States. She is an expert in the International Baccalaureate® model that the school uses and has trained other teachers in the model. Over 24 years of teaching at the school, she developed much of the curriculum for the lower school, which includes kindergarten through fifth grades. Her lessons are organized, scaffolded, and in line with the mission of the school. Over the better part of Sharon's career, the student body at Great Plains included socioeconomic diversity, but very little racial, linguistic, and cultural diversity. This changed after a large software company built its headquarters in town and a high number of families from China, India, and Bangladesh started enrolling their children at Great Plains. Given the past successes students had using the school's curriculum, Sharon has become increasingly frustrated by the fact that these new students do not experience the same successes and has concluded that they must not have strong family support like the other students in the school. These frustrations, which she has not felt before, lead her to consider early retirement, which she discusses frequently in the staff room with colleagues.*

A positive disposition toward working with multilingual learners of English (MLEs) is an essential characteristic in any teacher. Dispositions are perhaps the most difficult of the three areas necessary for serving students effectively (the other two being knowledge and skills) because they involve beliefs, mindset, and identity. For some adults, these areas are less malleable than others. Though there are a variety of teacher dispositions that are essential for working effectively and respectfully with MLEs, this chapter focuses on the following six critical teacher dispositions:

1. Educators empathize with circumstances related to immigration.
2. Educators are culturally sensitive and sustaining.
3. Educators believe that marginalization and oppression affect the educational experiences of multilingual learners of English.
4. Educators support their students' home language development.
5. Educators recognize the challenges of learning English and content simultaneously.
6. Educators are committed to ongoing professional development.

This chapter provides examples of how school-wide English learning (SWEL) coaches can support educators to develop the six critical dispositions needed to work effectively and respectfully with MLEs, with professional development (PD) plans attending to each disposition. Under each of the six dispositions, you will find engaging activities you can use when implementing PD with your colleagues.

> For additional videos and resources that highlight ways to address and cultivate dispositions for working with MLEs in the general education classroom, and for easy access to all of the resources used in these activities, see the companion site for this book, www.tesol.org/SWEL-book.

The PD plans are divided into parts that can be done as a whole or in segments over time, depending on the needs of the school context. Given the iterative nature of this work, it is also possible that the base components of a given PD activity have potential for a given school, but the details need to be tweaked to meet the needs of a specific school community. Teachers are experts at making these types of changes, and we encourage it. It is also worth noting that, with some small changes to the objective and focus, activities from the knowledge and skills chapters may also be used to address teacher dispositions.

## VOICES FROM THE FIELD

[The SWEL coach] has been so informative and helpful in sharing information and strategies. I appreciate how every PD meeting gave me something instantly tangible to put into practice and help my students. Every meeting with her was valuable and applicable to what was going on in my classroom at the time. *(SWEL coachee)*

# EDUCATORS EMPATHIZE WITH CIRCUMSTANCES RELATED TO IMMIGRATION

Currently, we are experiencing the greatest global refugee crisis in history. As mentioned in the introduction to this second edition, approximately 120 million people worldwide have been forcibly displaced due to persecution, conflict, and human rights violations. Around 43.4 million of them are refugees (UNHCR, 2024). Given this context, all educators are likely to work with immigrant students and their families at some point in their careers. Immigrants are in urban, suburban, and rural settings, where they enrich their communities socially and economically. Unfortunately, immigrants are not always warmly welcomed into communities, and this experience can have a traumatic impact on them. Unpleasant or offensive receptions compound trauma, particularly for those who left their countries of origin because of fear, war, poverty, or persecution.

Whenever choosing PD activities, it is critical to consider the needs of the communities that your school serves and to remind participants that, while the geopolitical conditions that influenced immigration may be similar within a given group of people, not all of your families will have the same experiences. There is tremendous diversity within the subgroup of students who fall into the MLE category, so this must be emphasized during any PD work on the subject. For example, not all immigrants are undocumented and not all immigrants experience trauma. The following activities are focused on how SWEL coaches can foster positive dispositions in their classroom/content teacher colleagues around immigrant and refugee families, as well as build a factual understanding of the immigrant experience and an appreciation for the individual ways in which immigration is experienced by MLEs and their families.

 **1. Immigration Facts**

| Objective | Participants will analyze common myths and realities related to immigration in order to develop a better understanding of the factual information related to those myths. |
|---|---|
| Time to Complete | 1 hour (10 minutes for small group discussions; 5 minutes per small group for large group presentation) |
| Materials and Resources | • Article: "Immigration Facts: The Positive Economic Impact of Immigration" (FWD.us, 2020; available at https://www.fwd.us/news/immigration-facts-the-positive-economic-impact-of-immigration/)<br>• Immigration Myth Cards (available on the companion site for this book, www.tesol.org/SWEL-book) |
| Preparation | Make front-and-back copies of the immigration myth cards. For each card, the myth should be on one side and the corresponding reality on the other. We recommend printing these cards in bright and different colors of paper. They can be standard printer paper, card stock, or laminated paper for reuse. You will print a total of 10 cards. |

**Directions**

1. Depending on the size of your group, give each participant a card or divide the participants into 10 small groups.

2. Provide enough time for each person or small group to read the front and back sides of their assigned card.

3. After a few minutes, ask them to stand up and hold their card with the myth facing outward. Then, they walk around the room, engage in conversations with colleagues or another small group, and insert the myth into their conversation, using the discussion questions on the back of the myth cards as prompts, if needed. The person holding the card is tasked with combating the myth as naturally as possible with the information on the "reality" side of the card. Continue for approximately 10 minutes or until all participants have discussed all myths. Participants should keep the same card for the duration of the exercise.

4. When finished with the walk-around, ask each individual or small group to return to their seats and go around the room sharing the myth and the reality of that myth with the whole group. This will ensure that all participants are able to learn about each myth.

 **2. Immigration Trauma Simulation**[1]

This activity can be difficult for some participants. We recommend the following trigger warning prior to starting the activity:

> TRIGGER WARNING: *This is a trauma simulation and can be very difficult, particularly for those who have experienced traumatic loss. We ask that you participate in the activity to the best of your ability. If at any point you are unable to continue participating in the activity, please feel free to move to the back of the room or step outside. You can rejoin the group when the simulation is completed.*

| Objective | Participants will develop a deeper understanding of the emotional effects of trauma. |
|---|---|
| Time to Complete | 30 minutes |
| Materials and Resources | • 1 sheet of paper for each participant<br>• Immigration Trauma Simulation Guide (available on the companion site for this book, www.tesol.org/SWEL-book, and printed in the Directions) |
| Preparation | None |

**Directions**

Use the following list as a guide to facilitate the simulation, but do not share it with participants. This activity is intended to build empathy for those who have lost loved ones and belongings as a result of tragedy. It is often emotional for participants and can make them very uncomfortable.

---

1 Based on York (2015).

Read each of the items on the following list. Repeat each one once and give participants a few minutes to complete each task.

1. On a piece of paper, make three columns.
2. In the first column, write the names of five people that you love and adore (pets can be included).
3. In the second column, write five things or objects that you love and adore—items with special meaning to you.
4. Share your list with your neighbor.
5. Cross off one item on each side. That person and thing are no longer in your life.
6. In the third column, write how it felt to cross that person and thing off your list.
7. Cross off another person and thing. Write another feeling.
8. Notice in your body where you are feeling what you are feeling.
9. Cross off number three. Discuss in your groups the feelings that you have written down.
10. Cross off one more person and one more thing. Write another feeling if you have one. Sit quietly and honor how you are feeling. Where/how do you feel that?
11. Cross the last person and thing off. Write down your feelings, unfiltered. You don't have to share.

**Discussion Questions**

1. How are the experiences of our students similar or different from this simulation?
2. What is the value of teachers understanding the physical effects of trauma?
3. How does this activity help you to gain perspective on some students you have taught?
4. What implications might students' traumatic experiences have for our instruction?

## EDUCATORS ARE CULTURALLY SENSITIVE AND SUSTAINING

Who we are culturally is so inherent to our sense of self that it is sometimes difficult to discern what is part of our personality and what is part of our cultural norms and practices. For students whose culture is not represented in schools—in the curricular materials, the posters on the walls, the language(s) spoken in the hallways, and the adults in charge of teaching and leading, among other ways—it can feel as if they do not belong or cannot succeed. It is the job of the adults in the school to ensure that all aspects of the school environment are both culturally sensitive and sustaining. Culturally sensitive spaces are ones that recognize that different cultures exist and that no one culture is better than or superior to another. Culturally sustaining schools are ones that recognize, value, and weave all cultures into the fabric of schooling (Paris & Alim, 2017). Drawing on the work of Ladson-Billings (1995) by honoring the rich experience and knowledge that MLEs bring to their classrooms, educators aim to build not only culturally sensitive, but also culturally sustaining learning communities.

**1. I Didn't Know . . .**

| Objective | Participants will reflect on situations in which their lack of familiarity with a given culture created misunderstanding or confused communication. |
|---|---|
| Time to Complete | 1 hour |
| Materials and Resources | • Video: "EDTalks: Kao Kalia Yang" (Achieve Twin Cities, 2015; www.youtube.com/watch?v=hCn84oHSl9g&t=241s)<br>• Handout: "I didn't know" Think, Pair, Share (available on the companion site for this book, www.tesol.org/SWEL-book)<br>• Laptop/computer, projector, screen, speakers |
| Preparation | Preview Yang's EDTalk and consider how you would respond to these prompts. If preferred, print reflection sheets for Part I and Part II. Alternatively, you could prepare a presentation slide with the prompts for each of the two sharing activities and have participants write their reflections on a piece of notebook paper. |

**Directions**

(The full handout is available for download on the companion site for this book, www.tesol.org/SWEL-book.)

*Part I*

Prior to watching Yang's EDTalk, ask participants to engage in the following think, pair, share prompts:

> A time when I was limited by my language or knowledge about a subject (e.g., when I filed my taxes, when I learned about a medical diagnosis, when I was at the auto mechanic):
>
> How I felt:
>
> How I reacted:
>
> How the "knower" responded to my lack of understanding:

*Part II*

After watching Yang's EDTalk, please fill in the blanks with examples of "not knowing" from your teaching experience. Include how you felt and how you reacted in each situation. When it is time to think, pair, share, include anecdotes about how you learned these lessons.

> I didn't know. . .
>
> I didn't know. . .
>
> I didn't know. . .

## 2. Making Sure Each Child Is Known

| Objective | Teachers can access, collect, and analyze qualitative and quantitative MLE data from multiple sources to inform instruction. |
|---|---|
| Time to Complete | 1 hour |
| Materials and Resources | • Video: "Making Sure Each Child Is Known" (Edutopia, 2017; youtu.be/xjZx0VdmgkE)<br>• Poster paper, tape, markers, student lists<br>• Laptop/computer, projector, screen, speakers |
| Preparation | Gather student and/or class lists, create posters or digital spreadsheets with every student's name (MLEs or all students).<br>Optional: Create a presentation slide with discussion questions. |

**Directions**

1. *Think, Pair, Share:* Open the activity by asking participants to consider why they think it is important for students to feel connected to at least one adult in the school. If time permits, ask several pairs to share out their ideas.

2. Show the video "Making Sure Each Child Is Known" (Edutopia, 2017), which models the activity they will be doing.

3. Choose **one** of the following options:

   a. Create premade grade or class-level lists of students.

   b. Have educators work in groups (by grade level, content-area team, a combination of those two groups, or in another small grouping that is logical and places together teachers who have a common group of students on their class lists), and they can create student lists on poster paper for hanging. This is a good option if your prep time is limited, but it will also require that you give more time for the activity.

4. Ask the participants to work in small groups to create charts. Have them list their students, place their initials next to students they know, and write one thing about that student that is an asset they bring to the classroom.

*Chart Sample*

| Student Name | I Know This Student Well. | Student Asset |
|:---:|:---:|:---:|
| Jose | AOS, MB | A good friend to other kids. |
|  |  |  |

5. Once a group is finished going through the list, identify the students who are not known. Designate one participant who will take the initiative during the first week of school to find out one or more asset(s) that the student brings to school.

6. As a whole group, debrief by asking one or more of the following questions or coming up with your own original debrief questions:

   a. How did this activity help to inform your understanding of the students we will be working with this school year?

   b. How might framing students through the lens of the assets they bring to the school shape the way you approach your classes this year?

7. Hang the posters in a common space used only by adults in the school (e.g., the teachers' lounge or conference room in the main office) so that the charts can be revisited to ensure that each student is known by an adult and has assets identified.

## EDUCATORS BELIEVE THAT MARGINALIZATION AND OPPRESSION AFFECT THE EDUCATIONAL EXPERIENCES OF MULTILINGUAL LEARNERS OF ENGLISH

Despite our best efforts to isolate schools from some of the more negative influences of the outside world and given our obligation to make schools a safe space for all students, it is imperative that we work to deepen our understanding of how systems of privilege and oppression play out in the ways that MLEs interact with and experience schooling. By systems of privilege, we are referring to the often unseen or unnamed ways in which the systems with which we interact every day grant advantages to one group of people over another, whether those people ask for these advantages or not. Often, privilege is difficult to discern because it is perceived as simply "how things are." For example, school vacations are often scheduled so that they fall during the holidays that are celebrated by the majority religion or culture. Like a fish, we do not necessarily see the water—it's just there. By design, systems of privilege create systems of oppression, where one or many groups of people are denied advantages because of their identity or identities. These systems are at play in the lives and education of our students, and we would be negligent to ignore them.

The work of learning about systems of privilege and oppression for the purpose of using them to inform our instructional decisions, with the ultimate aim of changing them to remodel inequitable systems, is ongoing and should be attended to throughout our careers. The following activities are designed to begin that work for those who are new to considering the relationship between privilege and oppression, and they can also build on the work that others have already done to help better understand the roles privilege and oppression play in our own lives and the lives of our students. Though the activities are not exhaustive, they each provide unique ways to shine a light on structures that are otherwise difficult to see—or, in other words, to become fish that are aware of the water in which we swim.

# 1. Critical Incidents in Immigrant Education

| Objective | Participants will analyze incidents in which cultural blind spots may affect a teacher's understanding of student behaviors and examine potential responses. |
|---|---|
| Time to Complete | 90 minutes |
| Materials and Resources | Handouts and coaching materials (available on the companion site for this book, www.tesol.org/SWEL-book): <br>• Critical Incidents in Immigrant Education Activity <br>• Critical Incidents in Immigrant Education Activity Teacher Trainer Guide |
| Preparation | Make copies of Part I of the handout and cut it into strips so that each slip of paper has one critical incident on it and make individual copies of Part II. <br><br>Optional: Prepare a presentation slide with discussion questions for Part III. |

**Introduction to the Activity; Background to Share With Participants**

There is no single definition for the concept of a cultural blind spot. For the purposes of this activity, we define a cultural blind spot as an area in which someone is unfamiliar with the lived experience of another person because of a lack of exposure. We all have cultural blind spots of one kind or another. Keep in mind that one of the many jobs of a teacher is to be an advocate for each and every student, but that is difficult to do without reflection on our own cultural blind spots, areas for learning and growth, and consideration of what an advocate for all students does.

The following activity, in full, is available for download on the companion site for this book, www.tesol.org/SWEL-book.

**Directions**

*Part I*

1. Divide the large group into small groups of three to four people.
2. Have small groups select one critical incident (slip of paper), discuss the incident, and then craft a response to the prompt. Each of these incidents has been chosen because they can or did really happen.
3. If time allows or some groups finish sooner than others, have small groups exchange slips of paper and discuss their new incident.

> **CRITICAL INCIDENTS**
>
> 1. You have planned an immigration unit that has been received really well by your fifth-grade students. As part of this unit, students are writing about the immigrant stories of their families. One of your highest achievers announces to the class that his mom came here from Mexico led by a man named "Coyote," and that she had to hide in the back of a van.
> **What might be happening here? What are your reasons for thinking this? What are some other possible interpretations? How might you respond? Why would you respond this way?**
>
> 2. After a new state law was passed, your district is now collecting information on the citizenship status of your students. Your immigrant students, regardless of their legal status, have stopped coming to school. **What might be happening here? What are your reasons for thinking this? Are there other possible interpretations? If so, what might they be? How might you respond? Why would you respond this way?**

*Part II*

1. Have participants, individually, write three critical incidents that they have experienced. Explain that a critical incident should be a time in which their own blind spots prevented them from understanding their students' experiences. Instruct them to leave the final questions (What might be happening here? How might you respond?) blank because their colleagues will be tasked with answering them.

2. Collect all of the critical incidents that were written by participants. Randomly distribute them to the group. Have each participant read over the incidents and spend 15–20 minutes writing a response.

3. When the time is up, ask participants to find the author of the critical incidents and compare their interpretation and reaction with that of the teacher that experienced it.

*Part III*

Conclude with a discussion using the following prompts:

1. What surprised you about your blind spots?

2. How can a blind spot result in implicit bias?

3. Though blind spots and implicit bias can never be entirely eliminated, how can educators work together toward providing an equitable education for all students?

**2. My Name Is Not**

| Objective | Participants self-reflect on the significance of their names as well as negative perceptions that others may have of them. |
|---|---|
| Time to Complete | 30 minutes |
| Materials and Resources | None |
| Preparation | Optional: Create a presentation slide with or put directions on the board for the three parts of this activity, listed under Part II. |

**Directions**

*Part I*

1. Ask participants to consider a name that others have called them or might call them that they dislike. It could be a negative descriptor, like "fat lady" or "stupid kid," or it could be a neutral descriptor but one that narrows their identity, like "immigrant" or "young man."

2. Next, ask them to consider their own name (any part of their name is fine) and what it means to them. They could think about the heritage behind their name, stories related to their name, the pronunciation of their name, or how their name makes them feel.

*Part II*

Ask participants to introduce themselves in small groups or a large group using the following sentence starters:

My name is not _____.

My name is _____.

My name reminds me of _____.

For example: *My name is not refugee. My name is Aminah. My name reminds me of my grandmother who used to take care of me when I was a baby. Her name was also Aminah.* This community-building activity serves as a nice icebreaker or warm-up activity, even in groups of colleagues who have known each other for a significant amount of time.

# EDUCATORS SUPPORT THEIR STUDENTS' HOME LANGUAGE DEVELOPMENT

It is well known that students' home language skills greatly influence the development of new languages. In our experience, this fact has felt counterintuitive to both teachers who are unfamiliar with research on language acquisition and even well-intentioned parents of MLEs, who push their children to use English to the exclusion of the home language because they think they will confuse their children if they encourage home language proficiency. Knowing that language and culture are strongly related to one another, it makes sense that attending to home language can help to cultivate and sustain a student's cultural identity, not to mention enrich the classroom environment.

The activities in this section are designed to bring attention to both the role of home language development in light of its relationship to culture, as well provide ways in which educators can allow for and even encourage the use of home language in the classroom, regardless of their own knowledge or proficiency in that language.

##  1. I Can't Speak My Mother Tongue

| Objective | Participants consider the impact of home language proficiency on student identity and experience. |
|---|---|
| Time to Complete | 1 hour |
| Materials and Resources | • Article: "Getting to Know Your ELLs: Six Steps for Success" (Breiseth, n.d.; www.colorincolorado.org/article/getting-know-your-ells-six-steps-success)<br><br>• Handout: Getting to Know the MLEs in Your Classroom (available on the companion site for this book, www.tesol.org/SWEL-book)<br><br>• Videos:<br><br>— "I CAN'T SPEAK MY MOTHER TONGUE (Music Video) - Fung Bros ft. Dough-Boy" (Fung Bros, 2016; www.youtube.com/watch?v=6luZyPv0mO0)<br><br>— Optional: "What to Do First in the ELL Classroom" (Prentice Jimenez, n.d.; www.colorincolorado.org/classroom-video/what-do-first-ell-classroom)<br><br>• Access to a computer, the internet, speakers, projector |
| Preparation | Make hard copies or share digital copies of the article, "Getting to Know Your ELLs: Six Steps for Success" and the Getting to Know the MLEs in Your Classroom handout.<br><br>Cue up the video.<br><br>Optional: Prepare presentation slides with discussion questions, student class lists. |

**Directions**

*Part I*

1. Begin by asking the group if a language other than English was spoken in their home when they were growing up or if their parents grew up in a home where a language other than English was spoken. Ask them to turn to the person next to them to share what that language was and if they are able to speak, read, or write it.

2. Show the music video. When finished, ask the group to divide into groups of three to four and discuss at least two of the following questions:

    a. What are the reasons students would not learn their mother tongue?

    b.   What are ways we can allow MLEs to bring home language into the classroom?

    c.   How do you think that home language proficiency impacts students' sense of identity? What does this video tell us about what our students want/need?

    d.   What does this say about the dichotomy of the world they live in?

    e.   How can we, as their teachers, support MLEs' linguistic and cultural backgrounds?

Part II

1. Share the Getting to Know the MLEs in your Classroom handout, in either hard or digital copy, with each teacher in the group. The handout can be adjusted to make it appropriate for a specific school setting.

**Getting to Know the ELs in Your Classroom**

Directions: After reading the Colorin Colorado article, fill out the following chart in order to make sure that you have key background information on the EL students in your classroom.

| Student Name | Where was my student born? | What brought my student and/or my student's family here? | What should I know about my student's family? | What language(s) does my student speak? | What kind of schooling has my student had? | What are my students' interests? |
|---|---|---|---|---|---|---|
| | | | | | | |
| | | | | | | |
| | | | | | | |
| | | | | | | |
| | | | | | | |
| | | | | | | |
| | | | | | | |
| | | | | | | |
| | | | | | | |
| | | | | | | |
| | | | | | | |

2. Working in grade-level teams or small groups composed of teachers who work with a similar or the same group of MLEs (e.g., third-grade teachers or the math department), fill out the chart with all of the MLEs in a given grade or class. It can be useful to have class lists available if this activity is being conducted during opening week or before school begins. Participants should be encouraged to use each other, and especially the ELD teachers, as resources to complete each column in the table.

Part III

Bring the group back together and ask them to reflect on, as a whole group, the following questions:

1. How will knowing this information on your MLEs' linguistic backgrounds help you better understand their work in your classroom?

2. What else do you need to know about your MLEs to attend to their home language learning?

3. What resources might you find in order to attend to your MLEs' home language in the classroom?

## 2. Crafting School Language Policies

| Objective | Participants craft school language policies that are aligned with their school values. |
|---|---|
| Time to Complete | 1 hour |
| Materials and Resources | • Video: "Importance of Students' Home Languages (First Languages)" (PeelSchools, 2017; www.youtube.com/watch?v=a1J-ftbFaMc) <br> • Handout: Crafting School Language Policies (available on the companion site for this book, www.tesol.org/SWEL-book) <br> • Access to a computer, the internet, speakers, projector <br> • Optional article: "It's Not Uncommon for Schools to Have Dozens of Home Languages—And Our Classrooms Need to Reflect That" (Blackley, 2019; www.weareteachers.com/many-different-home-languages) |
| Preparation | • Make hard copies or share digital copies of the Crafting School Language Policies handout. <br> • Cue up the video. |

**Directions**

*Part I*

1. Begin by asking the group to free-write and share responses to the following questions:
   a. Have you or a relative experienced language loss of, or exclusion from, a family language?
   b. If so, how did you or the family member experience this? If not, how would you imagine this experience feels?
2. Show the video. When finished, ask the group to divide into groups of three to four and discuss the following questions:
   a. What are some strategies presented in the video to support and maintain home language?
   b. How does your school currently work to preserve the home languages of students?
   c. How does your school collaborate with families to preserve home languages?

*Part II*

1. Distribute copies of the Crafting School Language Policies handout. Ask participants to fill out the first page of the document independently.
2. After all participants have filled out the first page, ask them to share their responses in groups of three or four.
3. On the second page of the guide, have each group collaboratively write five language policies for the school. When finished, ask a group representative to write their five policies on the board.

4. Cross off duplicates for any policies that appear more than once.
5. Ask participants to mark their top five policies with an X on the board.
6. Erase all policies but those five with the highest number of Xs. Transfer them to a new document and disseminate. Refer to these policies often.

## EDUCATORS RECOGNIZE THE CHALLENGES OF LEARNING ENGLISH AND CONTENT SIMULTANEOUSLY

MLEs in pre-K–12 schools, unless they are in a bilingual program that focuses on their home language, are doing double duty when it comes to learning. Not only are they learning the content-area materials and being measured against state and national standards, they are doing so at the same time they are learning the language in which all of the material is being taught. This greatly increases the cognitive load for MLEs as compared to most of their English-proficient peers and means that they are likely under even greater pressure than most students.

It is easy to forget what it feels like to learn a new language once proficiency in that language has been achieved, especially if the language was acquired as a child and over the course of a lifetime. The activities in this section aim to demonstrate the complexity of language learning and, in some cases, the English language in particular. Without having to use a language other than English, each activity sheds light on the ways in which unfamiliar language creates increased cognitive demand. Educators who participate in these activities may come to realize that English is simply one of many vehicles with which to deliver content and that even the most proficient English speaker can struggle with the English language.

 **1. Vowel Sort**[2]

| Objective | Participants will develop a deeper understanding of the complexity of English vowel sounds and spelling. |
|---|---|
| Time to Complete | 1 hour |
| Materials and Resources | Available on the companion site for this book (www.tesol.org/SWEL-book):<br>• Vowel Sort Cards<br>• Vowel Sort Answer Key |
| Preparation | • Print the cards and the answer key. Each group of 3–5 participants will need 1 set of word cards and 1 answer key.<br>• Cut out the vowel sort cards. Put each set of words together in a clear plastic bag and pair with an answer key.<br>• Optional: Prepare a presentation slide with the discussion questions from Part III. |

---

[2] Adapted from "Bringing the Applied Alive in an Online MA TESOL Program" [Conference session], by B. Parrish, 2017, March 21–24, TESOL International Convention, Seattle, WA, United States. Adapted with permission.

**Directions**

*Part I*

1. Divide participants into groups of three to five. They will need a large, flat surface to do this activity, so they should work at a table or on the floor.

2. Give each group one set of word cards. Instruct all participants to organize the words on the cards into groups of words that have the same vowel sound. Ask them to raise their hands when they believe that they have put all the words into the correct groups. Typically, groups need about 8–12 minutes to sort the cards. They include vowel groups like the following:

| red | meant | said | friend | many |
| white | height | kite | light | eye |
| turquoise | boys | noise | foil | toys |

*Part II*

Distribute the answer key to groups that have finished sorting. They may give themselves 1 point for each category that has all words included and no additional words. Note how many points each group has and announce the winner.

*Part III*

Ask participants to discuss the following questions in their small groups:

1. How did you experience this activity?
2. How were you able to determine which words belonged in which category?
3. Do you believe that your MLEs would have been able to use the same skills that you used to group the words? Why or why not?
4. Knowing that English spelling is very difficult, what scaffolds can you create for MLEs so that they are able to demonstrate mastery of content?
5. Knowing that English pronunciation is very difficult, what scaffolds, considerations, and accommodations can you create for MLEs so that they are able to demonstrate mastery of content?

##  2. Communication Simulation[3]

*This activity is an excellent icebreaker for the start of a session at the beginning of the day.*

| Objective | Participants will experience a dialogue simulation in which their need to focus on language is greater than their need to focus on content (what they want to say). |
|---|---|
| Time to Complete | 1 hour |

---

[3] Based on Newton (2017).

| Materials and Resources | • Image: My Morning Routine (McGuire, n.d.; available at pixabay.com/photos/woman-hair-drying-girl-female-586185. Use an alternate visual if you choose a different prompt)<br>• Computer, projector, screen |
|---|---|
| Preparation | • Prepare picture prompt on a presentation slide.<br>• Optional: Prepare a presentation slide with (or write on the board) discussion questions from Part II. |

**Directions**

*Part I*

1. Ask all participants to divide into partners, assigning one person the role of Partner A and the other Partner B. In the case of an odd number, one group can have two Partner As. Give the following instructions:

    This activity will happen in two parts. For the first part, Partner A will be given a task. For the second part, Partner B will be given a task. Do not move on until instructed to do so.

Project the My Morning Routine Image: Image Source: McGuire, R. (n.d.). Woman drying hair. pixabay.com/photos/woman-hair-drying-girl-female-586185

2. Let participants know that they will have 3 minutes to complete this task. Set a timer, if possible. You can also adjust the time to 2 minutes for each partner if you have less time or want to have more time for Part II. Ask Partner A to describe their typical morning routine for a work day. Partner B's only job is to listen.

3. After 3 minutes have passed, quiet the group and tell them that they will also have 3 minutes for the next task. Partner B will now take a turn describing their morning routine. However, when Partner B is talking, they may not use any words containing the letter *R*, *whether at the beginning, middle, or end of the word*. Emphasize that Partner A should just listen.

*Part II*

1. Lead a reflection on the experience using the following prompts:

   a. Partner As: How did you experience this activity? What did you feel when you were talking? What did you feel when you were listening?

   b. Partner Bs: How did you experience this activity? What did you feel when you were talking? What did you feel when you were listening?

   c. This was a simulation in which some had to think about language more than content. What connections can you make between this activity and the MLEs in your classes?

2. You will want to elicit responses that help participants to draw links between what MLEs might be experiencing in the content-area classroom. Typical responses from people who were Partner B include, "I knew more than I could say," and "It was exhausting." These are opportunities to make connections to possible feelings that MLEs have at school.

## EDUCATORS ARE COMMITTED TO ONGOING PROFESSIONAL DEVELOPMENT

A best-selling author on leadership and management, John C. Maxwell, has said that "Change is inevitable. Growth is optional." To that end, change is also a constant in education, given that we have yet to "perfect" or arrive at a fail-proof way of educating all students. Evolving in your teaching practice is ultimately a necessary choice. This means that a preservice teacher education program is simply the beginning of any teacher's professional learning journey. By entering the profession, teachers are essentially committing to lifelong learning because new dispositional frames, educational theories, and pedagogies are constantly being explored. Classrooms are the testing grounds for these developments, which means that they are, in a sense, laboratories for innovation and need teachers who embody the spirit of a social scientist and innovator. After all, what better place is there for lifelong learning than a school? The following activities provide concrete ways to attend to teacher dispositions on continuing their professional evolution.

---

### VOICES FROM THE FIELD

I think just being able to work with teachers as their peer and help them with areas of need in order to best support their MLEs was a success in itself. I felt that engaging in conversations during planning time or [professional learning communities], we, as a team, were able to dive deeper into our instruction the further into the year we went. . . . The biggest success was getting into the classroom of one young colleague who, though she did not particularly like having anybody "watch her teach," came to look forward to our times together because she knew she'd be getting some "reflection time and more good ideas to use with her kids." I am pleased that we'll continue to work together next year. *(SWEL coach)*

**1. Uncovering Education Myths**

| Objective | Participants will recognize some of the ways in which practices that were once deemed effective have changed over time. |
|---|---|
| Time to Complete | 40 minutes |
| Materials and Resources | • Handout: Uncovering Education Myths (available on the companion site for this book, www.tesol.org/SWEL-book)<br>• Optional: timer or watch to keep track of speed dating[4] rounds |
| Preparation | • Make hard copies or share digital copies of the handout.<br>• Set up the room so that there is space for movement.<br>• Optional: Create a presentation slide or write the discussion questions from Part III on the board. |

**Directions**

*Part I*

1. Hand out or share digital copies of the Uncovering Education Myths handout, which includes five practices that are no longer considered accurate and two blank spaces for additional myths to be added.

| We used to believe . . . | Now we believe . . . |
|---|---|
| More homework equals more learning. | |
| Students just need exposure to texts in order to learn how to read. | |

Full document available on the companion site at www.tesol.org/SWEL-book

2. Ask each participant to fill out the right-hand column of the form to complete the statement, "Now we believe . . ." for each of the debunked educational practices listed in the left-hand column.

3. Ask each participant to write one or two debunked practices in the blank rows in the left-hand column, and write what we now believe about those practices in the corresponding right-hand columns. Some may have trouble coming up with ideas, so feel free to give prompts and/or let participants know that they can leave it blank and save it for later.

---

[4] Speed dating, also known as speed networking, is an instructional method where participants spend just a few minutes talking with a partner before switching to a new partner.

*Part II*

Tell the participants that they are going to participate in seven 2-minute rounds of speed dating. The directions for speed dating are as follows:

1. Have everyone find a partner.

2. When everyone has a partner (or one group of three if there's an odd number), ask them to discuss the Debunked Practice #1 and their thoughts on what we believe today. Set the timer for 2 minutes.

3. After 2 minutes pass, call the group back to attention and tell them to find a new partner. Ask them to discuss the Debunked Practice #2 and their thoughts on what we believe about it today. Set the timer for 2 minutes. Continue like this through #5, always encouraging people to talk to someone new with each speed dating switch.

4. After the speed dating Round 5, tell the group that they are now going to exchange what they wrote for their own debunked practice or belief. Set the timer for 2 minutes and allow discussion for #6 and #7. For those who struggled to come up with one or two debunked practices, prompt the partners to discuss what has changed since they started teaching and why those changes were made.

*Part III*

After completing all seven rounds of speed dating, ask participants to return to their original seats and debrief with the following discussion questions:

1. What do all of the debunked practices have in common?

2. What makes an educational practice go from accepted to debunked?

3. Why is it important to stay informed as a teacher?

4. What implications does this have for your own professional learning?

##  2. Know Better, Do Better

| Objective | Participants understand that new learning leads to change. |
|---|---|
| Time to Complete | 30–60 minutes |
| Materials and Resources | Know Better, Do Better Conversation Cards (available on the companion site for this book, www.tesol.org/SWEL-book) |
| Preparation | Print out a conversation cards sheet for each group of educators. We recommend 3–4 people in each group. Cut all 8 cards and put decks on tables. |

**Directions**

This activity is based on Maya Angelou's famous quote, "I did then what I knew how to do. Now that I know better, I do better" (Winfrey, 2011). Teacher participants will engage in conversation about the ways in which the knowledge base of a variety of professions, including education, has evolved over time.

*Part I*

1. Ask each table group to discuss the prompts on the four cards with print. They are unrealistic examples of outdated knowledge from a variety of professions, such as the following:

   > You just learned that your blurred vision is due to an issue that will require surgery on both of your eyes. Your doctor explains that he was trained in the early 1990s and doesn't keep up with modern medical practices but assures you that all will go well.

2. After reading each card, the group should discuss:

   a. What has changed in this professional knowledge base?

   b. What impact could an out-of-date knowledge base have in this scenario?

   c. What would you recommend in this circumstance?

   d. Why is it important for each of these professionals to stay current in their knowledge?

*Part II*

1. Ask participants to choose a blank card and write a similar unrealistic scenario from the field of education. If they have a specialization in a particular content area or approach, encourage them to pull from that area.

2. After they have finished, ask them to complete the same exercise with the new cards. After reading each card, the group should discuss:

   a. What has changed in this professional knowledge base?

   b. What impact could an out-of-date knowledge base have in this scenario?

   c. What would you recommend in this circumstance?

   d. Why is PD important in the field of education?

   e. How do you seek out opportunities for PD?

---

**VOICES FROM THE FIELD**

Teachers at my building are asking how to support MLEs in their classes and giving a lot of positive feedback after the PD sessions. Teachers told me that they looked forward to the MLE professional development sessions and started using strategies in their classrooms right away. Giving English language development (ELD) teachers the space to offer professional development in our building gave us a lot more agency in our school, and helped [the classroom/content teachers] realize the urgency of the language need after looking at the data together. *(SWEL coach)*

**Discussion Questions**

1. Which of the six teacher dispositions is strongest in your school?
2. Which of the six teacher dispositions is most in need of development in your school?
3. Which PD plan stood out to you as one that you would like to use with your colleagues? Why?

**Takeaway Task**

Considering the teacher disposition that is in most need of development in your school, plan to deliver PD. Choose one of the PD plans that falls under that disposition or use one of your own. This can be for the whole staff or a small group and it can be facilitated by one or by many ELD teachers. Share out how it went.

## References

Achieve Twin Cities. (2015, April 6). *EDTalks: Kao Kalia Yang* [Video]. YouTube. https://www.youtube.com/watch?v=-gO1cDGTPdc

Blackley, A. (2019, April 16). *It's not uncommon for schools to have dozens of home languages—and our classrooms need to reflect that*. We Are Teachers. https://www.weareteachers.com/many-different-home-languages/

Breiseth, L. (n.d.). *Getting to know your ELLs: Six steps for success*. Colorín Colorado. https://www.colorincolorado.org/article/getting-know-your-ells-six-steps-success

Edutopia. (2017, October 27). *Making sure each child is known* [Video]. YouTube. https://www.youtube.com/watch?v=xjZx0VdmgkE&feature=youtu.be

Fung Bros ft. Dough-Boy (2016, August 4). *I can't speak my mother tongue (music video) - Fung Bros ft. Dough-Boy* [Video]. YouTube. https://www.youtube.com/watch?v=6IuZyPv0mO0

Fwd.us. (2020, July 21). *Immigration facts: The positive economic impact of immigration*. https://www.fwd.us/news/immigration-facts-the-positive-economic-impact-of-immigration

Ladson-Billings, G. (1995). Toward a theory of culturally relevant pedagogy. *American Education Research Journal, 32*(3), 465–491.

McGuire, R. (n.d.). Woman drying hair [Image]. Pixabay. https://pixabay.com/photos/woman-hair-drying-girl-female-586185/

Newton, A. (2017, August). *Purposeful lesson planning for linguistically diverse learners* [WIDA training presentation]. Minnesota Department of Education.

Paris, D., & Alim, H. M. (2017). *Culturally sustaining pedagogies: Teaching and learning for justice in a changing world*. Teachers College Press.

Parrish, B. (2017). *Bringing the applied alive in an online MA TESOL program* [Conference session]. TESOL International Convention, Seattle, WA, United States.

PeelSchools. (2017, November 8). *Importance of students' home languages (first languages)* [Video]. YouTube. https://www.youtube.com/watch?v=a1J-ftbFaMc

Prentice Jimenez, A. (n.d.). *What to do first in the ELL classroom*. Colorín Colorado. https://www.colorincolorado.org/classroom-video/what-do-first-ell-classroom

United Nations High Commissioner for Refugees (UNHCR). (n.d.). *Refugee facts*. https://www.unrefugees.org/refugee-facts/what-is-a-refugee/

Winfrey, O. (2011, October 19). *The powerful lesson Maya Angelou taught Oprah* [Video]. Oprah's Life Class. http://www.oprah.com/oprahs-lifeclass/the-powerful-lesson-maya-angelou-taught-oprah-video

York, S. G. (2015, March 27). *Trauma informed skills for educators—Stacy G. York, LCSW—1 of 3* [Video]. YouTube. https://youtu.be/bE_X8hOnT8A

# CHAPTER 5

# TEACHER KNOWLEDGE NEEDED TO EFFECTIVELY AND RESPECTFULLY SERVE MULTILINGUAL LEARNERS OF ENGLISH

*Marcus has been teaching high school algebra for 5 years in a rural school that has seen a significant influx of immigrant families from Latin America in recent years. Marcus is thrilled to welcome this new population to the community. In fact, he frequently attends community meetings and advocates for the families of his students. His students love him. In his time at Chapman High, he has fine-tuned his curriculum and it's become such a well-oiled machine that he has not needed to change it for the last 2 years. Multilingual learners of English (MLEs) express that they are embarrassed to tell him that they do not understand his lessons because they know that his heart is in the right place. Marcus has the disposition to work with MLEs and the skills to develop curriculum, but not the knowledge needed to craft culturally and linguistically responsive lessons.*

In many ways, Marcus is perfectly positioned to meet the needs of MLEs in his math classroom. His enthusiasm for working with MLEs and his ability to write and teach his own curriculum means that his professional development (PD) needs fit neatly within the frame of building background in language acquisition and developing a base of knowledge related to how MLEs experience schooling. This learning can be done through hands-on and engaging PD activities. This chapter focuses on the following six knowledge frames for educators:

1. Educators know about second language acquisition and approaches to teaching language through content.

2. Educators know about approaches to supporting home language development.
3. Educators know about the theories of cultural relevance and sustainability.
4. Educators know who immigrants are and how immigration happens.
5. Educators know systems of oppression and how they affect the educational experiences of multilingual learners of English.
6. Educators know approaches to advocacy and the legal requirements for adequately serving multilingual learners of English.

Each section in this chapter provides PD activities that will help to cultivate these knowledge areas for classroom/content teachers or for those who have not completed coursework that focused on second language teaching and learning. You will notice that all of the activities in this section begin with a task that asks teacher participants to read an informational text or watch an informational video. To build a knowledge base, it is critical that educators seek out ways to learn from other experts in the field. Like all of the PD activities provided in this book, adaptations can and should be made in order to best meet the needs of a specific staff and school setting. Where appropriate, we have included suggestions for adaptation or modification. It is also worth noting that, with some small changes to the objective and focus, activities from the dispositions and skills chapters may also be used to address teacher knowledge.

> For additional videos and resources that highlight ways to address and cultivate knowledge for working with MLEs in the general education classroom, and for easy access to all of the resources used in these activities, see the companion site for this book, www.tesol.org/SWEL-book.

## EDUCATORS KNOW ABOUT SECOND LANGUAGE ACQUISITION AND APPROACHES TO TEACHING LANGUAGE THROUGH CONTENT

### VOICES FROM THE FIELD

During our PD slide show, we showed and discussed more about how a second language is learned since almost all of our students speak a second language, and it's ideal to have that background knowledge while teaching. *(SWEL coach)*

For those of us who are monolingual English speakers, we have probably experienced what it is like to study or learn a language other than the one we speak in our homes. Whether this was a one-class-per-day requirement or enrollment in a dual immersion bilingual program during the K–12 schooling experience (or something else entirely), most people who completed their secondary education have had at least a smattering of exposure to second language learning, if for no other reason than world language credits were required for graduation. It would be remiss not to mention that such schooling is done within the security of being part of the linguistic majority, where leaving the world language classroom places you back into spaces where your home language is commonly used. Regardless, these experiences can serve as the groundwork for understanding how it feels to be working in an unfamiliar language.

Even with experience in language learning, few people outside of linguists, English language development (ELD) teachers, and world language teachers have given much attention to what the process of learning a second language is like. What is happening in the brain? What comes first or most easily? What are some challenges in language learning? Going even further, how many of us have thought about what that experience would have been like if our math or science classes were taught entirely in a new language and our grade depended on our ability to both comprehend and perform in the content area *through* the second language? The following activities are designed to help educators better understand the second language learning process by connecting it to their own learning experiences.

## 1. The Five Stages of Second Language Acquisition

| Objective | Participants will learn the five stages of second language acquisition and consider their classroom applications. |
|---|---|
| Time to Complete | 1 hour |
| Materials and Resources | • Video: "Stages of Second Language Acquisition: ELD, ELL, LEP & Bilingual" (Teachings in Education, 2016; www.youtube.com/watch?v=Hk7_lBaFC5w&feature=youtu.be)<br>• Handout: Five Stages of SLA Activity Sheet (available on the companion site for this book, www.tesol.org/SWEL-book)<br>• Large enough open space to form a circle of participants standing<br>• Laptop/computer, projector, screen, speakers |
| Preparation | Make copies of the handout for all participants (back-to-back and stapled). |

**Directions**

*Part I*

1. Tell participants that they will be learning about the five stages of second language acquisition (SLA). Distribute the Five Stages of SLA Activity Sheet and ask participants to take notes in the gray spaces of each sheet while watching the "Stages of Second Language Acquisition" video.

2. Show the video.

3. Once participants have finished watching the video, provide additional time for them to reflect on the questions relating to their experience at each stage. They can write their reflection in the space provided on the activity sheet.

*Part II*

1. For this activity, called "Inside-Outside Circle," the participants will discuss the responses that they just wrote down. They can bring their notes with them or speak from memory.

2. Divide the group in half. Instruct half of the group to stand up and form a circle, facing outward. Instruct the second half to form another circle around them, facing inward. Each person on the inside of the circle should face another person on the outside of the circle.

3. Inform the participants they will be discussing prompts with the person across from them (both listen and share). After each prompt, the outside circle will rotate one space clockwise. Provide the following prompts with 1–4 minutes of talk time per question, depending on the needs of the group.

   a. Share your personal experience with the silent period stage of second language acquisition.

   b. Share your personal experience with the early production stage of second language acquisition.

   c. Share your personal experience with the speech emergence stage of second language acquisition.

   d. Share your personal experience with the intermediate fluency stage of second language acquisition.

   e. Share your personal experience with the advanced fluency stage of second language acquisition.

   f. Share your experience teaching a student in the silent period stage of second language acquisition.

   g. Share your experience teaching a student in the early production stage of second language acquisition.

   h. Share your experience teaching a student in the speech emergence stage of second language acquisition.

   i. Share your experience teaching a student in the intermediate fluency stage of second language acquisition.

   j. Share your experience teaching a student in the advanced fluency stage of second language acquisition.

*Part III*

Ask participants to discuss the following questions in small groups or as a large group:

1. How did you experience each stage of second language acquisition? Were some stages more frustrating than others? More exciting or interesting? Why?

2. Consider your MLEs. Who is at each of these stages? How do you know?

3. Why does each stage take longer than the last? What implications does this have for teaching and assessing MLEs?

## 2. Content Area Language Challenge

| Objective | Participants will demonstrate their knowledge of ways to scaffold content-area materials for multiple English language levels. |
|---|---|
| Time to Complete | 1 hour |
| Materials and Resources | • Article: "ELD Matrix of Grammatical Forms" (Dutro et al., 2007); https://www.knoxeducation.com/sites/main/files/file-attachments/susana_dutro_eld_matrix_11x17.pdf) <br><br> • Handouts: <br>   — Vitamin D Passage (available on the companion site for this book, www.tesol.org/SWEL-book, and printed in Part I) <br>   — Content Area Language Challenge Sheet (available on the companion site for this book) <br><br> • A textbook or piece of text that is used in classroom/content instruction (this should reflect the content areas taught by the participants) <br><br> • Optional: poster board |
| Preparation | • Ask participants to bring a text from a subject or one of the subjects they teach. <br><br> • Print the Vitamin D Passage on half-sheets of paper and write it on the board or post on poster paper so that all participants can see it. <br><br> • Print or share the digital copy of the Content Area Language Challenge sheet. <br><br> • Prepare the guiding questions in Part II so that they can be posted during work time. |

**Directions**

*Part I*

1. As participants arrive, hand them a half-sheet with the Vitamin D passage printed on it. In addition, post the passage on a board, poster paper, or other type of screen so that all participants can see it:

    It turns out that people who live in northern climates may not get enough vitamin D because the sun is not strong during the long winter months. Sometimes referred to as the sunshine vitamin, our bodies create vitamin D when we are exposed to the sun, and it is important for keeping our bones strong. In fact, vitamin D helps our bodies make use of the calcium that we get in foods like cow's milk, cheese, yogurt, salmon, and beans. Rickets is a disease that can be caused by not getting enough vitamin D. Not getting enough sun is one possible reason why a person might not be getting enough vitamin D. An additional reason for having a vitamin D deficiency includes not consuming enough vitamin D rich foods. For people who live in northern climates with extended winters and short daylight hours, it may be necessary to take a vitamin D supplement. (Spritzler, 2018)

2. Ask participants to stand up and find a partner. They should bring their slip of paper and a writing utensil with them. When everyone has a partner, ask them to discuss the following question:

   *How would you teach the words that are bolded?*

3. After about 3 minutes, ask the participants to find a new partner. When ready, give them the following question prompt:

   *Now that you have discussed how to teach the words that are bolded, what do you notice about the ways that the sentences are structured and the text is put together?*

   You may invite the participants to jot down notes on their pieces of paper.

4. After about 4 minutes, ask the participants to find another new partner. When ready, give them the following question prompt:

   *Assuming this is a grade level–appropriate text, what might you need to teach in order to ensure comprehension for MLEs of all levels?*

5. After about 4 minutes, call the group back together.

Part II

1. Ask the participants to return to their seats. Share out key takeaways from the activity in Part I (approximately 5 minutes).

2. When finished, share or hand out hard copies of the "ELD Matrix of Grammatical Forms," which participants may refer to if they are unsure of which structures are developmentally appropriate for each language level. Tell the participants that they are going to examine their own curriculum materials, either individually or in small groups, and analyze their text, looking for ways to make it accessible for MLEs at Levels 1 (beginning), 2 (early intermediate), 3 (intermediate), and 4 (early advanced). They should fill out the Content Area Language Challenge sheet to document their analysis. It may be worth encouraging participants to consider using this activity to analyze the text for an upcoming lesson so that they can put their work to use sooner rather than later.

3. On the board or other screen, post the following guiding questions that individuals or small groups should consider while working:

   - Which words, including but not limited to the bolded vocabulary words, might be new to MLEs at Levels 1, 2, 3, and 4?

   - What syntax or sentence structures might be new to or require explicit instruction for MLEs at Levels 1, 2, 3, and 4?

   - What resources do you need in order to make the text more accessible to MLEs at Levels 1, 2, 3, and 4 (e.g., picture cards, sentence starters, sentence stems, outlines, home language translations)?

4. Provide enough work time for the participants to fill out most or all of the Content Area Language Challenge sheet, approximately 30 minutes. Float around the room and provide assistance where needed, ask probing questions, and track the progress being made by individuals or small groups.

*Part III*

Call the whole group back together and debrief using the following discussion questions:

- Describe how this exercise may have influenced or changed the way you understand the text you brought today.
- How did you decide to scaffold your text for MLEs who are working at Levels 1 and 2?
- How did you decide to scaffold your text for MLEs who are working at Levels 3 and 4?
- What are some of the key takeaways from this exercise in terms of understanding the language demands of the texts that you use in your teaching?

## EDUCATORS KNOW ABOUT APPROACHES TO SUPPORTING HOME LANGUAGE DEVELOPMENT

Recognizing the importance of home language maintenance and cultivation is a disposition that we hope all educators embody. Believing in the importance of supporting home language development and literacy, however, is very different from knowing why and how to do it. Experts in language learning know that literacy in a second language leverages the literacy skills in the home language and expedites the learning process for most students. We learn the act of reading once and then apply those skills to other languages in which we learn to read and write. This work of learning about the act of reading is much more efficient in the home language, which is why home language literacy is so valuable to our MLEs. Of course, this is just one of many examples of why home language development has such positive benefits. The following activities are designed to help classroom/content teachers or those without ELD training better understand the role of home language use, cultivation, and learning.

 **1. To Translate or Not To Translate, That Is the Question!**

| Objective | Teachers can name when direct translation in writing or speaking is useful and how to scaffold for students when translation does not provide enough support. |
|---|---|
| Time to Complete | 60 minutes (30 minutes if prereading assigned) |
| Materials and Resources | • Article: "When Is It OK to Use Google Translate in the English-Learner Classroom?" (Ferlazzo, 2024); www.edweek.org/teaching-learning/opinion-the-use-or-misuse-of-google-translate-in-the-ell-classroomwhen-is-it-ok-to-use-google-translate-in-the-english-learner-classroom/2024/06<br><br>• Handout: To Translate or Not To Translate, That Is the Question! Worksheet (available for download on the companion site for this book, www.tesol.org/SWEL-book) |

| Preparation | • Ask participants to bring a copy of an upcoming lesson plan in which they plan to use translation to support MLEs, to be taught at least 3 days after the PD session. |
|---|---|
| | • Print or share the digital copy of "When Is It OK to Use Google Translate in the English-Learner Classroom?" (If you would like participants to read the article before the PD session, share it digitally at least 3 days in advance.) |
| | • Print or share the digital copy of the To Translate or Not To Translate, That Is the Question! worksheet. |

**Directions**

Skip to Part II if you assigned prereading of the article.

*Part I*

1. Ask the participants to raise their hand if they use translation to support MLEs in their classroom. Ask them to contribute how they use translation (e.g., live translation through Google Translate [https://translate.google.com], written translation for school assignments, etc.).

2. Distribute hard copies of or share the link to the digital version of "When Is It OK to Use Google Translate in the English-Learner Classroom?" Be sure to give everyone enough time to complete the reading.

3. If some participants finish reading quickly, ask them to write down a few notes on what was familiar and what was new from the article.

*Part II*

1. Ask the participants to take out the lesson plan they brought and, working individually, consider the questions in the To Translate or Not To Translate, That Is the Question! worksheet and fill in their answers and thoughts.

2. Ask participants to turn and talk to a partner about the following questions:

    a. Will translation be a benefit to students in this particular lesson?

    b. Will translation enhance student understanding of the lesson content?

    c. What other scaffolds could be used in addition to or instead of translation?

*Part III*

1. Depending on the number of participants, create evenly sized small groups. (If the session is smaller, Part III can be completed as a whole group activity.)

2. Ask small groups to create posters with scaffolds that can be used in addition to or instead of translations.

3. Ask the groups to present their lists of ideas. Alternatively, the groups can hang their posters and do a gallery walk to see what the other groups brainstormed. It can be helpful to assign ELD teachers to each small group, if possible, to help direct the discussion.

*Part IV*

Call the whole group back together and debrief using the following discussion questions:

- What new thinking do you have about the use of translation as a scaffold for MLEs?
- How does this new knowledge influence the lesson plan you brought with you today?
- What questions do you have? Is there any additional information you need on this topic?

 **2. Benefits of Bilingualism**

| Objective | Participants will understand the cultural, social, and cognitive benefits of bilingualism and multilingualism. |
|---|---|
| **Time to Complete** | 45 minutes |
| **Materials and Resources** | Articles:<br>• "Why Bilinguals Are Smarter" (Bhattacharjee, 2012; www.nytimes.com/2012/03/18/opinion/sunday/the-benefits-of-bilingualism.html)<br>• "MIT Scientists Prove Adults Learn Language to Fluency Nearly as Well as Children" (Chacon, 2018; medium.com/@chacon/mit-scientists-prove-adults-learn-language-to-fluency-nearly-as-well-as-children-1de888d1d45f)<br>• "Bilingualism: What Happens in the Brain?" (Hewings-Martin, 2017; www.medicalnewstoday.com/articles/319642.php)<br>• Infographic: "10 Amazing Benefits of Being Bilingual" (Bilingual Kidspot, 2017; bilingualkidspot.com/2017/05/23/benefits-of-being-bilingual)<br>• Poster paper, markers |
| **Preparation** | • Print or electronically share the materials and resources with participants.<br>• Prepare poster paper by writing a prompt at the top of each (see Part II for prompts) |

**Directions**

*Part I*

1. Divide the participants into four groups by numbering off one through four. Explain that this is a jigsaw reading activity. Each person will be assigned to the following reading based on their group number:

    **Group 1:** "Why Bilinguals Are Smarter" (Bhattacharjee, 2012)

    **Group 2:** "MIT Scientists Prove Adults Learn Language to Fluency Nearly as Well as Children" (Chacon, 2018)

**Group 3:** "10 Amazing Benefits of Being Bilingual" infographic (Bilingual Kidspot, 2017)

**Group 4:** "Bilingualism: What Happens in the Brain?" (Hewings-Martin, 2017)

2. Once all of the participants are assigned to a group, give them approximately 5–10 minutes to read and reflect silently on their assigned article. About halfway through, check in and ask how many more minutes they need by show of fingers. Use this check to gauge how much additional time to give them.

3. When everyone has had a chance to read their assigned article, reconfigure the participants into groups with one person from each of the four groups. (An optional midpoint step would be to have all of the people in the same group get together and discuss the key takeaways from their assigned article before dividing into groups of four.)

4. Give each person in the new groups of four 3 minutes to present highlights from their article and 2 minutes to answer questions from the group, for a total of approximately 20 minutes. Feel free to adjust this timing as needed.

*Part II*

1. After everyone has had a chance to discuss and learn from one another during the jigsaw activity, ask the participants to do a gallery walk and write their responses to the prompts on the posters that are hung around the room. They should plan to respond to all of the questions that are posted. Poster prompts can include the following questions, but feel free to come up with questions that might be a better fit for the group.

    - What was new or unfamiliar in the articles about bilingualism?
    - What was something you already knew about bilingualism?
    - What benefits exist for bilingual or multilingual brains?
    - What can you do to help your students better understand the benefits of bilingualism?
    - What can you do to help the parents and guardians of your students better understand the benefits of bilingualism?

2. When it looks like most people have responded to all of the prompts, give them a 1-minute warning. Once the minute has passed, ask them to move around the room silently and read all of their colleagues' responses to each of the prompts. They do not need to do this in any particular order and can add to the posters if they think of something new.

3. Once sufficient time has been given for the silent gallery walk, call the group back together and ask for volunteers to share out key implications for their teaching.

## EDUCATORS KNOW ABOUT THE THEORIES OF CULTURAL RELEVANCE AND SUSTAINABILITY

In Chapter 4, we discussed the critical need for educators to be culturally sensitive and sustaining, but that requires knowledge of the reasoning behind these practices. There are many outstanding books dedicated to the topic, and one way to diffuse this knowledge across the staff is to lead a book study, perhaps in professional learning community groups, so that teachers are able to distill, through discussion and group reflection, the ways in which the knowledge applies to their classrooms.

Following are two additional activities that help to provide teachers with background knowledge on theories of cultural relevance and sustainability so that they can begin to examine their practices and decide where there is room for growth in their work toward building culturally sensitive and sustaining classrooms.

 **1. Funds of Knowledge: Reflection and Planning**

| Objective | Participants will reflect on how their curriculum integrates and attends to the background knowledge of all students. |
|---|---|
| Time to Complete | 1 hour |
| Materials and Resources | • Video: "Funds of Knowledge" (Administration for Children & Families, 2015; www.youtube.com/watch?v=aWS0YBpGkkE)<br>• Handouts (available on the companion site for this book, www.tesol.org/SWEL-book)<br>— Funds of Knowledge Activity Sheet<br>— Funds of Knowledge Plan<br>• Laptop/computer, projector, screen, speakers |
| Preparation | • Make hard copies of the Funds of Knowledge Activity Sheet and hard copies (or share digital copies) of the Funds of Knowledge Plan.<br>• Create a presentation slide with question prompts for Parts I and II. |

**Directions**

*Part I*

1. Show Luis Moll's brief video lecture ("Funds of Knowledge"; Administration for Children & Families, 2015) and share the definition of funds of knowledge:

   "... to refer to the historically accumulated and culturally developed bodies of knowledge and skills essential for household or individual functioning and well-being."

   —Moll et al. (2005)

2. Then, ask the teacher participants to engage in a discussion based on the following prompts:

   Consider a current or former student and reflect on how you brought their funds of knowledge—or their unique knowledge and expertise—into your curriculum. How did you learn of this student's fund of knowledge? Did you incorporate it into your curriculum? Your instruction? If so, how did you do this and what was the result? If not, what could you do in the future to ensure that this student's funds of knowledge are integrated into the curriculum?

3. As participants ask each other these questions, they should jot down their thoughts on the Funds of Knowledge Activity Sheet.

| Student's Fund of Knowledge | How I Learned About This Fund of Knowledge | Ideas for Integrating This Fund of Knowledge Into Instruction |
|---|---|---|
|  |  |  |

*Part II*

Use the Funds of Knowledge Plan handout to create a plan for how you will learn more about students' funds of knowledge. The plan should include the following:

1. In one page, summarize how you will learn more about your students' funds of knowledge.
2. State your goals(s): What would you like to see happen over the year as it relates to funds of knowledge and your classroom/teaching? Be specific.
3. Outline the process involved. What steps do you have to take to reach your goal? Include these steps in a timeline with tentative dates.

## 2. Windows and Mirrors Lesson Check

| Objective | Participants will consider how to design lessons that are culturally relevant to all of their students. |
|---|---|
| Time to Complete | 30–60 minutes (*NOTE: Teacher participants will need 30–60 minutes to read article prior to the activity*) |
| Materials and Resources | • Article: "Curriculum as Window and Mirror" (Style, 1996; nationalseedproject.org/images/documents/Curriculum_As_Window_and_Mirror.pdf)<br>• Handout: Windows and Mirrors Activity Sheet (available on the companion site for this book, www.tesol.org/SWEL-book)<br>• Blue and green Post-it notes (or other coordinated colors), blue and green markers (or other coordinated colors), poster paper<br>• Optional: computer/laptop, screen, projector |
| Preparation | • Ask all participants to read the article and consider implications in your school setting.<br>• Prepare Windows and Mirrors Activity Sheets to distribute to participants (hard copies or digital).<br>• Ask participants to bring a lesson plan for a class that they are going to teach within the next month.<br>• Optional: Prepare a presentation slide with (or write on the board) discussion question prompts from Part I and Part IV. |

**Directions**

*Part I*

Provide the following definitions in both writing and orally as a way to model teaching that uses multiple modalities:

> Curriculum as window: Classroom and instructional materials that allow students to see the world around and beyond themselves (Bishop, 1990).

> Curriculum as mirror: Classroom and instructional materials in which the students see themselves reflected (Bishop, 1990).

Ask participants to break into small or table groups and engage in discussion using the following questions:

1. "Curriculum as Window and Mirror" (Style) was originally written in 1988. What concepts from the article still feel relevant in the present day? How so?
2. What concepts from the article feel irrelevant in the present day? Why?

*Part II*

1. Draw windows in green marker and mirrors in blue marker on poster paper and place them around the room.
2. Ask participants to use the green Post-it notes to jot down times in which they provided their students windows in their curriculum and blue Post-it notes for times in which they provided their students mirrors in their curriculum. Participants may also be prompted to consider how a window for one student may actually be a mirror for another, which can be noted on the Post-it notes. They should then place these notes on the corresponding poster papers around the room.
3. Finally, participants can do a gallery walk of the posters, reading what each participant has shared and reflecting on how it might inform their teaching and/or work with MLEs.

*Part III*

1. Ask teachers to take out the lesson plans that they brought. Hand out the Windows and Mirrors Activity Sheet.
2. Ask each teacher to draw a grid (or prepare a handout with a blank grid and enough spaces for each student in a given class) and write the name of each student in class in small print at the top of each box in the grid (see example of grid).

| | Windows and Mirrors | | | | | | | | | | | | |
|---|---|---|---|---|---|---|---|---|---|---|---|---|---|
| Student Names | | | | | | | | | | | | | |
| Windows | | | | | | | | | | | | | |
| Mirrors | | | | | | | | | | | | | |

3. Finally, ask participants to consider the lesson plan that they prepared and write an example of a curricular window and mirror that the lesson provides for each student in the class.

*Part IV*

1. Ask the participants to find a partner to discuss how the lesson plan they chose provides curricular windows and mirrors for their students and share the following discussion questions:

    a. What takeaways do you have from completing Part III of this activity?

    b. Do you see new opportunities for providing more windows or mirrors in your lessons?

    c. How does this inform your choices for instructional materials and teaching activities?

2. Optional: Have the partners share out one key takeaway from the activity with the whole group.

## EDUCATORS KNOW WHO IMMIGRANTS ARE AND HOW IMMIGRATION HAPPENS

There is a great deal to know about immigrants. There are complex and evolving laws, region-specific circumstances, and factors like secondary migration (when an immigrant moves to a second or new location within the same country in which they reside) to understand. For example, one part of the country might have a large population of home language Portuguese speakers from Brazil while another part of the country might have very few Portuguese speakers, but the largest Somali-speaking population in the country. The circumstances of the two immigrant groups in this example are very different and the circumstances of immigration *within* each of those groups are also varied. This is why it is important for educators to know who the immigrants in their communities are and, at least generally, how they arrived in the country, state, and region. This background knowledge will help to provide a baseline understanding of the kind of prior school experiences the MLEs in their classroom, as well as the MLEs' families, may or may not have had. It will also provide a baseline knowledge of the stories that their students and families bring to the classroom.

The activities in this section are just the tip of the iceberg when it comes to building knowledge on immigration and *it cannot be overstated that facilitators of any activity related to immigration need to be clear that what one immigrant experiences may be very different from what another may experience, even for immigrants from the same country, language group, or region of the world.* The first activity, which attends to the trauma that some students or their families may have experienced as refugees fleeing their homelands, is one such case where it is critical to begin the activity noting that it should not be assumed that all immigrants have experienced trauma. With that said upfront, teachers will benefit greatly from understanding how trauma might play out in the classroom.

 **1. The Neurological Impacts of Trauma: Hand Model of the Brain**

A note from Chris Homiak, author of the "Hand Model of the Brain" video (2018) used in this activity:

> Trauma-informed education is connected to all content, to your way of being and the systems of your school. If offered in isolation, a "lesson" like this brain video can cause additional harm. This video should be offered in the context of anti-oppression equity analysis, which impacts everything from curricular choices to classroom agreements/expectations to "discipline" systems, and in conjunction with balanced lessons about brain chemistry and structural trauma.

We encourage you to read more about trauma and the effects it has on the brain, schooling, and the lives of people who are survivors of traumatic experiences. For scholarly articles on trauma as it relates to immigrants, you may consider the following:

- Putnam, F. W. (2006). The impact of trauma on child development. *Juvenile and Family Court Journal, 57*(1), 1–11. https://doi.org/10.1111/j.1755-6988.2006.tb00110.x

- van Der Kolk, B. A. (2005). Developmental trauma disorder: Toward a rational diagnosis for children with complex trauma histories. *Psychiatric Annals, 35*(5), 401–408. https://doi.org/10.3928/00485713-20050501-06

- Vaughn, M. G., Salas-Wright, C. P., Huang, J., Qian, Z., Terzis, L. D., & Helton, J. J. (2017). Adverse childhood experiences among immigrants to the United States. *Journal of Interpersonal Violence, 32*(10), 1543–1564. https://doi.org/10.1177/0886260515589568

A plethora of resources can also be found through The National Childhood Traumatic Stress Network (www.nctsn.org). It is worth noting that the resources on their website are also available in Spanish.

| Objective | Participants will identify the parts of the brain that react to traumatic experiences, triggers, and memories. |
|---|---|
| Time to Complete | 20 minutes |
| Materials and Resources | • Video: "Hand Model of the Brain" (Homiak, 2018; www.youtube.com/watch?v=8Tn62r1K-0M)<br>• Laptop/computer, projector, screen, speakers |
| Preparation | Cue video and either prepare a presentation slide with the discussion questions or provide table tents with printed versions of the discussion questions. |

### Directions

1. Ask participants to stand to watch the video. In this video, North Kansas City ELD teacher Chris Homiak demonstrates Siegel's hand model of the brain. Participants should follow along with the video.

2. Divide into pairs or small groups of three to four people. Discuss the following questions. Recommended time for discussion is 15–20 minutes, with an optional 5 minutes for small groups to share out in the larger group at the end.

    - Share an example of a student going into the fight mode of lizard brain. How does this impact the student's ability to learn?

    - Share an example of a student going into the flight mode of lizard brain. How does this impact the student's ability to learn?

    - Share an example of a student going into the freeze mode of lizard brain. How does this impact the student's ability to learn?

- After a student has "flipped their lid," what are some ways that you can bring them back into their wizard brain?
- Share an example of a time when you witnessed the same student functioning in both the lizard and wizard brains. What implications does this have for teaching?

 ## 2. History of Immigration to the United States

| Objective | Participants know how geopolitical circumstances have shifted immigration over time in the United States. |
|---|---|
| Time to Complete | 45 minutes |
| Materials and Resources | • Video: "Animated Map Shows History of Immigration to the US" (*Business Insider*, 2017; www.youtube.com/watch?v=Fe79i1mu-mc)<br>• Computer, screen, projector, time keeper (watch, phone, etc.)<br>• Optional: speakers |
| Preparation | • Cue up video of the animated map.<br>• Optional: Write or create a presentation slide with the think, pair, share prompt.<br>• Optional: Write on the board or create a presentation slide deck with prompts for each concentric circle rotation. |

**Directions**

*Part I*

Think, Pair, Share: Ask participants to find a partner, think about, and then discuss the following question: *The immigration issues we face today have never been experienced in U.S. history.* Decide how much time to dedicate to this opening activity based on the amount of time you have for the PD session.

*Part II*

1. Watch the video of *Business Insider's* animated map that shows the history of immigration to the United States.

2. Ask the participants to number off to form two groups.

3. Concentric Circles/Inside-Outside Circles Discussion Activity: Ask the participants in Group 1 to form a circle facing outward. Then have the participants in Group 2 form a circle facing inward, around the circle made by the participants in Group 1. This should form two concentric circles where each person from Group 1 is facing a partner from Group 2.

4. Tell the two groups that they are going to share their family's immigration story, noting that you may have some participants who are Native American and do not have a history of immigration in their family. If that is the case, they can participate by telling a family story that feels relevant, such as moving from one place to another within the country. Each person

in the pair will have 2 or 3 minutes (depending on how much time you have) to share their story. Using a timer, cue Partner 1 to begin. After a designated amount of time, cue Partner 2 to begin.

5. Now ask the interior circle to rotate one person to their left. The participants in the outer circle should remain where they are. For this rotation, ask the participants to share what is similar and what is different from their family's immigration story when compared to the MLEs they teach.

6. Ask the interior circle to rotate one person to their left for a final time. For this discussion, ask them to share one thing from the video that they already knew about immigration and one thing that was unfamiliar. An alternative to this discussion question is to ask them to consider the common themes of immigration over time (e.g., war and poverty).

*Part III*

Ask participants to return to their seats and debrief as a whole group using the following questions or create questions that feel more relevant to your school site.

- Why is knowing about immigration important for educators?
- What implications does this knowledge have for our teaching?

## EDUCATORS KNOW SYSTEMS OF OPPRESSION AND HOW THEY AFFECT THE EDUCATIONAL EXPERIENCES OF MULTILINGUAL LEARNERS OF ENGLISH

As discussed in Chapter 4, providing an education for all students that is founded on principles of equity and an understanding that the classroom is not free of outside influences depends on educators' knowledge of the systems of oppression that are at play in society as well as the history of those oppressive systems. Given the interplay between teacher dispositions, knowledge, and skills, *knowing* about these systems can have a tremendous impact on a teacher's dispositions and their development of culturally relevant and sustaining pedagogies. The PD activities in this section are designed to bridge the space between dispositions and knowledge, with an aim to make sure we are aware of ways that the cultural contexts in which we live impact our work as teachers.

 ### 1. What I Should Have Said: Calling Out and Calling In

This activity can be difficult for some participants. We recommend the following trigger warning prior to starting the activity:

TRIGGER WARNING: *This activity attends to bigotry and bias and requires participants to perform acts of bigotry and bias. This activity may cause discomfort for participants. Judgment is encouraged about the appropriateness of this activity for a given group.*

| Objective | Participants will recall personal experiences with bias and develop possible "calling in" responses to those situations to practice advocating for students. |
|---|---|
| Time to Complete | 60–90 minutes |

| Materials and Resources | • Video: "Standing Up: What Is Calling in vs. Calling Out?" (PROJECT ROCKIT, 2018; www.youtube.com/watch?v=zYX2CHFT4EM) |
| --- | --- |
| | • Handout: What I Should Have Said (available on the companion site for this book, www.tesol.org/SWEL-book) |
| | • Laptop/computer, projector, screen, speakers, a device or paper for free-writing |
| Preparation | • Make hard copies or share digital copies of the handout. |
| | • Set up the room so that all participants can see the performances. |
| | • Either make handouts with definitions of *calling out* and *calling in* or prepare a presentation slide to show all participants when giving background on the activity. |
| | • Optional: Make a presentation slide with the discussion questions from Part IV of the activity. |

### Background

A critical role of an educator is to be an advocate. However, many feel unprepared for this role. We have all experienced moments in which we encountered bias and did not respond in a way we would have liked. This full activity can be found on the What I Should Have Said handout.

### Directions

*Part I*

1. Show the video to teacher participants and share the following definitions (adapted from Rodriguez-Cayro, 2018):

   *Calling out*: Publicly giving feedback to someone about their potentially problematic, biased, and/or oppressive behavior; performative in nature.

   *Calling in*: Talking with someone privately about their problematic, biased and/or oppressive behavior. Considered less reactionary than "calling out."

2. Hand out the What I Should Have Said handout and ask participants to independently free-write about a time in which they encountered bias in a personal (nonwork) setting. The handout contains the following prompts:

   - Describe the context. Where were you? Who was there? When did this happen?
   - What happened?
   - How did you respond?
   - How could you have "called out" the person enacting bias or oppression?
   - How could you have "called in" the person enacting bias or oppression?

*Part II*

Ask participants to form groups of four to five. In their groups, they will do the following:

1. Discuss the experience that they wrote about.

2. Choose one of the experiences to act out.
3. Create a short performance with a narrator and actors. The performance will have four parts: (1) the event, (2) what I said, (3) a reenactment of the event in which the main character "calls out" the offender, and (4) a reenactment of the event in which the main character "calls in" the offender.

*Part III*

Each group will perform all four acts of their skit in front of the larger group. Each will be followed by a discussion using the following prompt:

*Which of the three endings would have been most likely to end in positive change?*

*Part IV*

Ask each small group from the performances to discuss the following questions (also found on the handout). When finished, pose the questions to the large group as a debriefing exercise.

1. What is the rationale for "calling out"? What is the result of "calling out"?
2. What is the rationale for "calling in"? What is the result of "calling in"?
3. How can we decide when to do which?
4. How can we overcome the tendency to remain silent?
5. What impact does this have on our students?

##  2. Understanding Privilege

| Objective | Participants know that privilege plays a role in the schooling experiences their students have. |
|---|---|
| **Time to Complete** | 60–90 minutes |
| **Materials and Resources** | • Videos:<br>  — "Students Learn a Powerful Lesson About Privilege" (BuzzFeedVideo, 2014; www.youtube.com/watch?v=2KlmvmuxzYE)<br>  — "What Is Privilege?" (As/Is, 2015; www.youtube.com/watch?time_continue=239&v=hD5f8GuNuGQ)<br>  — "Why Does Privilege Make People So Angry? | Decoded | MTV News" (MTV Decoded, 2016; www.youtube.com/watch?time_continue=146&v=qeYpvV3eRhY)<br>• Handout: Understanding Privilege: Reflection (available on the companion site for this book, www.tesol.org/SWEL-book)<br>• Computer, screen, projector, speakers |

| Preparation | • Cue up the videos. |
| --- | --- |
| | • Make hard copies or share digital copies of the reflection handout. |
| | • Write on the board or prepare a presentation slide with a list of the lesson plan components for Part II. |

**Directions**

*Part I*

1. Pass out or share the reflection handout and tell the group that you will be watching three short videos. These videos provide different ways to understand privilege and how it plays a role in our lives and the lives of our students. They are also student appropriate and might be used for a lesson in the classroom. After each video, everyone will be asked to pause to reflect, write, and share.

2. Show the first video. When finished, give the group 3 minutes to quietly reflect and write on their reflection handouts.

3. After enough time has passed for everyone to jot down some thoughts, ask them to turn to a partner and discuss their reflections, as well as how they or another teacher might be able to use the video in their classroom. Repeat this process with the remaining two videos, asking the participants to discuss with a new partner after each reflection time.

*Part II*

Divide the participants into three groups. Assign each group one of the three videos and ask them to write a lesson plan on privilege that uses the assigned video as an anchor for the activities. You can ask the group to use a common lesson plan format that is used in the school or they can use a template of their own choosing. Ask the three groups to include most or all of the following:

1. A state or national standard from an appropriate content area (this topic can be addressed across most content areas with the appropriate adjustments and activities)

2. A content objective

3. A language objective (if teachers have been trained to create language objectives)

4. An activities sequence

5. A formative assessment

# EDUCATORS KNOW APPROACHES TO ADVOCACY AND THE LEGAL REQUIREMENTS FOR ADEQUATELY SERVING MULTILINGUAL LEARNERS OF ENGLISH

Going into the profession already knowing the legal requirements for serving MLEs is imperative to ensuring that schools continue and even improve their support for MLEs. However, many practicing teachers graduate from their teacher preparation programs without this background knowledge. For this reason, we need to ensure there are PD opportunities for those teachers to learn what they are legally obligated to provide in terms of language learning support, how to advocate for students, and how to engage with families of MLEs.

The activities in this section offer some ways to develop this knowledge, either as a refresher for more recent teacher preparation graduates or as an introduction for those teachers who were not afforded the opportunity to take courses related to MLEs. Many of these activities can be refined to include only one part of the activities listed or tailored to best meet the needs of the local context. We encourage this.

 **1. Multilingual Learner of English Engagement**

| Objective | Participants will consider the needs of MLE families in their school community and develop a school event or process that will serve those needs. |
|---|---|
| Time to Complete | 1–2 hours |
| Materials and Resources | • Article: "ABCs of Family Engagement: Key Considerations for Building Relationships With Families and Strengthening Family Engagement Practices" (Mancilla et al., n.d.; wida.wisc.edu/sites/default/files/resource/ABCs-Family-Engagement.pdf)<br>• Optional: chart paper |
| Preparation | • Share the "ABCs of Family Engagement" article or print hard copies.<br>• Write discussion questions on the board or create a presentation slide.<br>• Pass out sticky notes.<br>• Optional: Create a shared Google document for Part III. |

**Directions**

*Part I*

1. Ask participants what they think MLE families need to know about the school and community. Write their answers on chart paper (if you want to save the answers for future reference, this is a helpful choice) or on the board.

2. Once you have established a thoughtful list of responses, have the participants number off into groups of three using letters A, B, and C. Once everyone has an assigned letter, ask them to read the corresponding section in the "ABCs of Family Engagement" (Mancilla, Blair, &

Cuéllar, n.d.) article. This will take about 5 minutes, and you may invite people who finish early to read other sections in the article.

3. After everyone has read their assigned section, ask the expert groups to meet by designating a space in the room for all of the As, another for all of the Bs, and a third for all of the Cs. Ask the expert groups to discuss the following questions:

- What are four key takeaways from our assigned section that most apply to our school setting and need to be shared with the other groups?
- Given our specific setting, is there anything else we should add?

4. Give the expert groups 5–7 minutes to meet and come up with the key points to share with the people who read different sections.

5. When finished, divide the group into triads (or groups of six, if you have a very large group) that include at least one person from each of the three expert groups. Give the new small groups time to share out the key takeaways from their assigned section, discussing, reflecting, and asking questions as they go.

*Part II*

1. Plan a family gathering for the families of your MLEs. This can be done in small groups that consist of grade-level or department teams or as a large group for a single event that will happen at some point during the course of the school year. You may also want to have three or four small groups plan separate family nights that will take place during the school year.

2. Divide the group in the appropriate way for your setting. Once they have gathered together, ask them to assign a notetaker to capture the details of the plan. Have them address the following in their plan:

- Objective and purpose of the event
- Location of the event
- Invitation list
- Recruitment for attendance plan (e.g., phone calls home from a bilingual staff member)
- Transportation plan, if needed
- Translation plan, if needed
- Agenda for the event

3. Encourage participants to use resources acquired online, in person, through expert staff members, and so on.

4. After enough time has been given to plan an event, gather the groups back together and share highlights from their plans with the whole group.

*Part III*

Schedule the family gathering and hold, as planned. Be sure to set a time to debrief soon after the event takes place so that the following questions can be addressed:

1. Describe three key successes.
2. Describe three changes that you will make for the next family gathering.
3. Describe how you will follow up with families and assign these tasks to specific people.

##  2. What Does the Law Say About Serving Multilingual Learners of English?

| Objective | Participants will know the laws that direct the ways in which schools are obligated to serve MLEs. |
|---|---|
| Time to Complete | 1 hour |
| Materials and Resources | • Online resources for each group (see Table 1)<br>• Handout: Influential Court Cases: Summaries (available on the companion site for this book, www.tesol.org/SWEL-book)<br>• Optional: laptops or tablets for all participants |
| Preparation | • Make hard copies of the court case summary sheet or share it digitally.<br>• Write on the board or prepare a presentation slide with the discussion questions from Part III. |

**Directions**

*Part I*

1. Divide the participants into three small groups in a way that feels appropriate for the setting (e.g., by numbering off or by grade level taught).
2. Tell the groups that they will be looking closely at court cases that are directly related to how schools are legally obligated to meet the needs of MLEs. Each group will put together a 3-minute presentation on their assigned case to present to the whole group.
3. To get the groups started, assign them each a case and share the resources from Table 1, but encourage them to search for additional and useful resources on their assigned legal decision. Give the groups 15–20 minutes to put together their presentations, checking in after 12 minutes to see how far along each group is in the process.

**TABLE 1.** Court Cases Related to Multilingual Learners of English: Online Resources

| Influential Court Decision | Resources |
|---|---|
| Guey Heung Lee v. Johnson, 1971 | **Wikipedia Entry**<br>https://en.wikipedia.org/wiki/Guey_Heung_Lee_v._Johnson<br><br>**Opinion (FindLaw)**<br>https://caselaw.findlaw.com/us-supreme-court/404/1215.html |
| Lau v. Nichols, 1974 | **Summary (PBS)**<br>https://www-tc.pbs.org/beyondbrown/brownpdfs/launichols.pdf<br><br>**Supreme Court Ruling (Google Scholar)**<br>https://scholar.google.com/scholar_case?case=5046768322576386473&hl=en&as_sdt=6&as_vis=1&oi=scholarr<br><br>**Video (Colorín Colorado)**<br>https://www.youtube.com/watch?v=iYH_Cj9aRUM |
| Plyler v. Doe, 1982 | **Summary of Ruling (United States Courts)**<br>https://www.uscourts.gov/educational-resources/educational-activities/access-education-rule-law<br><br>**Fact Sheet (American Immigration Council)**<br>https://www.americanimmigrationcouncil.org/research/plyler-v-doe-public-education-immigrant-students<br><br>**Video (Colorín Colorado)**<br>https://www.youtube.com/watch?v=cSutYJ9mvuk |

*Part II*

1. Distribute the court case summary handout or share it digitally with all participants. Give the group a few minutes to fill in the notes section for their assigned group.

2. When finished, have the groups take turns presenting their assigned case, going in chronological order to show how each case leads to the next.

3. When finished, each participant should have a sheet with notes on how each case creates the legal framework for serving MLEs in schools.

*Part III*

As a whole group, discuss the following questions:

- How does this information align with what you already know about serving MLEs?
- How is our school meeting these requirements?

**Discussion Questions**

1. Which of the six teacher knowledge areas is the strongest in your school?
2. Which of the six teacher knowledge areas is most in need of development in your school?
3. Which PD plan stood out to you as one that you would like to use with your colleagues? Why?

**Takeaway Task**

Considering the teacher knowledge area that is in most need of development in your school, plan to deliver PD. Choose one of the PD plans that falls under that knowledge area or use one of your own. This can be for the whole staff or a small group and it can be facilitated by one or many ELD teachers. Share out how it went.

**References**

Administration for Children & Families [usgovACF]. (2015, May 12). *Funds of knowledge* [Video]. YouTube. https://www.youtube.com/watch?v=aWS0YBpGkkE

As/Is. (2015, July 4). *What is privilege?* [Video]. YouTube. https://www.youtube.com/watch?time_continue=239&v=hD5f8GuNuGQ

Bhattacharjee, Y. (2012, March 17). Why bilinguals are smarter [Opinion]. *The New York Times*. https://www.nytimes.com/2012/03/18/opinion/sunday/the-benefits-of-bilingualism.html

Bilingual Kidspot. (2017, May 23). *10 amazing benefits of being bilingual*. https://bilingualkidspot.com/2017/05/23/benefits-of-being-bilingual/

Bishop, R. S. (1990). Mirrors, windows, and sliding glass doors. *Perspectives*, 6(3), ix–xi.

Business Insider. (2017, August 8). *Animated map shows history of immigration to the US*. https://www.businessinsider.com/animated-map-shows-history-immigration-us-america-2017-8

BuzzFeedVideo. (2014, December 9). *Students learn a powerful lesson about privilege* [Video]. YouTube. https://www.youtube.com/watch?v=2KlmvmuxzYE

Chacon, S. (2018, May 3). *MIT scientists prove adults learn language to fluency nearly as well as children*. Medium. https://medium.com/@chacon/mit-scientists-prove-adults-learn-language-to-fluency-nearly-as-well-as-children-1de888d1d45f

Dutro, S., Prestridge, K., & Herrick, J. (2007). *ELD matrix of grammatical forms*. EL Achieve. https://www.knoxeducation.com/sites/main/files/file-attachments/susana_dutro_eld_matrix_11x17.pdf

Ferlazzo, L. (2024, June 25). When Is It OK to Use Google Translate in the English-Learner Classroom? Education Week. https://www.edweek.org/teaching-learning/opinion-the-use-or-misuse-of-google-translate-in-the-ell-classroomwhen-is-it-ok-to-use-google-translate-in-the-english-learner-classroom/2024/06

Guey Heung Lee v. Johnson, 404 U.S. 1215 (1971). https://caselaw.findlaw.com/us-supreme-court/404/1215.html

Hewings-Martin, Y. (2017, October 4). Bilingualism: What happens in the brain? *Medical News Today*. https://www.medicalnewstoday.com/articles/319642.php

Homiak, C. (2018, March 2). *Hand model of the brain* [Video]. YouTube. https://www.youtube.com/watch?v=8Tn62r1K-0M

Lau v. Nichols. 414 U.S. 563 (1974). https://scholar.google.com/scholar_case?case=5046768322576386473&hl=en&as_sdt=6,24&as_vis=1

Mancilla, L., Blair, A., & Cuéllar, D. (n.d.). *WIDA ABCs of family engagement: Key considerations for building relationships with families and strengthening family engagement practices*. Wisconsin Center for Education Research. https://wida.wisc.edu/sites/default/files/resource/ABCs-Family-Engagement.pdf

Moll, L. C., Amanti, C., Neff, D., & González, N. (2005). Funds of knowledge for teaching: Using a qualitative approach to connect homes and classrooms. In N. González, L. C. Moll, & C. Amanti (Eds.), *Funds of knowledge: Theorizing practices in households, communities, and classrooms* (pp. 71–88). Lawrence Erlbaum Associates.

MTV Decoded. (2016, January 13). *Why does privilege make people so angry? | Decoded | MTV News* [Video]. YouTube. https://www.youtube.com/watch?time_continue=146&v=qeYpvV3eRhY

Plyler v. Doe, 457 U.S. 202 (1982).

PROJECT ROCKIT. (2018, March 11). *Standing up: What is calling in versus calling out?* [Video]. YouTube. https://www.youtube.com/watch?v=zYX2CHFT4EM

Rodriguez-Cayro, K. (2018, May 15). *What does call-in mean? When call-out culture feels toxic, this method can be used instead*. Bustle. https://www.bustle.com/p/what-does-call-in-mean-when-call-out-culture-feels-toxic-this-method-can-be-used-instead-9056343

Spritzler, F. (2018, July 23). *Common symptoms of vitamin D deficiency and how to treat them*. Healthline. https://www.healthline.com/nutrition/vitamin-d-deficiency-symptoms

Style, E. (1996). Curriculum as window and mirror. *Social Science Record*, Fall. https://nationalseedproject.org/images/documents/Curriculum_As_Window_and_Mirror.pdf

Teachings in Education. (2016, September 27). *Stages of second language acquisition: ELD, ELL, LEP & bilingual* [Video]. YouTube. https://www.youtube.com/watch?v=Hk7_lBaFC5w&feature=youtu.be%5D%2C+Five+Stages+of+SLA+Activity+Sheet

# CHAPTER 6

# TEACHER SKILLS NEEDED TO EFFECTIVELY AND RESPECTFULLY SERVE MULTILINGUAL LEARNERS OF ENGLISH

*Jean is a career changer. She shares that she left her job as an engineer because it was not fulfilling. She recently completed a fast-track teacher licensure program and is thrilled to have a new position as a science specialist in an urban elementary school that serves 42% multilingual learners of English (MLEs). She is thoughtful, empathetic, and sensitive to her students' needs. Being fresh out of school, she is also knowledgeable about second language acquisition theories and schooling models for MLEs because her program included a dedicated class for this. However, she is frustrated. Jean's lessons seldom go as planned and she struggles with classroom management. Her MLEs score poorly on assessments and students complain that "science is boring." Jean has the disposition to work with MLEs as well as the content knowledge, but she needs to build her skills in order to be an effective teacher of MLEs.*

We have established that all teachers *are* language teachers, and it's clear that Jean is keeping language learning in her sights as she thinks about the needs of her students. Given that all teachers are tasked with teaching language in context, Jean would benefit greatly from the support of a school-wide English learning (SWEL) coach to help her identify areas in which she is already attending to language and ways in which she can provide more explicit instruction, which will likely help to create lessons that are more engaging for students. Working with a SWEL coach will also help Jean to meet her students' language learning needs, and planning for language levels will ensure that Jean's lessons are interesting to the students, in large part because the content will be accessible.

This chapter focuses on the following five critical skills for educators:

1. Educators can plan for language instruction.
2. Educators can teach and assess language development.
3. Educators can differentiate for multilingual learners of English.
4. Educators can support home language development.
5. Educators can enact culturally relevant practices.
6. Educators can advocate for immigrant families.

The activities in this chapter are designed to help classroom/content teachers hone their practical skills so they are able to teach content and language simultaneously, as well as support MLEs as whole learners. You will note that every activity attends to a skill that teachers need to effectively and respectfully serve MLEs. As in previous chapters, it is also worth noting that, with some small changes to the objective and focus, activities from the dispositions and knowledge chapters may also be used to address teacher skills. We encourage you to refine these activities to best meet the needs of your school setting.

> For additional videos and resources that highlight ways to address and cultivate skills for working with MLEs in the content-area classroom, and for easy access to all of the resources used in these activities, see the companion site for this book, www.tesol.org/SWEL-book.

## EDUCATORS CAN PLAN FOR LANGUAGE INSTRUCTION

Our experience working with both preservice and in-service teachers underscores the call for explicit attention to language learning across the entire school day in all classrooms and content areas. It has become clear that, without systematic and habitual attention to language learning, content learning priorities often overshadow the areas where language instruction is needed, even in classrooms that are cotaught with English language development (ELD) teachers. Of course, this is self-defeating because the vehicle for teaching content is language. For this reason, professional development (PD) that helps teachers learn new pedagogies related to language instruction is key to creating school-wide focus on and continuous attention to the double duty that MLEs are responsible for as they learn content and language simultaneously. The activities in this section address planning for language instruction by making explicit the language learning needs that our own proficiency in English often prevents us from seeing.

## VOICES FROM THE FIELD

Teachers now have a sense that language development isn't outside their realm of understanding . . . A lot of the teachers that I have interacted with had initial ideas about what it means to provide oral language activities or written language development in the classroom. They felt like it was going to be an overwhelming thing and overtake everything that they were going to be doing. Once they started to see that it could be integrated into their current instruction in such a way that it not only benefited the MLEs but also benefited most of the other students, particularly the struggling students, that was the moment that they seemed to say, "Oh I actually want to do this on a regular basis as opposed to just learning about it". . . . So it's kind of like that light bulb. This is common sense when you start to integrate it in the curriculum. *(SWEL coach)*

### 1. Professional Discourse Challenge[1]

| Objective | Participants will gain clarity on the discourse level of language (also known as text type) by describing an image using the language of a particular profession. |
|---|---|
| Time to Complete | 30 minutes |
| Materials and Resources | • Image: "Mulberry Street, New York City" (Detroit Publishing Company, 1900; available at images.app.goo.gl/himhxdq5TPaba3az8)<br>• Profession Cards (available on the companion site for this book, www.tesol.org/SWEL-book)<br>• Small plastic or paper bags for card sets<br>• Paper or devices for writing |
| Preparation | Print and cut out the profession cards. Brightly colored paper is best. If you plan to use them many times, laminate them for reuse. |

### Directions

*Part I*

1. Arrange participants in groups of four to six. Hand out the profession cards so that each participant has one. Ask them not to share their profession with anyone.
2. Tell participants that they will be required to write about an image you will show them from the perspective of the profession noted on the card. It can be useful to give an example, such as "If I am an artist, I might write about color saturation and sepia treatments." They will have 5 minutes, and they can use any resources that they have at their disposal. Internet searches are permitted and encouraged.

---

[1] Based on Newton, 2017

*Part II*

1. Show the image. The image and professions can be changed to reflect your school or community. This image was chosen because of its relevance to the topic of immigration. You may choose a visual that includes the school mascot or a scene from your community. Be sure to change professions on the profession cards accordingly. The key to finding an alternate picture is that there needs to be a great deal of detail in the photo or painting. Be sure to check usage rights.

2. Give participants 5 minutes to write about the image using the language that a professional from the discipline on their profession card would use.

"Mulberry Street, New York City." Detroit Publishing Company, 1900. In the public domain.

*Part III*

1. Ask participants to read what they have written aloud to their group. After each person has read what they wrote, ask the group to guess what profession they thought it was.

2. Once everyone has had a chance to read, return to the large group and discuss the following questions:

- How did you decide what and how to write about the image?
- What did you identify as language norms of the discipline that you had?
- We know that students are often unaware of the language norms of text types that we take for granted.
    — What are some examples of text types that you ask your students to produce or interact with?
    — What are some language norms in those text types?
    — How could you teach those norms explicitly?

##  2. Building Leveled Language Objectives

| Objective | Participants will modify existing lesson plans so that they include relevant language objectives. |
|---|---|
| Time to Complete | 60–90 minutes |
| Materials and Resources | - Building Leveled Language Objectives (Appendix D, available on the companion site for this book, www.tesol.org/SWEL-book)<br>- Academic Language Video Lecture 1: "Bricks, Mortar, and Buildings: A Metaphor for Understanding Academic Language" (MichelleBenegas, 2020a; https://www.youtube.com/watch?v=HtUn_UI9AS8&t=3s)<br>- Academic Language Video Lecture 2: "Writing Academic Language Objectives (ALOs)" (MichelleBenegas, 2020b; https://www.youtube.com/watch?v=6yIBY0zL8ig)<br>- Timer or watch |
| Preparation | - Print hard copies or share a digital copy of Appendix D.<br>- Ask teacher participants to come to this session with a lesson plan that they have previously taught. There is no required format for the lesson plan and it does not need to be detailed.<br>- Become very familiar with the Building Leveled Language Objectives tool in order to efficiently assist participants as they create their own leveled objectives. |

### Directions

*Part I*

1. Using the lesson plan that participants have brought to the session, ask them to fill out Sections A and B of the Building Leveled Language Objectives tool.

    a. Identify your **content objective(s)**.

b. **Language Function(s):** What are you asking students to do with language? (e.g., analyze, compare/contrast, explain, interpret, argue, persuade, categorize, describe, predict, question, retell, summarize, justify with evidence)

2. Before moving on, review the levels of language with teacher participants using the Academic Language video lectures.

3. After showing the video, have them discuss Sections C, D, and E with a partner and fill in those sections for their specific lesson plan. Refer to the Building Leveled Language Objectives Tool for a chart that shows each of the language functions, along with examples of language, supports, and sample language objectives at each of the three levels of language.

   a. **Content Vocabulary:** What key vocabulary (word level—"the bricks") do you need to introduce/review with students? How will students engage with that vocabulary in the lesson? How is this vocabulary being introduced, developed, or reviewed in this lesson?

   b. **Syntax:** What syntax (sentence level—"the mortar") is present in the materials that you are going to teach?

   c. **Discourse:** What text type (discourse level—"the building") will students need to produce?

4. Finally, ask them to use the sentence frames and examples to write three language objectives that could be used in this lesson or a subsequent lesson (e.g., not all lessons attend to the discourse level). They will need to have one language objective at the word level, one at the sentence level, and one at the discourse level. Of course, in practice you would not have three language objectives for a single lesson plan. However, it is important to see how language can be taught at three levels for a given content area.

*Part II*

1. Language Objectives Speed Dating! Ask teacher participants to stand up, walk toward another side of the room, and find a colleague with whom to share their content objective (learning target) and their newly created word-level language objective. Set your timer so that they have 4 minutes per partner.

2. Partners should be listening closely to make sure that the language objective has all of the required components. You may invite participants to edit their language objectives if needed.

3. When the 4 minutes have passed, announce that they should find a new partner and share their content objective (learning target) and sentence-level language objective. Partners should be listening to make sure that the language objective has all of the required components.

4. Repeat this process for a final round of speed dating, focusing on sharing out the content objective (learning target) and the discourse-level language objective.

## EDUCATORS CAN TEACH AND ASSESS LANGUAGE

In keeping with the belief that all teachers are language teachers, it stands to reason that teachers would also need skills related to teaching and assessing language. Teaching content-specific language can be viewed through a variety of lenses and might be addressed through scaffolding techniques, such as providing additional visuals, giving students structured opportunities for academic discussions, and breaking down activities into explicit steps, to name just a few.

Assessing language growth has the same breadth in terms of skills, but it is imperative that classroom/content teachers continually check their assessments to ensure that they are not inadvertently assessing language that is unfamiliar or has not been explicitly taught. To help build teacher understanding of the ways that assessments can sometimes be a test of language rather than content, it can be useful to recreate experiences that are similar to those of MLEs in the general education classroom. The following PD activities aim to do just that. They help teachers to answer such questions as "What does it feel like to listen in a second language?" and "What does it feel like to be assessed in a second language?"

---

## VOICES FROM THE FIELD

From previous experience, writing and implementing language objectives effectively was something a lot of teachers at our school struggled with. We wanted to give workshops that would not only introduce function-driven language objectives, but give them time to practice writing and revising them, as well as opportunities to look at their lessons and think of what it would look like to incorporate activities explicitly related to the language objectives. . . . Teachers seemed to really appreciate them [PD sessions on language objectives], especially the way they built on each other. They commented often about how it was great to keep returning to language objectives and to have opportunities to practice writing them for their own lessons. *(SWEL coach)*

---

 **1. Listening in a Second Language: A Shock Language Experience**

| | |
|---|---|
| Objective | Participants know how to create supports for students that help to ensure comprehension when listening in English. |
| Time to Complete | 30 minutes |
| Materials and Resources | • Worksheet: Venn Diagram Listening Activity (available on the companion site for this book, www.tesol.org/SWEL-book)<br>• Video: "Said Salah Ahmed: The Lion's Share in Somali" (MN Original, 2012; www.youtube.com/watch?v=f7EHQRd7JJI)<br>• Laptop/computer, projector, screen, speakers |
| Preparation | • Cue up the video.<br>• Make hard copies or share digital copies of the Venn diagram.<br>• Optional: Write the discussion questions on the board or a presentation slide. |

**Directions**

1. Tell the group that language is conveyed through the four modalities: reading, writing, listening, and speaking. These modalities are either receptive (reading and listening) or productive (speaking and writing). These modalities are reflected in the ways that MLEs are assessed and

can be found in the WIDA ACCESS, ELPA21, LAS Links, or equivalent language assessment scores. Tell the participants that they are going to go through a simulation activity that helps to demonstrate what it might mean to listen in an unfamiliar language.

2. Pass out or share a digital copy of the Venn Diagram Listening Activity and tell the group that they are going to listen to the same story twice. The first time, they are just going to focus on listening. Ask the participants to write down what they comprehend about the story they are hearing in the circle on the left-hand side of the Venn diagram.

3. *Turn off the projector screen* and play a minute or more of the Somali folktale. After turning off the audio from the video, give participants a minute or so to finish jotting down their notes, recognizing that many will have nothing to write if they are unfamiliar with the Somali language. You may also invite them to write down how it *felt* to listen to the story without the visuals.

4. Cue the video at the beginning and *turn the projector back on*. This time, show the visuals of the story reader and the story book. Play the same amount of the Somali folktale that you did the first time. Ask the participants to write down what they comprehend about the story they are hearing and seeing in the circle on the right-hand side of the Venn diagram.

5. When finished listening and viewing the second round of the Somali folktale, give the participants a couple of minutes to fill in the overlapping portions of the Venn diagram with their thoughts on what was similar about the two experiences.

6. Divide into small groups and discuss the following prompts:

    a. Describe what you already do in your teaching to support student listening comprehension.

    b. Describe what you might add to your instruction in order to support student listening comprehension.

##  2. Plargs (Second Edition): Assessing Content-Area Learning

*This revised edition of the Plargs PD plan includes additional resources created by Hawaii SWEL coach, Jeremiah Brown (the Engineered Assessment and the Amplified Text). Dividing the participants into three groups creates additional opportunities for thoughtful reflection on how students can learn new language and meet learning standards at the same time with the right level of support in place.*

| Objective | Participants will know how to write assessment questions that address content without inadvertently assessing language knowledge. |
|---|---|
| Time to Complete | 45 minutes |
| Materials and Resources | • Handouts (as shown in this section and available on the companion site for this book, www.tesol.org/SWEL-book):<br>— Plargs Quiz and Answer Key<br>— Plargs Vocabulary Cards<br>— Plargs Engineered Assessment<br>— Plargs Amplified Text (online only)<br>• Laptop/computer, projector, screen |
| Preparation | • Make paper copies of the Plargs Quiz, the Plargs Engineered Assessment, and the Plargs Answer Key<br>• Create sets of the Plargs flashcards with vocabulary words (one set per small group)<br>• Be prepared to share a digital copy of the Plargs Amplified Text (created by Jeremiah Brown) during Part II<br>• Optional: Write the discussion questions from Part IV on the board or create a presentation slide.<br>• Optional: For Part V, ask teachers to bring a quiz, short assessment, or rubric that they use in their teaching. |

### Directions

*Part I*

1. Divide the participants into groups of three and ask the groups to sit together. Ask each group to number off again so that each group has a Person 1, Person 2, and a Person 3.
2. Distribute paper copies in the following way:
    - Person 1: Plargs Quiz
    - Person 2: Plargs Quiz and Vocabulary Cards
    - Person 3: Plargs Engineered Assessment

3. Each small group member should have different version of the assessment at this point. Now, tell participants that this is a quiz and that it needs to be worked on independently because it will count toward their grade in the PD session.

**PERSON 1: PLARGS QUIZ**

### Plargs

Plargs are important traptors that many jarbles misunderstand. First, some jarbles think they are floptans, but they are not. Even though they splog, plargs do not have talalas. Instead, they have chotnas like many other ligariths. Plargs do not have actual trammas, either.

Second, plargs are nochips. Most plargs come out only at norla, although some may splog at morgena. Because they are barl at norla, they underbarl during the norlana.

Finally, some jarbles believe that plargs are fliptan and temb. Actually, they are very uddle and koff themselves frequently. They are also very helpful to jarbles because they eat skeys. They do not elry jarble's blog!

1. Plargs are important traptors because
    a. Plargs are nochips.
    b. Plargs splog.
    c. Plargs eat skeys.
2. Plargs do not have chotnas.
    a. True
    b. False
3. Ligarths have
    a. Talalas, not chotnas
    b. Chotnas, not talalas
    c. None of the above
4. Plargs are
    a. Fliptan
    b. Temb
    c. Uddle
5. Plargs elry jarble's blog.
    a. True
    b. False

# PERSON 2: PLARGS QUIZ (AS IN PERSON 1) + VOCABULARY CARDS

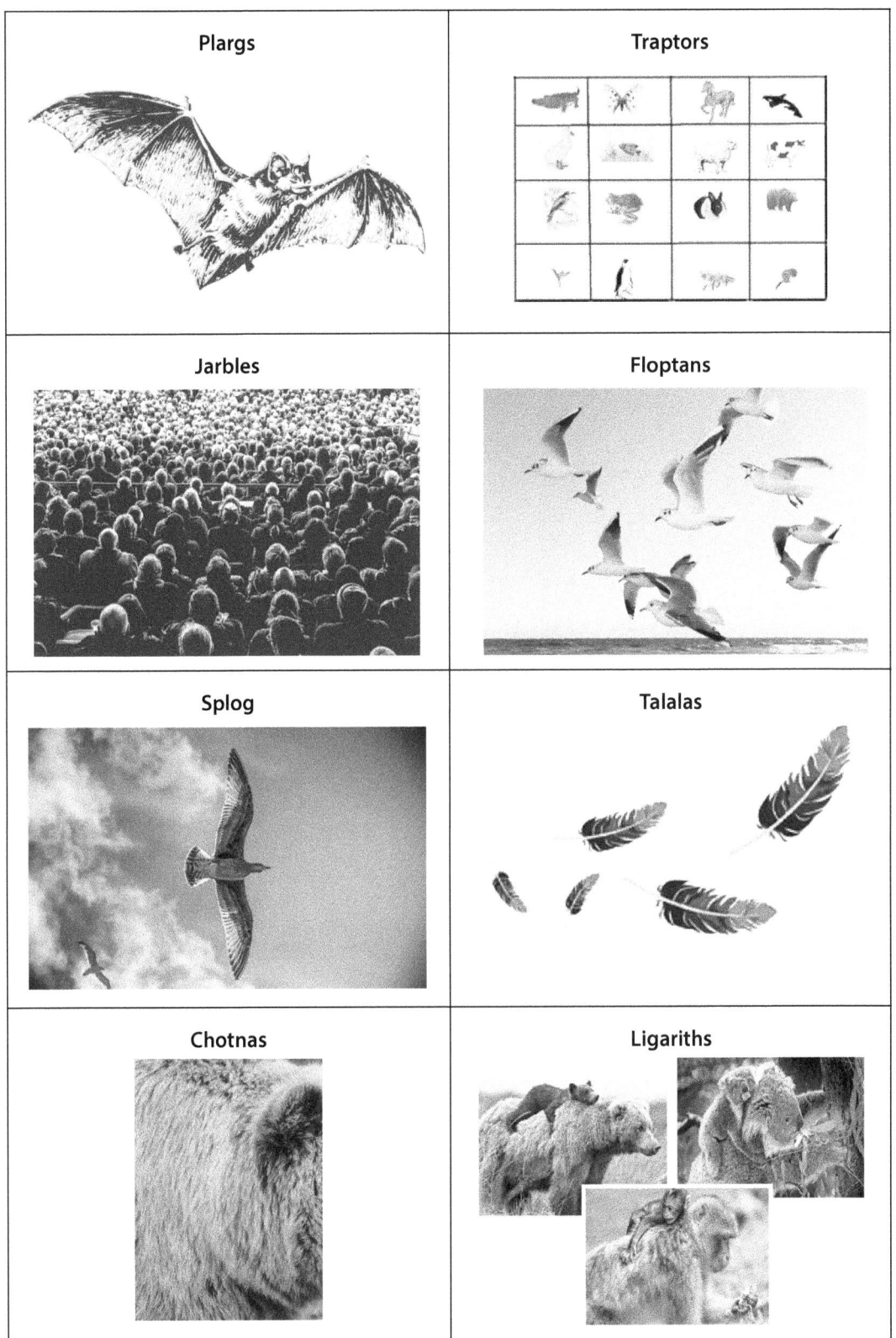

Teacher Skills Needed to Effectively and Respectfully Serve Multilingual Learners of English

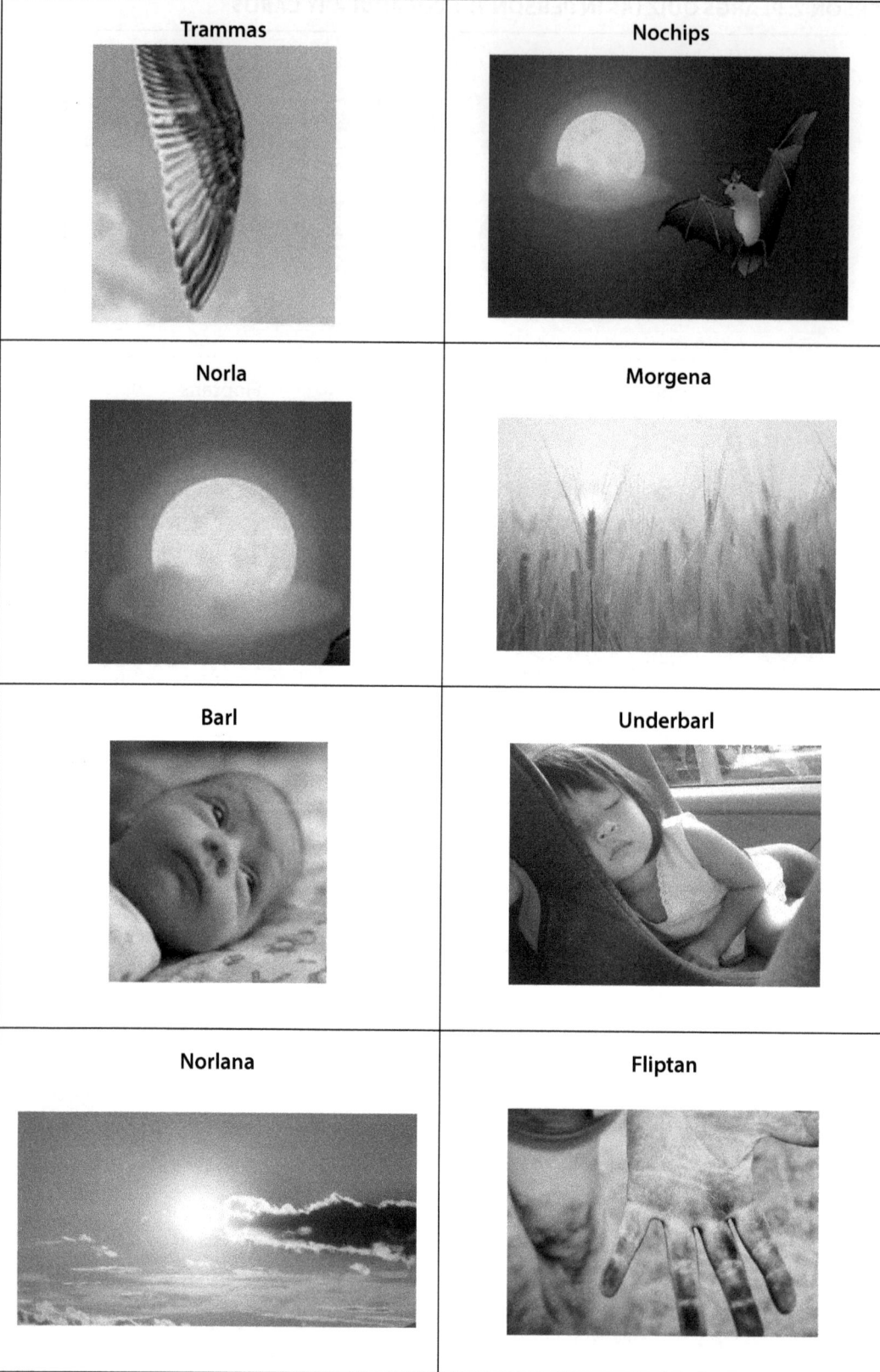

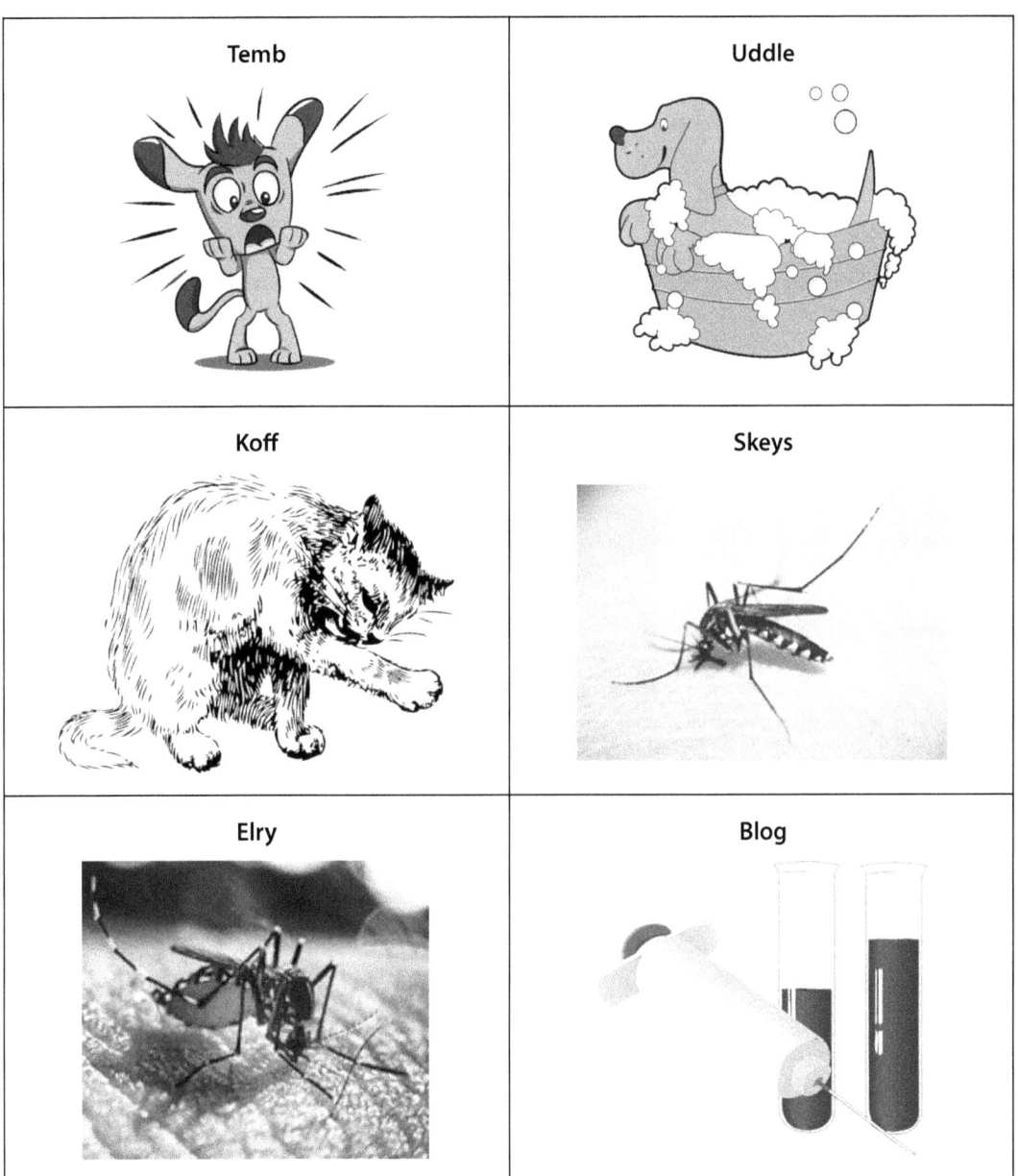

## PERSON 3: PLARGS ENGINEERED ASSESSMENT

**Word Sort-** Write each word or phrase in the correct column.

| traptors | ligarths | koff | splog | nochips |
|---|---|---|---|---|
| eat skeys | chotnas | uddle | trammas | talalas |
| floptans | temb | helpful | elry blog | fliptan |

| Characteristics of plargs | Behavior of plargs | Misconceptions of plargs |
|---|---|---|
| Plargs are _____. | Plargs can _____. | Plargs are not _____ |
| Plargs have _____. | Plargs [verb]. | Plargs do not_____ |
| | | Plargs do not have _____. |
| | | |

**Fill in the Blank-** write the correct word from the word bank in the blank spaces below.

<u>Word Bank</u>- temb, splog, floptans, uddle, fliptan, helpful, blog

Plargs can _____, but they are not _____.

Some jarbles think plargs are _____, but they are actually very _____.

Some jarbles think plargs elry _____, but that's not true.

Plargs are neither _____ nor _____. Instead, they are both _____ and _____.

**Short Answer-**
How are plargs and floptans similar? How are they different?
*Both plargs and floptans... However, plargs....*

What is one misconception (wrong idea) that many jarbles have about plargs?
*One misconception is that...*

While participants are completing the Plargs quiz, remind them that their work needs to be done independently and silently and that cheating is against the rules. You might also ask them to sound out words if they are struggling. After about 4 minutes (or before it looks like everyone is finished) give participants a 1-minute warning and ask them to turn their quizzes over when the minute has passed.

**PLARGS ANSWER KEY:**

**Bats**

Bats are important animals that many people misunderstand. First, some people think they are birds, but they are not. Even though they fly, bats do not have feathers. Instead, they have fur like many other mammals. Bats do not have actual wings, either.

Second, bats are nocturnal. Most bats come out only at night, although some may fly at sunset. Because they are awake at night, they sleep during the day.

Finally, some people believe that bats are dirty and scary. Actually, they are very clean and groom themselves frequently. They are also very helpful to people because they eat mosquitoes. They do not suck people's blood!

1. Bats are important creatures because
    a. Bats are nocturnal.
    b. Bats fly.
    c. Bats eat mosquitoes.

2. Bats do not have fur.
    a. True
    b. False

3. Mammals have
    a. feathers, not fur.
    b. fur, not feathers.
    c. None of the above

4. Bats are
    a. dirty
    b. scary
    c. clean

5. Bats suck people's blood.
    a. True
    b. False

*Part II:*

Ask the small groups to share their version of the quiz and look at the Plargs Amplified Text. Provide the following discussion prompts for their review and discussion:

- What is the same and what is unique about each version?
- How did you feel as you were taking your version of the quiz?
- What would have been different for you if you had been assigned to a different version of the quiz?
- How would the Plargs Amplified Text have helped you take the quiz if you had been able to read it in advance?

*Part III:*

Call the groups back together to debrief their experiences and discussions as a whole group, using the following discussion questions:

- What specific tools are being used to support learners in each version of the Plargs quiz and the Plargs Amplified Text?
- What might be similar and what might be different about how you experienced the Plargs quiz and how one of your MLEs might experience it?
- What implications does this have for your lesson planning, teaching, and assessment in terms of how you ensure that MLEs are fully comprehending the content you teach?

*Part V:*

Ask participants to take out the assessment or rubric sample that they brought with them to the PD session. Working in the same small groups as in Parts I and II, ask the participants to take turns analyzing their assessments or rubrics for the following:

1. Are there any areas in the assessment that inadvertently test language knowledge that has not been explicitly taught? If so, what can be changed in instruction or changed in the assessment to ensure that what is assessed was also taught?

2. Are there any places in the assessment where students might be able to respond correctly without actually comprehending the content, in the same way that many were able to answer the questions on the Plargs quiz correctly without actually knowing what the passage was about? How can you write your classroom assessments so that they actually measure student learning?

Provide enough time for this activity so that each of the participants in the small group is able to share and discuss the assessment they brought.

When finished, bring the whole group back together and ask each small group to share some key takeaways from the session. Lead a discussion on how they might use what they learned to inform their instruction and assessment.

## EDUCATORS CAN DIFFERENTIATE FOR MULTILINGUAL LEARNERS OF ENGLISH

Most teachers are familiar with the concept of differentiation, but we still hear from many that it feels like writing a separate lesson plan for each student. When practiced as intended, differentiation might take a little extra time on the front end, but it is actually just a matter of adding some variety to a lesson. Like many teaching skills, the more it is practiced, the more efficient the process of differentiating lessons and unit plans becomes. The following activities are meant to provide some foundational information for how to differentiate for MLEs based on what they are able to do at a given language development level and where they are aiming to go based on the next level. As always, readers should feel free to refine these PD activities so that they best meet the needs of the local context.

*Note: The WIDA resources used in this section are open source and available publicly. They serve as an excellent way to establish an understanding of the meaning behind language levels in the four modalities (reading, writing, listening, and speaking). If you are in a state that is not affiliated with WIDA, you may want to adjust this activity to reflect the language assessment used locally.*

## VOICES FROM THE FIELD

[My colleagues] have talked about seeing students more engaged and more able to participate. In my coaching, we focus on academic discussions; specifically, the oral language piece . . . The teachers really felt strongly that a lot of students, particularly MLEs, gained confidence. When they gained that confidence, they were more willing to engage. A lot of teachers previously would do activities like turn-and-talks and a lot of our MLEs would just not participate or just sit there silently when they're supposed to be speaking.

The teachers felt like after designing some of these more in-depth activities and some assessments related to those activities, that the students were able to engage more in oral discussions with them and help them access the content so much more. And so they really saw those students growing in confidence becoming leaders and their content knowledge increased. *(SWEL coach)*

 **1. Using WIDA Can Do Descriptors to Make Content Accessible**

| Objective | Participants will be able to articulate what an MLE at a given language level is generally able to do in each of the four modalities (reading, writing, listening, and speaking) and identify ways in which to push MLEs to the next level. |
|---|---|
| Time to Complete | 90 minutes |
| Materials and Resources | • Handout: Modality Audit (available on the companion site for this book, www.tesol.org/SWEL-book)<br>• Grade level–appropriate WIDA Can Do Descriptors (WIDA Consortium, 2016a; wida.wisc.edu/teach/can-do/descriptors)<br>• Video: "WIDA Can Do Philosophy" (WIDA Consortium, 2019; wida.wisc.edu/resources/can-do-philosophy-video)<br>• Student/class lists<br>• Laptop/computer, projector, screen, speakers |
| Preparation | • Make hard copies or share digital copies of the Modality Audit handout.<br>• Create or share lists of MLEs that include their assessed language levels in each of the four domains.<br>• Optional: Write the discussion questions from Part IV on the board or prepare a presentation slide. |

**Directions**

*Part I*

Begin this activity by asking teachers to fill out the Modality Audit handout (either on paper or digitally) for a recent lesson they taught:

---

**MODALITY AUDIT**

Consider the last class that you taught that was not a test or student presentation day. From the students' perspective, estimate how much time they spend in each of the four modalities:

**Input:**

Listening _____

Reading _____

**Output:**

Speaking _____

Writing _____

---

Ask the participants to set their Modality Audit aside and tell them that you will return to it later.

*Part II*

1. Show the "WIDA Can Do Philosophy" video.
2. Divide the teachers into small groups based on grade level or content area taught.
3. Ask the ELD teacher(s) to serve as a small group support by floating around the room.
    a. Have each teacher download the appropriate grade level Can Do Descriptors document from WIDA's website.
    b. In small groups, discuss the following:
        - What is familiar?
        - What is new?
        - How can you use the Can Do Descriptors to inform instruction throughout the school year?

*Part III*

Ask the groups to look at the assessed language levels of the MLEs on their assigned lists and compare them to the Can Do Descriptors for the given language levels *and the next level up*. Emphasize that we should be looking for ways in which to move students to the next language level. Have each group fill out a chart paper with three columns: the students' names, their assessed language levels, and activity ideas for differentiating.

## DIFFERENTIATION IDEA CHART EXAMPLE

| Student Name | Language Level | Ideas for Differentiating |
|---|---|---|
| Ahmed A. | Reading: 2.8<br>Writing: 2.1<br>Listening: 4.2<br>Speaking: 1.7 | Create academic discussion starters and sentence frames for pair and small group discussions and writing assignments.<br><br>Ahmed's mom is bilingual and biliterate in Somali and English, so enlist her to help with writing and reading assignments in both languages.<br><br>Create more opportunities for academic talk in the classroom.<br><br>Assign audio books for homework (in English and Somali, when possible) so that Ahmed can listen to a reading assignment before it is assigned to the whole class to read. He should listen first, while looking at the text, and then read without the audio support. |

*Part IV*

Bring the whole group back together. Ask the teachers to take their modality audit sheet out again and to turn and talk about their breakdown for each modality using the following discussion prompts:

- Given what you know about language levels in the four modalities and differentiation, would you make any changes to this lesson in the future? If so, what changes would you make?
- How does examining your MLEs' language assessment data help you make instructional decisions?

## VOICES FROM THE FIELD

A lot of the teachers who I worked with said that these were things that were not covered in their teacher training program—which may have been 5 years ago or may have been 25 years ago. They felt like it was really helpful for them to learn some concrete strategies related to those different areas. *(SWEL coach)*

## 2. WIDA Can Do Name Charts

| Objective | Teachers can access, collect, and analyze qualitative and quantitative MLE data from multiple sources to inform instruction. |
|---|---|
| Time to Complete | 45 minutes |
| Materials and Resources | • Video: "WIDA Can Do Philosophy" (WIDA Consortium, 2019; wida.wisc.edu/resources/can-do-philosophy-video)<br>• Grade level–appropriate WIDA Can Do Descriptors (WIDA Consortium, 2016a; wida.wisc.edu/teach/can-do/descriptors)<br>• Grade level–appropriate WIDA Can Do Name Charts (WIDA Consortium, 2016b; wida.wisc.edu/teach/can-do/descriptors)<br>• Student/class lists<br>• Laptop/computer, projector, screen, speakers<br>• Notecards |
| Preparation | • Cue up the "WIDA Can Do Philosophy" video, if using.<br>• Make hard copies or share digital copies of the WIDA Can Do Name Chart.<br>• Print or share student language level assessment data, such as WIDA ACCESS scores (composite score and all four modalities). |

### Directions

*Part I*

1. Show the "WIDA Can Do Philosophy" video.

    *Note: If you already used this video during the "Using WIDA Can Do Descriptors to Make Content Accessible" activity, you do not need to show it again unless you think it would be useful.*

2. Afterwards, divide the teachers into small groups based on grade level or content area taught. Ask the ELD teacher(s) to serve as a small group support by floating around the room.

3. Using a blank Can Do Name Chart and a commonly used source for student language assessment data (please ensure that classroom/content teachers will also have the ability to use the source), model the ways in which a teacher can transpose individual student data into the name chart. If a digital platform for student data is unavailable, you may need to print hard copies of student language levels on assessments, such as the WIDA ACCESS.

4. Think aloud what it means for a student to have a given score in a given modality and how that might inform instruction. For example, you could say, "Now that I know Maria has an ACCESS score of 4.5 in listening and a 2.2 in speaking, I realize that I am going to need to create opportunities for her to practice using content-area language orally."

Part II

1. Have each group work to place students who they teach or students from their classroom on the grade level–appropriate Can Do Name Chart.

2. When all MLEs are placed on the Can Do Name Charts, ask teachers to discuss what this information might tell them about instruction. Facilitators and/or ELD teachers can float to the various groups to help support the teachers' processing of this information.

3. Bring the whole group back together. Have each teacher fill out an exit ticket on a notecard to share how this activity will inform their instruction, then ask each small group to share one key takeaway from this exercise. When finished, collect the exit tickets in order to assess what may need to be addressed in future PD sessions.

## EDUCATORS CAN SUPPORT HOME LANGUAGE DEVELOPMENT

Understanding why we need to support home language literacy is key to teacher knowledge for working with MLEs. Believing that it is important to support home language literacy is a disposition we want to see in all teachers, but particularly those who have MLEs in their classrooms. Understanding *how* to support home language literacy is a skill that requires most teachers, or at least those who are not proficient in the home languages of all of the MLEs they teach, to give up some control. It can be very uncomfortable for people who identify as "knowers of things" to not understand everything that is being said or written. It takes time, practice, exposure, and a lot of self-reflection to cultivate these skills. The activities in this section are designed to help build the skills to support home language literacy by giving teachers a chance to practice in a safe and controlled environment.

 ### 1. Translanguaging Activity

| Objective | Participants will learn new techniques for embedding home language use within classroom lessons and units of instruction. |
|---|---|
| Time to Complete | 1 hour |
| Materials and Resources | • Handout: Translanguaging: A CUNY-NYSIEB Guide for Educators (Celic & Seltzer, 2013; www.cuny-nysieb.org/wp-content/uploads/2016/04/Translanguaging-Guide-March-2013.pdf)<br>• Videos:<br>— "04 Andy Brown Translanguaging A multilingual Learning" (CUNY-NYSIEB, 2017; www.youtube.com/watch?v=O6DBPbDT_GE)<br>— "Session 5: Classroom Examples" (CUNY-NYSIEB, 2016; www.youtube.com/watch?v=b6z1u1ivlWY&t=78s)<br>• Laptop/computer, projector, screen, speakers<br>• Participants will need access to an internet-enabled mobile device, such as a laptop or tablet.<br>• Optional: If using Part III of this activity, participants should be asked to bring a copy of a lesson plan. |

| Preparation | • Download the translanguaging guide and share digital copies with participants.
• Cue up both videos.
• Ask participants to bring a laptop or tablet.
• Create a poster for Part III, if completing.
• Optional: Create presentation slides with directions for the activities and include the link to view the translanguaging guide (you can also create a free QR code through a website, such as www.qr-code-generator.com, instead of listing the entire URL). |
|---|---|

**Directions**

*Part I*

1. Tell the participants that you will be doing a jigsaw reading and ask them to open the translanguaging guide that you shared on their laptop or mobile device. Create two small groups by numbering off the participants as either Group 1 or 2. Ask Group 1 to read pages 1–6 and Group 2 to read pages 7–12.

2. Fast readers or early finishers can read the section for the alternate group or look through the remainder of the guide, which includes a large number of classroom activities for translanguaging.

3. When everyone is finished reading their assigned section, ask all of the participants assigned to Group 1 to find a partner from Group 2. If you have an odd number of participants, have one group of three participants work as a small group instead of a pair. Each pair should take turns summarizing their assigned section of the translanguaging guide. This will take approximately 10 minutes. Those who finish early can browse the activities section of the guide.

*Part II*

1. Bring the group back together after all of the pairs have finished sharing in the jigsaw activity. Tell the participants that you are going to show them an example of what translanguaging looks like in practice, first from the planning perspective and then from the classroom perspective. Show the "Session 5: Classroom Examples" video.

2. Ask the participants to turn and talk to a partner for 2 minutes about the following questions:

    a. How would this kind of planning work in your teaching, whether or not you have a coteacher?

    b. How would this kind of planning for the use of home languages affect your students?

3. After the partner discussion, show the "04 Andy Brown Translanguaging A multilingual Learning" video.

4. When finished, ask participants to turn and talk to a partner about the following reflection questions:

a. How does Andy Brown encourage students to use their home languages in the classroom?
   b. What do you feel you would need to do to engage in the kind of translanguaging instruction that Andy Brown uses?
5. After the second partner discussion, debrief with the whole group by asking participants to share out some of their key takeaways.

*Part III (Optional)*

1. Divide the participants into small groups based on grade level or content area taught (e.g., second grade, science) and ask them to walk through the activities for translanguaging in the translanguaging guide, pages 13–193, with attention focused on those activities that apply to the contexts and age levels in which they teach. Have them write a list or mark the activities that they would like to try with their students.
2. After giving the group 15–20 minutes to look through the activities in the guide, ask them to take out the lesson plan they brought to the PD session. Working together and sharing resources, have the participants find places in their lesson plans where they might consider adding one or more activities from the translanguaging guide that would leverage their MLEs' home languages.
3. Facilitators can circulate the room, offering ideas and suggestions to those who might be stuck or want to talk through their own ideas with an ELD teacher.
4. Call the group back together and tell them that you will be hanging a poster paper in the staff lounge or other teacher-dedicated space with a translanguaging chart that includes the following:
   a. Student name: You may decide not to include student names on the chart.
   b. Translanguaging activity used: They should include the name of the activity used and the page number from the translanguaging guide, if possible.
   c. Glows: What went well when the activity was used.
   d. Grows: What could be improved or what the teacher will change the next time the activity is used.

An example of a possible response is shown in Figure 1.

| Name | Translanguaging Activity Used | Glows: Things That Went Well | Grows: Areas for Improvement |
|---|---|---|---|
| Amy | multilingual collaborative work, p. 62 | The students were really excited to do their research in their home language so that they could present in English later. I let them search the internet for resources in Somali and they were totally engaged with what they found. | Some of the students were confused by the directions I gave them and thought that they were going to have to do the presentation in Somali, too. They were worried that the other students wouldn't understand. Next time, I will write the directions on the board so that they get directions orally and in writing. |

**FIGURE 1.** Example translanguaging activity chart.

5. Over the course of a specified period of time (e.g., 6 weeks), encourage teachers to take a few minutes to jot down notes on the chart so that others can learn from their experience using translanguaging. It may be beneficial to include one of your own experiences with a translanguaging activity to model how to use the chart. You can leave the poster up for as long as it is relevant and useful. In schools launching equity or literacy initiatives, among others, this work may be incorporated into the larger initiative and become part of a school year–long focus.

 ## 2. The Benefits of Multilingualism

| Objective | Participants will create classroom posters that highlight the benefits of multilingualism. |
|---|---|
| Time to Complete | 1 hour |
| Materials and Resources | • Article: "Dispelling the Myth of 'English Only': Understanding the Importance of the First Language in Second Language Learning" (Billings & Walqui, n.d.; www.nysed.gov/common/nysed/files/dispelling_myth_rev-2.pdf) <br> • Poster paper, art supplies (e.g., markers, bulletin board borders, stickers) |
| Preparation | • Make hard copies or share digital copies of the article. <br> • Set up poster paper and art supply materials at tables or in a convenient location so that participants can access them. |

### Directions

*Part I*

1. Ask everyone to stand up. Tell the group that they are going to be spending time thinking about the benefits of knowing more than one language.

2. Ask the participants who speak more than one language to sit down. Once those people are seated, ask the participants whose parents speak more than one language to sit down. Follow this by asking people whose grandparents speak/spoke more than one language to sit down and then those whose great-grandparents spoke more than one language to sit down.

3. At this point, nearly everyone in the room will be sitting. For those who are standing, you can invite them to sit down and point out that, even for those who are monolingual, it is typical for most people to have a family history of bilingualism or multilingualism.

4. Hand out the article, or ask participants to open digital copies, and tell them that they are going to read the article quietly to themselves. Provide enough time for each participant to get through the article. You may also assign the reading of this article ahead of time; however, this can result in a variety of completion rates, so we have found it easiest to provide time to read during the PD session itself.

5. When everyone is finished reading, divide the participants into groups of three to four based on the grade levels that they teach and ask them to discuss the following questions:
   - How would you explain the cognitive benefits of multilingualism to your students?
   - How would you explain the social-emotional benefits of multilingualism to your students?
   - How would you explain the academic benefits of multilingualism to your students?
6. As the groups are discussing, have one person take notes on a piece of poster paper with three rows and two columns. The language should be aimed at the age of the students taught by the participants in each group:

| Cognitive benefits of multilingualism | |
| --- | --- |
| Social-emotional benefits of multilingualism | |
| Academic benefits of multilingualism | |

*Part II*

1. Once each of the small groups has sufficiently discussed and filled out their poster paper, have them post their brainstorms on the wall for everyone to see.
2. Tell the participants that they are going to create posters for their classrooms that highlight the benefits of bilingualism. Distribute another piece of poster paper to everyone and tell them that they can choose from the various supplies and draw from the ideas generated in the small-group discussions. (Alternative: Participants can create a poster online and print it out to hang on the wall.) Provide enough time for people to create their posters or come very close to finishing. This will help to ensure that the posters are used in the classrooms and reduce the amount of time that teachers need to work on them outside of the time provided for PD.

*Part III*

Bring everyone back together and ask them to take turns sharing their posters with the whole group. If the whole group is very large, smaller groups can be created for sharing.

## EDUCATORS CAN ENACT CULTURALLY RELEVANT PRACTICES

Most educators today would agree that the best way to effectively and respectfully teach students from diverse backgrounds is to design culturally relevant lessons. However, many educators report that PD about the topic of culturally relevant practice tends to dive deep into knowledge (the theory of culturally relevant practice) and dispositions (the mindset needed to enact it), but few attend to the skills needed to design lessons and engage with learners in culturally relevant ways. This section presents two activities that provide concrete frameworks for developing culturally relevant practices. Some of these activities are designed to be completed over time, so it is worthwhile to consider how they might be woven into the PD framework for the school year.

# 1. Multilingual Learner of English Profile

*This activity has six parts. After Part I, the parts can be done in any order. It can take time to fill out a Multilingual Learner of English Profile (MLEP), so it is helpful to scaffold it over time.*

| Objective | Teachers can access, collect, and analyze qualitative and quantitative MLE data from multiple sources to inform instruction. |
|---|---|
| Time to Complete | 1 hour to get started, then ongoing |
| Materials and Resources | • Handouts (available on the companion site for this book, www.tesol.org/SWEL-book): <br>  — Multilingual Learner of English Profile Template (Kiran, 2018a) <br>  — Sample Multilingual Learner of English Profile (Kiran, 2018b) <br> • Class lists (by class and/or grade level), MLE language assessment scores, laptops or tablets for each participant <br> • A copy of the language level definitions used in your state |
| Preparation | • Make hard copies or share digital copies of MLE student lists, student language assessment scores, language level definitions, and the Sample Multilingual Learner of English Profile. <br> • Share digital copies of the Multilingual Learner of English Profile Template. <br> • Ask participants to bring a laptop or tablet. |

**Directions**

*Part I*

1. Divide the group of teacher participants into grade levels. Distribute names of MLEs in the grade to all teacher participants to avoid duplication. This may vary by setting.

2. Ask the participants to open the digital copy of the MLEP template.

3. Ask the teacher participants to create a new MLEP file for each of the MLEs on their lists and fill in the Student Information, Home Information, and ELD Teacher Contact sections. If they do not have all of the information requested, they can leave areas blank and fill them in at a later date. In the event that participants have a very large number of MLEs in their classes, they can choose to focus on a smaller number of MLEs, perhaps even focusing only on the MLEs who are new to the school community.

4. Upload a student photo to the top of the MLEP.

*Part II*

Ask the teacher participants to fill out the Cultural Background and Assets sections of the MLEP. Cultural Background information can feature any cultural practices or perspectives that would be helpful to teachers. An example of this might be religious holidays observed by the student and family. Assets are funds of knowledge that students bring with them to school. An example of an asset would be the ability to play a musical instrument or carpentry skills. Allow teachers time to get to know their MLEs so that they are able to include adequate detail.

*Part III*

Ask the teacher participants to fill out the Language Proficiency Levels section using the appropriate student language assessment data. When finished, participants should fill out the language level definitions that reflect the levels of each student in the section on the MLEP form titled "WIDA Can Do Descriptors." You may also choose to use an alternate set of standards or descriptors, depending on the kind of language assessment used in your region. Refer to the Sample Multilingual Learner of English Profile handout to see how this is done.

*Part IV*

1. Ask teacher participants to develop three to five long-term goals for each MLE. This can be done in conversation with an ELD teacher and should be based on needed areas for growth based on student data. Include recommendations in the Recommendations section to help the MLE achieve these goals.

2. Ask teacher participants to develop three to five short-term goals for each MLE. This can be done in conversation with an ELD teacher and should be based on areas for growth determined from student data. Include recommendations in the Recommendations section to help the MLE achieve these goals.

*Part V*

Consult with the ELD teacher to fill out the following sections: Classroom Modifications and Accommodations, Modifications and Accommodations for Assessment, Helpful Strategies, and Resources.

*Part VI*

It is likely that a single PD session will not provide enough time for an MLEP form to be filled out for every MLE in the school. As such, it is useful to store the MLEP forms on a shared drive or server so that they can be accessed by all teachers and completed over time. When the time you have allotted for this session is near the end, provide 10 minutes for the following whole group debrief discussion. Alternatively, you could have small groups discuss.

1. Filling out an MLEP form for every MLE in the school is a time-consuming task, but one that can be built upon year after year. How do you see this information as beneficial to your teaching in the near term?

2. How do you see the MLEP form as beneficial in the long term?

3. Describe one or two things that you learned today about an MLE you teach.

Be sure to consider how you will complete the MLEP forms, who will "own" them, how you will follow up on this PD session, and how the staff will utilize the MLEP forms going forward.

## 2. Mirrors in the Classroom

*This PD activity is a natural follow-up to the Windows and Mirrors Lesson Check activity in Chapter 5.*

| Objective | Participants will gather classroom resources that reflect the cultural and linguistic diversity of the students they teach. |
|---|---|
| Time to Complete | 1 hour |
| Materials and Resources | • List of the cultural and linguistic groups represented by MLEs in the school<br>• Notecards, poster paper, markers<br>• Computer, screen, projector |
| Preparation | Create a spreadsheet (using tabs) with the cultural and linguistic groups represented in the student body at the school. Google docs or sheets work well for this, but any format that allows multiple people to access and write in the same document will work. |

**Directions**

*Part I*

1. Remind the participants that it is important for students to "see" themselves in the curricula. Tell them that they are going to do an activity together to develop a comprehensive resource bank for the cultural and linguistic groups represented in the MLE student population. (Note that you could expand this activity to include an even broader group of students.)

2. Number off the participant group to create as many groups as you have cultural and linguistic groups represented in your school. For example, if you have a Google sheet with tabs for Somali language and culture, Hmong language and culture, Ojibwe language and culture, Karen language and culture, and Oromo language and culture, then you would divide the larger group into five small groups. Ask the groups to find a place to sit together.

3. Assign each group to one of the cultural and/or linguistic groups. Tell them that they are going to spend time working together to add resources to the corresponding tab on the spreadsheet. They should add items such as

    - book titles that reflect the students' languages and cultures;
    - online resources, such as informative articles about the language structures (e.g., order of subject-verb-object or direction of text);
    - links to audio books in the home language; and
    - any other useful information.

4. The small groups should use their professional judgment to vet the quality, validity, and integrity of the materials and resources they find.

*Part II*

Once sufficient time has been given for the small groups to generate a list of five or more resources, have the groups take turns sharing two or three of the best resources they found with the whole group. This can be done as a presentation with the document projected. Participants will also have a copy and can follow along on their laptops or tablets, asking questions when they have them.

*Part III*

1. Invite the group to continue adding to this document over time. Hand out notecards to each participant and ask them to jot down responses to the following:

    - What was useful about creating this bank of resources?

    - What else do you want or need to know about providing mirrors for your students?

2. Collect the notecards as exit tickets and use them to inform future PD presentations and/or to add additional information to the shared resource bank.

## EDUCATORS CAN ADVOCATE FOR IMMIGRANT FAMILIES

Perhaps the skill that educators feel least prepared to enact is advocacy, although educators frequently advocate for their students whether it's systematic and intentional or not. In the case of serving MLEs, it is a particularly critical skill. MLEs experience widening opportunity gaps and they and their families often lack the resources and infrastructure to self-advocate in ways that other student groups and their families do. The following activities prepare educators to advocate for MLEs and their education through writing opinion editorials and lobbying. The local context will play a significant role in shaping how these activities are realized.

---

**VOICES FROM THE FIELD**

We have a large population of students who have experienced trauma. Our students often come from families who have immigrated and are dealing with the challenges of citizenship. I feel that understanding the emotional impacts of events on students, we can better meet their academic needs. *(SWEL coach)*

---

 ### 1. Opinion Editorial (Op-Ed) How-To

| Objective | Teachers can identify a problem that impacts MLEs and write an opinion editorial to inform the public on the issue. |
|---|---|
| Time to Complete | 30 minutes, then ongoing (*NOTE: Participants will need 1–2 weeks between Parts II and III*) |
| Materials and Resources | Participants will need to bring a device and have internet access. |
| Preparation | Optional: Write discussion prompts from Part III on the board or create a presentation slide. |

**Directions**

*Part I*

Lead teacher participants in a group discussion around the question: "What are some issues that impact MLEs?" Share the following list to get them started. Encourage teacher participants to include issues that are local and impact their MLE populations.

- Unavailability of assessments in home language
- Need for more cultural events and celebrations in schools
- Teacher training needed for how to address racism
- Teacher training needed in trauma-informed practice
- Accommodations needed for Muslim students (prayer and fasting)
- Increased availability of interpreters for phone calls and meetings
- Opportunities to support home language development
- Issues related to Deferred Action for Childhood Arrivals (DACA)
- Student access to healthcare, including dental care and mental health resources
- Students experiencing food insecurity
- Need for training all teachers to teach MLEs

*Part II*

Explain to the teacher participants that they will be tasked with writing an opinion editorial advocating on behalf of MLEs. They can choose one of the topics previously identified, they can choose a new topic, or they can choose to respond to an existing article. They will share this op-ed with their colleagues. They may also choose to send it to a local or national newspaper, but that is dependent on their comfort level. In the op-ed, they should introduce themselves, including their credentials, experience, and place of employment. They should also include at least one reference to the benefits of bilingualism and one anecdote from their professional experience.

*Part III*

Bring teacher participants together to share their op-eds with each other. In pairs, have them exchange op-eds and discuss the following questions:

- How did you experience writing this op-ed?
- Where would you send this if you were to submit it for publication?
- What do you hope to achieve with this op-ed?

They can change partners and have this conversation with a new partner as time allows.

## 2. White Papers for Mock Legislative Meetings

This activity prepares participants to lobby policymakers. It could be used in a meeting with a legislator or a policymaker in your school. We know policymakers in our greater community to be legislators. Policymakers in a school are people who make decisions relating to the school community. This could be a superintendent, principal, or ELD lead teacher, for example. This activity can be done on three separate days or in one long session and is ideally for 12–24 participants.

| Objective | Teachers can draft white papers that make issues impacting MLEs clear to policymakers and lobby policymakers on behalf of their MLEs. |
|---|---|
| Time to Complete | 1–2 hours |
| Materials and Resources | • Handout: Issues That Impact MLEs (available on the companion site for this book, www.tesol.org/SWEL-book) <br> • Participants will need to bring a device and have internet access. <br> • Notecards |
| Preparation | • Make hard copies or share digital copies of the handout. <br> • For the lobbying simulation, you will need a large empty space in which participants can stand in two lines, facing each other. |

**Directions**

*Part I*

1. Let participants know that Parts I and II of the activity are preparation for a speed dating lobbying experience.
2. Ask them to use the Issues That Impact MLEs handout to brainstorm a list of issues that impact MLEs and their education. These issues can be from the handout or from their professional experience. At the end of the document, they will be asked to choose three focal issues. They should work on this independently.

*Part II*

*This portion of the PD can be assigned as work between sessions, if that is preferable. If completing in person, the group will need 45 minutes to an hour in order to create their white paper drafts.*

Participants will draft white papers on each of the three issues that they identified. A white paper is a succinct, one-page document that provides accessible information on a particular issue with the intent of influencing policy change. Remember—a policy is just a rule. It can be a law or a school rule. They will finish with one to three separate white papers using the following format:

- Title: Identified issue
- Talking point: One sentence that highlights the issue. Be sure to use language that is understandable to someone outside of the field.
- Anecdote: Support this talking point with a brief story (two to three paragraphs) that illustrates the issue.

- Ask: Clarify whether you are asking for funding or policy change. Clearly state what you are requesting to resolve by addressing this issue.

## Part III

*If Part II was completed in a separate PD session, be sure to remind participants that they should bring their white paper drafts for Part III.*

1. This activity can be done sitting or standing.

    a. If you prefer to have the group standing, organize them in two rows. Each participant should turn to face someone in the row opposite them for their first lobbying session.

    b. If you prefer to have the group sitting, arrange desks or tables in one long row. Participants will sit across from each other.

2. Explain to the group that for the first round, all of the participants on Side A will be policymakers and all of the participants on Side B will be lobbyists. Explain that the row of policymakers will be allies and adversaries (ally, adversary, ally, adversary, alternating all the way down the row). Allies will show genuine interest and support for the issue and adversaries will challenge the issue and/or their ability to resolve it.

3. Lobbyists will take out their first white paper draft. Their task will be to make a compelling case to the policymaker by presenting all of the information on the white paper without reading directly from it. Before sharing their issue, it will be important that the lobbyists professionally greet (handshake or otherwise) the policymakers and introduce themselves, including sharing their educational background and position in the school community.

    *NOTE: Each lobbying session will be only 4 minutes. Actual legislative lobbying often happens in hallways and under time constraints, so it is important to develop the skill of clearly and efficiently presenting an issue and a proposed solution.*

4. Before the first pairs begin, ask the participants who are acting as lobbyists to tell the participants acting as policymakers who they are (senator, governor, school board member, head of the PTO, etc.). Alternatively, you could assign these positions to them. Set a timer for 4 minutes. When you say "Go," participants should get started. Circulate the room. Feel free to show participants the timer as you walk around so that they can budget their time. When the timer goes off, remind lobbyists to thank their policymakers.

5. After completing the first round, ask lobbyists to move one spot to the right and pull out their second white paper draft (or use the same draft if they only wrote one). *In practice, lobbyists are the ones that move from policymaker to policymaker, not the other way around.* Lobbyists should tell policymakers who they are before they get started. For Round 2, policymakers should keep the same role of "ally" or "adversary." In Round 3, lobbyists will rotate once more and policymakers should take on the role of their choice (ally or adversary).

6. After the lobbyists have shared three times with three policymakers, let participants know that Side A is now made up of lobbyists and Side B is made up of policymakers. Lobbyists will now rotate to the left. They will complete the same cycle three times with these new roles until all participants have had three opportunities to be a lobbyist and three opportunities to be a policymaker.

*Part IV*

When finished with the rotations, call the group back together and provide an exit ticket notecard to each person. Ask them to answer the following questions on their cards before leaving.

1. What is one strength you have when it comes to lobbying or convincing someone of your position on an issue?
2. What is one area for growth you have when it comes to lobbying or convincing someone of your position on an issue?
3. What else would you like to learn about advocating for MLEs?

**Discussion Questions**

1. Which of the six teacher skills is the strongest in your school?
2. Which of the six teacher skills is most in need of development in your school?
3. Which PD plan stood out to you as one that you would like to use with your colleagues? Why?

**Takeaway Task**

Considering the teacher skill that is in most need of development in your school, plan to deliver PD. Choose one of the PD plans that falls under that skill or use one of your own. This can be for the whole staff or a small group and it can be facilitated by one or by many ELD teachers. Share out how it went.

**References**

Benegas, M. (2020a, March 24). *Bricks, mortar, and buildings: A metaphor for understanding academic language* [Video]. YouTube. https://www.youtube.com/watch?v=HtUn_UI9AS8&t=3s

Benegas, M. (2020b, March 24). *Writing academic language objectives (ALOs)* [Video]. YouTube. https://www.youtube.com/watch?v=6yIBY0zL8ig

Billings, E., & Walqui, A. (n.d.). *Dispelling the myth of "English only": Understanding the importance of the first language in second language learning.* New York State Education Department. http://www.nysed.gov/common/nysed/files/dispelling_myth_rev-2.pdf

Celic, C., & Seltzer, K. (2013). *Translanguaging: A CUNY-NYSIEB guide for educators.* CUNY-NYSIEB. http://www.cuny-nysieb.org/wp-content/uploads/2016/04/Translanguaging-Guide-March-2013.pdf

CUNY-NYSIEB. (2016, February 11). *Translanguaging: Classroom examples* [Video]. YouTube. https://www.youtube.com/watch?v=b6z1u1ivIWY&t=78s

CUNY-NYSIEB (2017, February 11). *04 Andy Brown translanguaging a multilingual learning* [Video]. YouTube. https://www.youtube.com/watch?v=O6DBPbDT_GE

Detroit Publishing Company. (1900). *"Mulberry Street, New York City."* https://www.loc.gov/item/2016794146/

Kiran, A. (2018a). *English learner profile template.* Unpublished resource materials.

Kiran, A. (2018b). *Sample English learner profile.* Unpublished resource materials.

MN Original. (2012, February 8). *Said Salah Ahmed: The lion's share in Somali* [Video]. YouTube. https://www.youtube.com/watch?v=f7EHQRd7JJI

Newton, A. (2017, August). *Purposeful lesson planning for linguistically diverse learners* [WIDA training presentation]. Minnesota Department of Education.

WIDA Consortium. (2016a). Can do descriptors, key uses. https://wida.wisc.edu/teach/can-do/descriptors

WIDA Consortium. (2016b). Can do descriptors name charts. https://wida.wisc.edu/teach/can-do/descriptors

WIDA Consortium. (2019). WIDA can do philosophy (video) [Video]. https://wida.wisc.edu/resources/can-do-philosophy-video

# PART C

# Application of Peer Coaching Using a Directed, Cyclical Approach

# CHAPTER 7

# SETTING UP TEACHERS FOR SUCCESS

It is wise to always keep the end in mind when working on an initiative that is meant to turn the ship or alter the ways in which we conceptualize and actualize the work we do. In the case of English language development (ELD) teachers working as teacher leaders through peer coaching and professional development (PD) delivery, the end goal is ultimately about supporting the success of multilingual learners of English (MLEs). Given that instructional practices—from planning to assessing—are tremendously influential to student success, peer coaching and ongoing, continuous, on-site PD are the means by which we are working to meet that ultimate goal. Making these changes thoughtfully requires us to be intentional in everything we do to cultivate teaching practices—the desired dispositions, knowledge, and skills that are addressed in Chapters 4, 5, and 6—that attend to the academic and social needs of MLEs.

This chapter presents two tools that are meant to support the structural shifts that the schoolwide English learning (SWEL) model asks teachers to make. The tools are designed to provide clarity around those practices deemed effective for MLEs and structures for organizing the work. Most important, they are nonevaluative in nature and are set up to drive professional dialogue forward rather than serve as checklists or documentation for what teachers are and are not doing. For the ELD teachers serving as peer coaches, they are tools that give purpose and structure to coaching conversations. For the classroom/content teachers who are participating in peer coaching, the tools shed light on promising practices and serve as references for planning, instruction, and assessment.

New to this section of the book are considerations for how the psychology of change, or how humans enact and react to change, impacts the work of SWEL coaches. We discuss how to use the research on change management to build a successful system of supporting MLEs through SWEL coaching. As you read, keep in mind that you are also being asked to change understandings of your role within the school and of how you spend some of your time, so the psychology of change applies to your experiences, too. We will also share updated planning tools for conducting PD within the SWEL model, all of which can be found in the appendixes and in digital form on the companion website. Feel free to use (or not!) the tools as is or modify them so that they are a better fit for your setting; your professional discretion and knowledge of your local context is paramount.

Before sharing the tools to support teacher success, we introduce the coaching cycle for SWEL coaches. Like all of the resources in this book, we encourage you to make professional decisions around what will work for your specific setting. We will provide some examples of how to tailor the coaching cycle based on what existing SWEL coaches are doing in their work and provide some ideas for how you might do this in your own setting. As experts in your field, your professional judgment is an important part of making sure that classroom/content teachers are able to get the most out of your support. Simultaneously, building a colearning environment will surely help to expand your own teaching practice.

## The Role of Change Management in SWEL Coaching

Roughly 2500 years ago, the Greek philosopher Heraclitus said that "there is nothing permanent except change." And yet, humans naturally struggle with change, teachers included. Not only do most people resist change, but there are also collective misunderstandings of what will affect change. Cross (2013) identified three common myths of behavior change in her research, including (1) education will change behaviors, (2) changing attitudes is necessary in order to change behaviors, and (3) people know what motivates them to change. Conversely, what Cross learned is that more education does not necessarily convince people to change what they are doing. Instead, people need to see tangible, net benefits in order to make changes. Rather than pushing for attitude change, the most effective way to go about influencing behavior change is to figure out what that person values most. For example, some teachers might change their teaching practices because they strongly believe in immigrant rights, while others might value having the best test scores in their grade level or content area. For SWEL coaches, this could mean focusing on the knowledge or skills PD plans rather than those for teacher dispositions. As we have emphasized many times throughout the book, SWEL coaches know their schools and colleagues best, and these decisions should be made according to their expertise.

The psychology of change also reveals that we are most influenced and motivated by what others are doing—and we often fail to see that. This bodes well for SWEL coaches who start slowly with a small number of colleagues because their successes will ultimately influence others to join. We have seen this happen with SWEL coaches over the years. In one instance, two coaches in the same school struggled mightily to find even one classroom/content teacher to work with them in their 1st year of SWEL coaching. By the end of the year, those reluctant volunteers became vocal champions not only for the benefits they realized as the result of SWEL coaching, but also for the success of their students (MLEs and proficient English speakers alike). When it was time to plan for the 2nd year of SWEL coaching at that school, so many classroom/content teachers asked to take part that they had to create a waitlist!

### VOICES FROM THE FIELD

Since I was already coteaching and teaching small groups in classrooms around the school, I was a familiar face. This role has given teachers a chance to meet with an ELD teacher and get support that another ELD colleague doesn't have extra time to [provide]. I have been approached by almost every type of employee in the school regarding a variety of questions or elicited support. I think [SWEL coaching has] made our ELD department more visible and given school employees a safe place to ask questions. The role is a bit elevated from our other ELD team roles and has given me a leadership position that teachers have capitalized on when they need help. *(SWEL Coach)*

# THE SWEL PEER COACHING CYCLE

As previously mentioned, there is no prescribed timeline for the SWEL peer coaching cycle. Rather, it is often more a matter of systemic structures, such as the availability of dedicated time to complete the process, than a matter of any set deadlines for completion. For instance, a SWEL coach who has a full prep period dedicated to peer coaching and PD delivery may be able to complete two or three peer coaching cycles with a given classroom/content teacher colleague over the course of a school year. However, a SWEL coach who uses their only prep period to support three classroom/content coteachers will likely only complete one peer coaching cycle per teacher over the course of the academic year. This section of the book offers a step-by-step guide through the SWEL peer coaching cycle.

Once the SWEL coaches have identified the classroom/content teacher or teachers that they will be working with one-on-one or in small groups (professional learning communities have been useful for this), they can begin the seven-step SWEL peer coaching cycle (see Figure 1). Each step can be interpreted in a way that best suits a school or even an individual teacher.

## Set Instructional Goals

This cycle begins with a coaching conversation in which the classroom/content teacher being coached (the coachee) sets a goal. Ideally, these conversations are held in person or online with cameras on, because it is much easier to read communication cues this way. If the SWEL coach and the coachee have the same work or preparation time during the school day, this might be a good opportunity for goal setting and coaching conversations. Some teachers like to set up meetings either before or after school, over lunch, or on designated professional development days.

Of course, there are instances where the coachees are unsure where they want to focus their efforts; in these cases, the coach should conduct an initial observation using one of the SWEL Support Tools (Appendixes A-C, described in detail later in this chapter). Note in Figure 1 the circular arrow between setting instructional goals and the precoaching observation, indicating that either step can be used as a jumping-off point for goal setting. It may be useful to offer the order in which to begin as a choice to coachees.

As discussed in Chapter 2, key SWEL coaching principles for observation discussions were derived from the work of Knight (2011), Garmston and Wellman (2016), and Aguilar (2013), and they were informed by our own experiences working with in-service ELD teacher leaders. These principles include the following:

1. Parity
2. Shared learning
3. Presuming positive intentions
4. Asking questions
5. Goal-driven decision making

Following these five principles will help to ensure that the coaching conversations and relationships get off to a positive start and may even be helpful in setting a baseline of expectations for a new type of relationship between colleagues who have been working together for many years. We encourage SWEL coaches to explicitly share these principles with the classroom/content teachers they work with so that everyone is aware of and agrees to adhere to them.

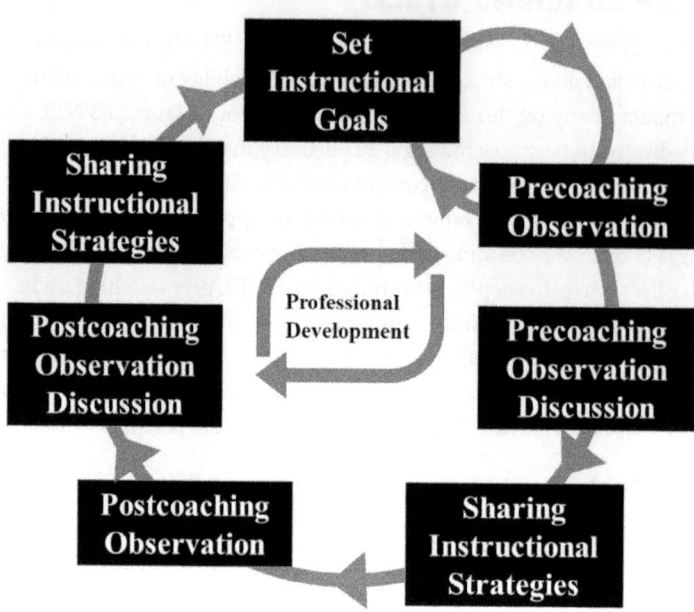

**FIGURE 1.** The school-wide English learning model coaching cycle.

Finally, this part of the coaching cycle is an important time to ask your classroom/content teaching colleague (1) how they currently attend to language in their instruction, and (2) what challenges they have when it comes to meeting MLEs' needs. Though there might be other practices you have noticed about the teacher's work with MLEs, you should write those down in your notes for another time and focus during this initial goal-setting conversation on what the teacher has identified as an area for growth. By doing so, you ensure a sense of ownership over the goal and help to cultivate a relationship of trust—one where you honor another teacher's ability to reflect on and analyze their own practice.

### Precoaching Observation

With the SWEL Support Tools (see Appendixes A, B, and C), the precoaching observation can serve as a baseline to show growth and change in instructional practices as well as serve as a peer coaching conversation outline. It is not evaluative, but rather provides a road map for productive discussions around how to support MLEs in the general education classroom.

You can also record video while conducting this observation, because it creates opportunities for the coachee to conduct a self-observation and the video can be revisited individually or as a coaching pair. Additionally, a single video can be used for multiple purposes in addition to SWEL coaching observations, such as principal "walkthroughs" or demonstrations for PD sessions. Several brave SWEL coaches and their coachees have shown videos of their own teaching in PD sessions on specific teaching strategies for MLEs, and this has been met with a great deal of respect and interest from colleagues who are not working directly with a SWEL coach. In addition, video observations can be useful in future years of SWEL implementation.

For the purposes of the coaching cycle, the SWEL coach will either focus closely on practices related to the coachee's instructional goal or, if the coachee has asked for help setting goals, look for opportunities to help establish an instructional goal.

> **VOICES FROM THE FIELD**
>
> Observing classroom teachers connected us with the immediate needs of our fellow teachers. We were able to know their strengths and areas of improvement. This guided our school-wide staff development—an advantage an off-campus consultant might not have. *(SWEL coach)*

## Precoaching Observation Discussion

Continuing to use the five principles for peer coaching conversations, SWEL coaches should strive to find a time to meet with the coachee shortly after the initial precoaching observation so that the experience and notes stay fresh in everyone's mind. This does not mean that the meeting needs to take place immediately after the observation, which is often difficult or impossible to schedule because of teaching obligations. Instead, finding a time to meet within a week will allow for some reflection and help to ensure that the details have not been forgotten. Of course, using video can also relieve some of the pressure for scheduling a precoaching observation conversation and creating detailed notes.

Key considerations for the precoaching observation discussion include the following:

- Ask questions. Let the coachee drive the discussion. This will set a reflective tone for the conversation.
- What did you learn from observing that you might add to your own teaching? We all appreciate recognition for the skills we have.
- What went really well?
- What do you want to work on related to the instructional goal? Asking your coachees to refer back to their instructional goals and reflect on them is a natural entry into a discussion that focuses on ways to work toward the goal.

This conversation is an opportunity to revisit the instructional goal that was set at the beginning of the coaching cycle or work together to create a focus goal if that has not been done yet. Whichever situation you find yourself in, leading with questions is usually a good strategy for conducting this conversation. Ask questions like, "What went well in the lesson?," "If you teach this lesson again, what will you change?," and "What did you notice about the MLEs' engagement during this lesson?" Each of these questions allows the classroom/content teacher (who was in the somewhat uncomfortable role of being observed by a peer) to control the direction of the discussion. You can also ask how you can be helpful; some teachers want direct advice and ideas, while others would like to be guided to their own ideas through discussion. In the end, the precoaching observation discussion is an important opportunity for the coach and coachee to think about the successes of the lesson and where there are opportunities for improvement based on the goal that was set in the first meeting.

## Sharing Instructional Strategies

After the precoaching observation discussion, the SWEL coach works to gather resources for the classroom/content teacher that will assist in meeting their instructional goal. The coach provides those resources to the teacher or points their colleague toward readings that address second language acquisition pedagogy or even theory, if that fits the situation. Coachees usually appreciate activities and articles with relevant teaching ideas; when time is short, it can be useful to have someone gather and share specific teaching resources and strategies to experiment with in lesson plans. Likewise, providing information on the research that justifies the use of such strategies and how to use them will help to build knowledge and skills that support MLEs. Another option that many SWEL coaches use is coplanning, either together in person, in an online meeting, or even through a shared Google document. Some ideas for resources might be lesson plans, books, articles, websites, and activities for the classroom. These resources can be shared all at once during a meeting or more slowly over time between observations. This is also a time for the SWEL coach to invite the coachee to observe their own teaching, where the coach might model instructional strategies directly tied to the coachee's goal and explain why they were used.

If the coach is struggling to think of resources to share, the following options work generally across a number of audiences and can be a good start for this portion of the coaching cycle.

- Coplanning for language objectives
- Scaffolding language demands of text
- Developing language level–appropriate questions
- Embedding graphic organizers and other learning strategies into instruction (not just as a worksheet)
- Tips for increasing oral language use

Though this is not nearly an exhaustive list, it does give some concrete and productive ways in which to begin the pedagogy and strategy sharing until the SWEL coach gets more comfortable in the teacher leadership role.

## Postcoaching Observation

Whether it's at the end of a term or near the end of the school year, scheduling a postcoaching observation to see how the classroom/content teacher has attended to the instructional goal they set is an important part of the coaching cycle. In this phase, the SWEL coach should use the established instructional goal as a guidepost for the observation. The SWEL coach will look for the same instructional actions that were focused on during the initial observation. Of course, the idea here is that the coach will see positive changes in the teaching since the coaching pair started working together toward the goal. During the observation, the SWEL coach should look for new instructional strategies in use and for how MLEs are responding to the instruction, particularly as compared to the first observation.

## Postcoaching Observation Discussion

Much like the discussion that takes place after the first observation, the postcoaching observation discussion should be driven by questions that allow for reflection on practice. The following questions are designed to elicit a thoughtful conversation about professional practice as it relates to serving MLEs and the instructional goal that was set.

- Do you believe that you have met your instructional goal?
- If yes, what did you do differently that helped you meet this goal?
- If not, what will you try next time to help you meet your goal?
- What did you learn about your students in this process?
- What did you learn about yourself?
- What will you do differently in the future?
- Would you like to continue working on this goal?

The final question in this list indicates how the cycle will continue. Some teachers may feel that they want to keep refining their instructional practices related to the goal they originally set, which has been the case for a number of the teachers working with the SWEL coaches we have trained. Others may be ready to move on to a new goal and start the coaching cycle anew. Finally, there may be a need to move on to peer coaching with a new set of teachers, so the coaching cycle with this individual teacher might be put on pause to begin working with another colleague.

## Sharing Instructional Strategies

Regardless of how the coaching cycle does or does not continue, sharing instructional strategies is another way in which the SWEL coach can continue to serve as a PD facilitator to classroom/content teacher colleagues, even when there isn't an opportunity to work in a one-on-one setting. In addition to facilitating PD sessions that address dispositions, knowledge, and skills, such as those provided in Chapters 4, 5, and 6, a SWEL coach may want to look for books, articles, and lesson plans or activities that are related to or expand on the original goal. This might involve sharing teaching videos or modeling a new teaching strategy during coteaching. There are myriad ways in which the sharing of dispositions, knowledge, and skills for working with MLEs can continue both formally and informally. Chances are, teachers are already doing this in quick conversations in the hallways and lunchroom. The coaching cycle simply adds some structure to an otherwise typical way for teachers to share ideas. SWEL coaching is designed to be ongoing in nature and provide opportunities for reciprocity. The final stage of the coaching cycle exemplifies this.

## Professional Development

Centered in the SWEL peer coaching cycle is PD. Delivering ongoing, relevant, site-based PD to classroom/content teacher colleagues (such as the sample PD plans presented in Chapters 4, 5, and 6) is critical to transforming instruction for MLEs throughout the school day. PD sessions can be offered frequently to the entire staff and tailored to the needs of the greater school community, while one-on-one coaching focuses on the goals of an individual teacher. Some SWEL coaches also deliver PD in the professional learning community (PLC) setting, where small groups of teachers can name a shared goal and work together to accomplish it.

# THE SWEL LESSON PLAN INVENTORY

The SWEL Lesson Plan Inventory (Appendix H) can be used in multiple ways. Regardless of how it is used, SWEL coaches benefit from taking the time to walk through it with their coachees so that each criterion on the list makes sense to the classroom/content teachers. Given that much of the list attends to writing language objectives at the word, sentence, and discourse levels, it also means this topic should be addressed either in PD session(s), one-on-one peer coaching sessions, or both. We have also added three appendixes (E, F, and G) that detail the process of planning for word, sentence, and discourse level language instruction, respectively. Some SWEL coaches wait until later in the school year to introduce the Lesson Plan Inventory so that the peer coaching relationship has some roots and coachees are ready to tackle it in their planning. The SWEL coach must use their professional discretion and knowledge of the teaching context to decide exactly when the introduction of this tool is appropriate.

The SWEL Lesson Plan Inventory, available on the companion site for this book (www.tesol.org/SWEL-book), is intended to help classroom/content teachers strengthen their lesson plans so that all learners improve their English while mastering critical content-area knowledge, including but not limited to science, social studies, English language arts, and mathematics. It includes the following criteria:

- The lesson plan has a clear content objective (learning target).

- The lesson has an area of language to focus on in this lesson through
  - noticing students' areas of language needs and/or
  - forecasting areas of language need in lesson text, tasks, or tests.
- The lesson plan has a clear language objective.
- The language objective begins with a function (what students will be doing with language) that supports the content objective.
- The language objective ends with a support (a tool to support students with the language that you are teaching).
- Language objective focal area:
  - If the language objective is at the word level, there is a focal area of phonology (how words sound), morphology (parts of words), or semantics (vocabulary). At least three examples are included.
  - If the language objective is at the sentence level, there is a focal area of syntax (grammar, how words fit together). At least three examples are included.
  - If the language objective is at the discourse level, there is a named text type.
- The lesson plan includes instructional strategies and activities aimed at learning the language of the language objective.
- The lesson plan includes an assessment (formative or summative) of the language of the language objective.

The first way in which the lesson plan inventory can be used is as a resource for coplanning between the ELD and classroom/content teachers. For those SWEL coaches who are already working in coteaching structures, the introduction of the inventory is relatively seamless; the SWEL coach can take the lead on using the inventory for planning collaborative lessons and encourage their teaching partner to use it for planning the rest of the instructional day when coteaching is not taking place. In this situation, the SWEL coach can model how to use the lesson plan inventory. This might take the form of thinking out loud once a complete draft of the lesson or unit plan is done. A SWEL coach might say something like, "Now that we're done with the lesson plan draft, I'm going to walk through the lesson plan inventory to make sure we've included components that will help to make the content more accessible to MLEs." If components of the checklist are missing from the plan, then the SWEL coach can talk through areas where changes can be made and what those changes would do to help ensure MLEs' participation in the lesson.

A second way to use the lesson plan inventory is to share it with teachers at the end of a PD session that addresses language levels or writing language objectives. Rather than simply sharing it out with classroom/content teachers, it is a worthwhile exercise to go through each item on the checklist and include time for participants to ask questions and get feedback on how they can incorporate the checklist into their regular planning routine. If your school uses a common lesson plan template, then consider getting permission from administrators to add the inventory, or a link to it, to the end of the template. In schools where lesson plans are not standardized, a laminated copy of the checklist that can be kept in a planning book (for those who use paper) or a shared digital copy might be an effective way to get teachers to add the checklist to their planning routine. For SWEL coaches with dedicated time in their schedules for coaching, the checklist can be introduced in a PD session and then addressed in one-on-one coaching sessions.

Regardless of when it is used—and each SWEL coach should use their professional judgment to decide when that will be—the lesson plan inventory is meant to serve as a reminder to include language instruction in all content-area lessons throughout the school day and across all classrooms and content areas. It is not intended to be exhaustive, and once the items are consistently attended to or become automatic for classroom/content teachers, this tool no longer needs to be used.

## THE SWEL SUPPORT TOOLS: LANGUAGE-BASED TEACHER OBSERVATION FORMS

Though the SWEL Support Tools resemble observation forms in many ways, they are also designed to be nonevaluative ways to structure SWEL coaching and measure change in instructional practice over time. Dialogic or professional conversation focuses on the relationship that exists between two teachers with different areas of expertise, and the SWEL Support Tools provide a baseline for where instructional practices are and a roadmap for where they could go. This section presents the SWEL Support Tools in their entirety and breaks down each of their components. You can download the three full SWEL Support Tools, which are editable, on the companion site for this book (www.tesol.org/SWEL-book).

> In the resources, you will find three versions of the SWEL Support Tool: one for multimodal instruction, one for English language development, and one for supporting the language of identity.

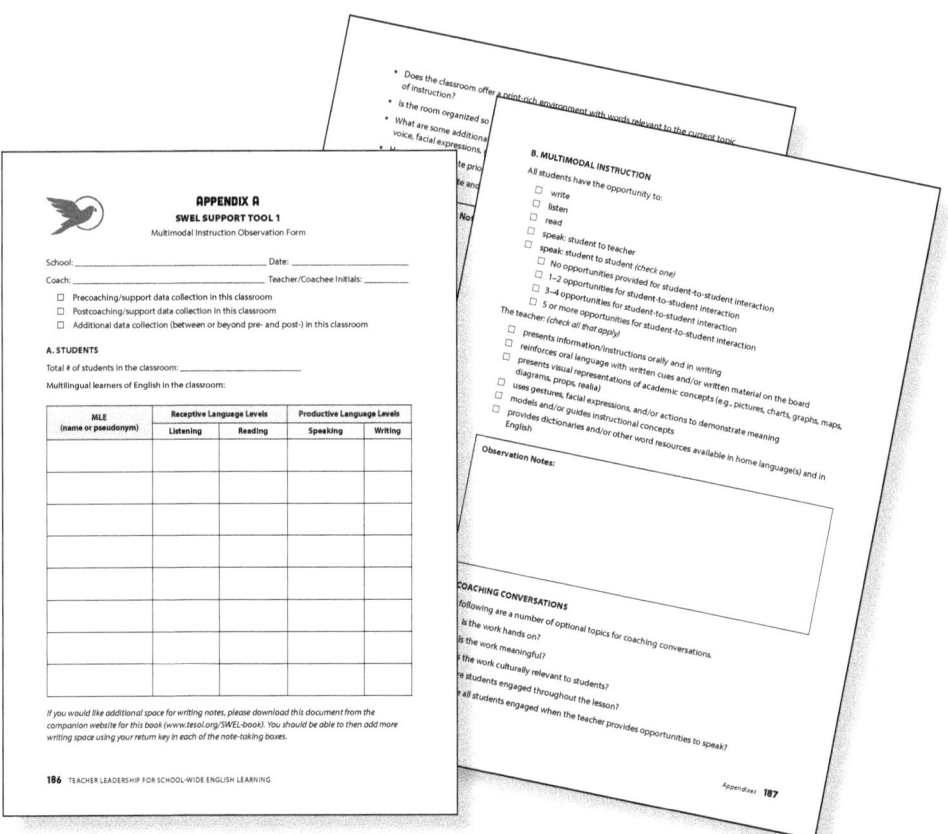

*Setting Up Teachers for Success* **155**

For teachers who would like to collect data related to change in practices and growth, the opening section of each SWEL Support Tool captures where the coachee is in the peer coaching cycle, which is described earlier in this chapter (see Figure 1). In a nonevaluative peer coaching relationship, this section would be explained and explicitly understood by the coachee. The SWEL Support Tools can also be used by classroom/content teachers to observe the SWEL coach, who would then be able to model the instructional strategies highlighted in the SWEL Support Tools. Alternatively, any teacher who has MLEs in their classroom can use any of the SWEL Support Tools to self-evaluate, perhaps filling it out while watching a video recording of their own teaching.

---

**VOICES FROM THE FIELD**

After our preobservation, I worked with the two other SWEL coaches and we looked at areas of weakness in all of the observations. We tried to compile some of those together to decide if they were areas that would be helpful for the all-staff professional development sessions. We also looked at the student population and thought about what they are lacking right now from their teachers. What could we give them more of? Are strategies being used effectively or do they need to be changed a little bit? With all of those pieces, we tried to figure out what could we teach or expand on that's already there. That's what we found by looking at the [SWEL Support Tools]. *(SWEL coach)*

---

### A. Students: Who Is in the Classroom?

The first section of each SWEL Support Tool provides background on the students in the room. This is useful for a number of reasons. As SWEL coaches and classroom/content teachers walk through the data that was collected with this tool, having student information readily available will help to make suggestions more concrete and individualized. It also helps to point toward the kind of scaffolding and differentiation strategies, in which a SWEL coach is well versed, that would be useful for the specific group of students being taught. Each SWEL Support Tool includes a place for naming specific students and listing their assessed language levels in each modality. In our experience, there are times when the classroom/content teacher is not aware of these assessed language levels or what they indicate. In these situations, it is worthwhile to fold a description of these levels into the pre- and postcoaching observation conversations.

Understanding the number of MLEs as a percentage of the total classroom population is also useful as teachers work together to decide on strategies that are best suited for the environment. For example, in classes where 80% of the students are MLEs and the vast majority of those students fall within the intermediate to advanced English levels, it makes sense to aim instruction at those levels and focus differentiation strategies on those who do not fall within that middle range (including monolingual English-speaking students). In classrooms with fewer than 5% MLEs, station work or small group instruction might be the better way to tailor the lesson to meet their needs.

## VOICES FROM THE FIELD

We sat down together with the [SWEL Support Tool] and looked for areas where teachers wanted to improve and make goals. From there on, most of the year naturally came from that goal. For example, the kindergarten teacher really had a lot of knowledge of teaching MLEs but she looked more deeply at the students and said "You know a lot of the MLEs don't talk and it's so hard to get them to talk. How can we get them to do that?" So we made oral sentence starters. The fifth-grade teacher was similar because a lot of times her MLEs couldn't produce responses in writing to their reading. So, we would make sentence frames and display them around the room to make more visuals. With another teacher, she and I were teaching fourth-grade writing together in the middle of the year and she was like, "You know they're doing great in writing but they are really struggling in math." So, we switched over to math ... We started talking about math, thinking out loud, and having discussions about numbers and making real-world scenarios for the kids through math because that's sometimes disconnected ... *(SWEL coach)*

### B. Lesson Plan Objectives: Content and Language

As mentioned in previous chapters, language objectives are created from the content objectives for a given lesson or unit plan. They may go by a variety of names, such as objective, learning target, learning focus, or learning goal. For our purposes, we use the terms *content objectives* and *language objectives*. Regardless of what they're called, most school settings require objectives for every lesson and it is fairly typical to see those objectives posted in the form of "I can" statements on the board, in a presentation slide, or somewhere that is visible to the students. Because of the relationship between content objectives and language objectives, the SWEL Support Tools provide a space for the content objective (Part B of each form). Many SWEL coaches have reported concerns about overwhelming their colleagues with PD on language objectives, so it may be that language objectives are set aside until SWEL coaching is fully integrated into the school culture. There are plenty of other strategies to focus on in the meantime!

> Rely on your expertise to decide if introducing language objectives should be set aside for the future. Consider starting with concepts such as "bricks, mortar, and buildings" and other aspects of language first.

### C. Language Objectives

Following the content objective is an area to note one of three language objectives, either at the word, sentence, or discourse/text type level (Part C of each SWEL Support Tool). Because it is seldom realistic to both teach and assess more than one language objective in a given lesson, the SWEL Support Tools are set up in such a way that the SWEL coach or teacher who is using a tool would only fill out the language objective at the language level that is targeted in the instruction. For example, if a science lesson is teaching students about density, the SWEL coach would record the following at the discourse level and leave blank the word- and sentence-level areas on the SWEL Support Tool: *I can describe density in a science lab report with the support of Cornell Notes and an outline.*

> **Discourse-Level Language Objective:** *(check all that apply)*
>
> ☑ Language Structure: Discourse level (text type)
>   ☑ Includes a function
>   ☑ Includes a text type
>   ☑ Includes supports
>
> **Please write the discourse-level academic language objective here:**
>
> *I can describe density in a science lab report with the support of Cornell Notes and an outline.*

It is worth noting that, in many cases, SWEL coaches who are working with classroom/content teachers to gather data on growth may not list a language objective for the precoaching observation or the first step in the coaching cycle. This is very common and not a cause for alarm or shame for not attending to the needs of MLEs. Writing language objectives takes a great deal of practice and is a relatively new process in ELD teaching. In fact, neither of us learned how to do this in our teacher preparation programs. Instead, we learned how to write language objectives over a number of years and through a number of processes that evolved over time. For that reason, it is important for the SWEL coach to reassure their coachee(s), and possibly themselves, that including language objectives in every lesson plan is a process that takes time, consultation with an ELD teacher, and a lot of practice. This is why we offer the SWEL Support Tools in three versions: one for multimodal instruction, one for ELD, and one for supporting the language of identity.

## D. Student Awareness of Language Learning

The more we can help students to be aware of their own learning, the better. It can help to increase student self-efficacy (Bandura, 1978), or their belief that they are capable of learning language, and give students a sense of ownership of their learning. Section D of each SWEL Support Tool builds on the prior section related to language objectives. It asks the teacher who is filling out the form, in most cases the SWEL coach, to analyze the content objective and language objective to see that they are related to one another and congruent.

For example, if a fifth-grade classroom/content teacher is working on a unit about the Titanic in which students are expected to write a five-paragraph editorial article as the summative assessment, then it would make sense that a given lesson in that unit attends to the discourse-level language learning related to editorials. However, if the language objective in the same lesson on the Titanic addresses generic or unrelated sight word recognition that may or may not be present in the readings for the lesson, then the first box in this section would not be checked.

> **D. STUDENT AWARENESS OF LANGUAGE LEARNING (METALINGUISTIC AWARENESS)**
> *Check all that apply.*
>
> ☐ Language objective is derived from the content objective/learning target.
> ☐ Language objective is written for students to see.
> ☐ Language objective is read out loud for students to hear.

The second two boxes in Section D go even further toward ensuring that students are consciously attending to their own language learning. In other words, the teacher is providing opportunities for students to develop their metalinguistic awareness, or their ability to think about their language learning. Check the second box if the language objective is written somewhere in the classroom where students can easily see and refer to it. Check the third box if the language objective is read aloud to the students or if it is read chorally by the students. If the educator being observed does not attend to any of these components of the SWEL Support Tool, they may serve as a good starting point for goal setting and peer coaching once language objectives have been introduced.

## E. Multimodal Instruction

In Chapters 4 through 6, the four language modalities of reading, writing, listening, and speaking were addressed in a number of PD activities. To become proficient in a language, students need to demonstrate sufficient skills in all four modalities, including the receptive modalities of reading and listening and the productive modalities of writing and speaking. Of course, there can be tremendous variety in a single MLE's language levels across each of the four modalities, and this should be made clear to classroom/content teachers who have not completed coursework or PD in language acquisition. It will help these educators to better understand why a given MLE can "sound fluent" in English but still qualifies for ELD support, to name just one of many potential misperceptions related to MLEs.

Multimodal instruction, or attending to all four modalities of language in teaching, is essential to working toward language proficiency. SWEL Support Tool 1: Multimodal Instruction (Appendix A) addresses the many ways in which teachers ensure that students have opportunities to not just read and listen, modalities which tend to be more heavily focused on in the typical classroom, but also write and speak. This is why the box under speaking is drawn out in a number of ways. It is also a nod toward potential PD and peer coaching work if it is observed that MLEs rarely have opportunities to speak in class, much less have conversations about the content being taught.

Though the SWEL Support Tools are not exhaustive in their coverage of pedagogies for MLEs, they provide both focus areas for instructional growth and a glimpse at what is happening in a classroom in terms of making content accessible for MLEs.

> **B. MULTIMODAL INSTRUCTION**
>
> All students have the opportunity to:
>
> - ☐ write
> - ☐ listen
> - ☐ read
> - ☐ speak: student to teacher
> - ☐ speak: student to student *(check one)*
>   - ☐ No opportunities provided for student-to-student interaction
>   - ☐ 1–2 opportunities for student-to-student interaction
>   - ☐ 3–4 opportunities for student-to-student interaction
>   - ☐ 5 or more opportunities for student-to-student interaction
>
> The teacher: *(check all that apply)*
>
> - ☐ presents information/instructions orally and in writing
> - ☐ reinforces oral language with written cues and/or written material on the board
> - ☐ presents visual representations of academic concepts (e.g., pictures, charts, graphs, maps, diagrams, props, realia)
> - ☐ uses gestures, facial expressions, and/or actions to demonstrate meaning
> - ☐ models and/or guides instructional concepts
> - ☐ provides dictionaries and/or other word resources available in home language(s) and in English

## F. Coaching Conversations

Each SWEL Support Tool indicates a number of topics that the SWEL coach could take up with classroom/content teachers, both in one-on-one peer coaching and in PD delivery. In addition, each SWEL Support Tool includes a number of additional topics that address instructional techniques which are typically used by ELD teachers but may not be part of regular practice for classroom/content teachers. For those who struggle to come up with a goal for the coaching cycle, these coaching conversation tips also provide ideas for focus areas.

The SWEL Support Tools help SWEL coaches to ensure meaningful coaching conversations, provide a means by which to measure growth and change, and add a nonevaluative structure to the work of ELD teacher leadership.

---

### VOICES FROM THE FIELD

There was a lot of teacher learning around specific strategies for MLE engagement and also ways to assess things that are perhaps more difficult to assess, like student conversation or student oral language. *(SWEL coach)*

**Discussion Questions**

1. How do you generally approach change when it comes to your teaching and professional learning?

2. How is instructional change generally viewed in your school or work setting?

3. What aspects of the SWEL peer coaching cycle may require adjustment in order to implement SWEL coaching in your setting?

**Takeaway Task**

Review the three SWEL Support Tools: the Multimodal Instruction Support Tool, the English Language Development Support Tool, and the Language of Identity Support Tool. How might each of these tools work in your setting? Would they require adjustments in order to be effective at your site?

## References

Aguilar, E. (2013). *The art of coaching: Effective strategies for school transformation.* John Wiley & Sons.

Bandura, A. (1978). Self-efficacy: Toward a unifying theory of behavioral change. *Advances in Behaviour Research and Therapy, 1*(4), 139–161.

Cross, Jeni. (2013, March). Three myths of behavior change - What you think you know that you don't [Video]. TEDx Talks. https://youtu.be/l5d8GW6GdR0?feature=shared

Garmston, R. J., & Wellman, B. M. (2016). *The adaptive school: A sourcebook for developing collaborative groups.* Rowman & Littlefield.

Knight, J. (2011). What good coaches do. *Educational Leadership, 69*(2), 18–22.

# PART D

**Putting SWEL to Work in Your School: Setting the Stage With Intentional Planning**

# CHAPTER 8

# DRAFTING AN ANNUAL SWEL ACTION PLAN

Critical to the success of any initiative is good planning. Just like when we teach, going in without a plan is risky business and often means that we have murky objectives or leave meeting the standards for student learning to chance. The same applies for delivering professional development (PD) and school-wide English learning (SWEL) coaching: Without a plan, the chances of meeting the ultimate goal of increasing multilingual learner of English (MLE) achievement through consistent attention to language learning are haphazard, at best.

With an aim for coaching to be as well planned as possible so that goals related to instructional change are achieved, this chapter presents the SWEL Action Plan (Appendix K) and a step-by-step guide that includes a rationale, how-to, and sample text for each section. In this edition, we are also including SWEL Planning for Professional Development (Appendix I), a tool with which SWEL coaches can focus exclusively on their PD work and which serves as a companion to the SWEL Action Plan.

## NEEDS ANALYSIS

At the onset of the action plan, it is important to clearly spell out the school context and its needs. The needs analysis is the "driver of the action plan" and provides the foundation on which all other components of the action plan are built. It is important to know the home languages of students, as well as their language levels and learner type. This matters because action plans will be tailored to the populations being served. For example, in a school with a high population of long-term English learners, staff may have a goal to better understand why students are not progressing in English language development (ELD). Alternatively, in a school with a high number of students with limited or interrupted formal education, the teachers may place more importance on the role of home language literacy or approaches to language instruction when home language literacy is not in place.

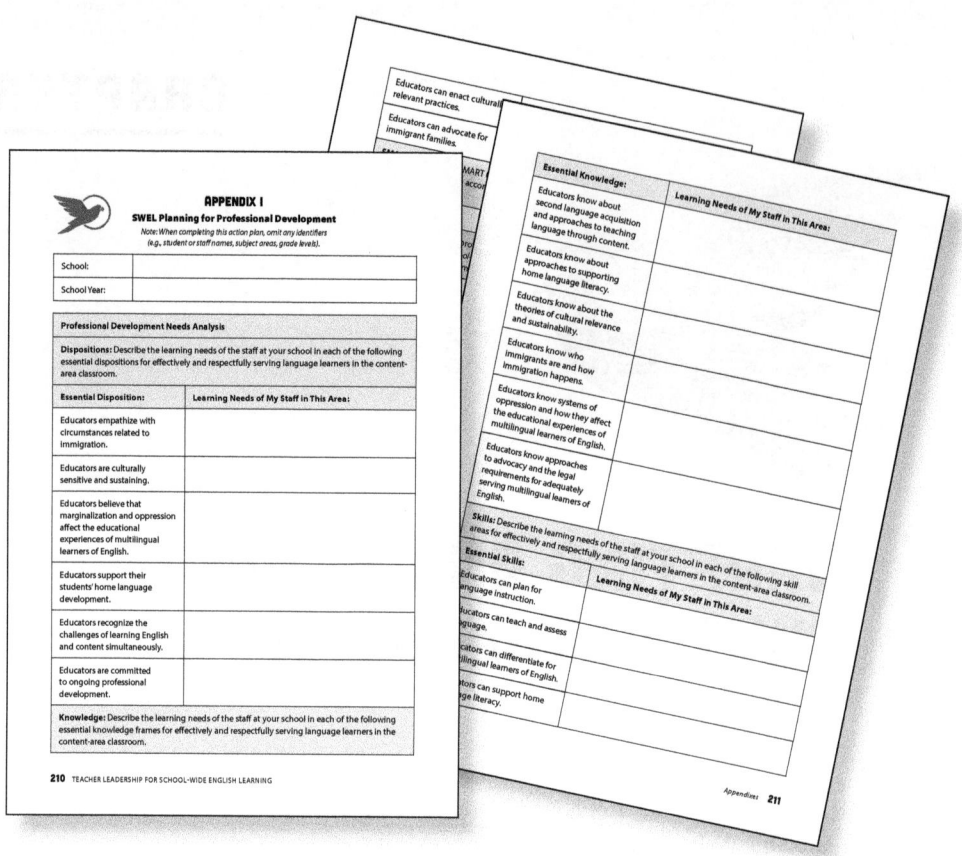

Appendix I: SWEL Planning for Professional Development can be used to evaluate whole-staff needs for PD. SWEL Coach Michelle Tornga developed an alternative to this activity. The SWEL Survey: A Diagnostic to Determine Staff Needs (tinyurl.com/bdewr9zu), is intended to be distributed to all educators in a school to determine where they perceive the most need for PD. The data are very helpful in annual action planning. These two tools could be used in tandem as well.

For this section, you will need to respond to three prompts:

1. A description of the language backgrounds, language levels, and types of MLEs at your school (e.g., highly literate newcomers, long-term English learners, students with limited or interrupted formal education)

2. The unique needs of your MLE populations

3. The challenges that your classroom/content teacher colleagues encounter

## 1. Learner Backgrounds

You may need to access a variety of resources in order to get all of this information. State and district data can be a good source for this. Some teachers include graphics from these databases, such as pie charts, to display student data, which can be useful when sharing the plan with administrators or other teachers. If data on subpopulations of MLEs are unknown, you can estimate based on your knowledge of the student population at a specific school site. This is also an appropriate place to list language levels or other composite standardized language test scores, as well as home languages as they are listed on student home language survey forms. See Sample Text A for an example of the first section of the Needs Analysis. The team of teachers that developed this action plan used a variety of data points to analyze the needs of the MLE population.

## SAMPLE TEXT A. NEEDS ANALYSIS PROMPT 1
(Adapted from Defrance Schmidt & Rich, 2019)

**Tracy Lake**

Tracy Lake Elementary contains the following two programs: the Hmong Dual Immersion Program (taught in Hmong) and the Hmong Studies program (taught in English). Demographically, 87.9% of our students are Asian, 5.0% Latinx, 3.8% Black, 2.3% Biracial/Multiracial, and 0.9% White. A large majority of our students (80.5%) qualify for free and reduced lunch.

**Description of MLEs at Tracy Lake**

A majority of our students (70%) are MLEs, with a greater percentage of MLEs in the primary grades as a result of students exiting services. Our students' primary home languages include Hmong, Karen, and Spanish. We also have students who speak Kiswahili, Nepali, Burmese, Sudanese Arabic, Somali, and Oromo. We have a Language Academy (LA) program, which provides targeted support for students in our classrooms who are newly arrived in the United States. However, with recent demographic changes based on U.S. immigration/refugee policy, we currently have far fewer students who qualify for the LA program. Although our LA students are too young to qualify as students with limited or interrupted formal education under state law, many of the newcomer students in our intermediate grades have had interrupted school and some have never been in school before. Currently, in Grades 3–5, we have three newcomers, two of whom have literacy in Arabic and are similar to highly literate newcomers, whereas the additional student is similar to a student with limited or interrupted formal education.

Most of our MLEs have been attending Tracy Lake or other U.S. schools since kindergarten. Many of our students are Generation 1.5 or second-generation students. In the past, LA students were often a primary focus for MLE and classroom teachers. With fewer LA students, we are shifting to focusing more on students at language Levels 3–5 to help them move toward proficiency. A majority of our students are at Levels 3 and 4, and we notice students often plateau at these levels. We hope to support students sufficiently so that they are able to exit services by fifth grade, before they become long-term English learners.

| WIDA Levels Based on Access Scores |
|---|
| Level 1:  7.4% (27) |
| Level 2:  20.9% (74) |
| Level 3:  43.1% (154) |
| Level 4:  24.2 (87) |
| Level 5:  3.8% (14) |

Tracy Lake has long focused on PD designed to support classroom teachers in teaching MLEs in the content areas. Because Tracy Lake has worked to have MLE strategies embedded in our PD work, our school outperforms the state and district in our average target toward their English language learning goals:

| State Progress Toward English Language Proficiency | Tracy Lake | District | State |
|---|---|---|---|
| Progress Toward Growth Target | 81.6% (367 Students) | 63% | 67% |
| Met Growth Target | 62.9% | 43.6% | 48.5% |

## 2. Learner Needs

The second prompt under the Needs Analysis is "Explain the unique needs of your multilingual learner of English populations." This can be answered in a variety of ways. It is important to consider the concerns that you and your colleagues have about areas in which MLEs are not making adequate progress. The team of teachers that developed the following Sample Text B considered the populations that they serve and their concerns about long-term English learners (also known as experienced multilinguals) as well as a need to focus more intentionally on productive modalities.

### SAMPLE TEXT B. NEEDS ANALYSIS PROMPT 2

**Unique Multilingual Learner of English Needs at Tracy Lake**

Our growth scores are promising and reflective of our deep work. However, until 100% of students meet their growth targets, we need to continue to refine our practice. In addition, we have students who are on track to becoming experienced multilinguals. Last year, 47 students had 6 years of ELD service and will be considered experienced multilinguals if they do not exit by the end of sixth grade. We had 34 students who showed a loss in their ACCESS scores.

At Tracy Lake, 49 students were proficient on last year's ACCESS test. Our productive modalities (writing and speaking) show the most need for improvement. Our students need more focused instruction on writing, including targeted support in meeting grade-level standards.

- In Grades 2–5, only one student scored at Levels 5 or 6.
- In Grade 1, nine students were at Levels 5 and 6 in writing.
- In kindergarten, 12 students were at Levels 5 and 6.
- In speaking: Only one student from Grades 2–5 was at Levels 5–6, one Grade 1 student was at Level 5, and 12 kindergartners were Level 5+.
- When our students exit services, they often still have a score of 3.5 or 4.0 on writing.

As we adapt to new demographics with fewer newcomers, it is a good time to refocus on intermediate and advanced MLEs to move them toward proficiency.

## 3. Educator Challenges

The third prompt under the Needs Analysis is "Explain the challenges that your classroom/content teacher colleagues encounter." Similar to the last prompt, this will depend greatly on the populations that you serve and the context in which you work. It is important to consider where your colleagues are and where they need to be when it comes to adequately serving MLEs. One consideration to keep in mind is any kind of demographic shift that has occurred in the MLE population. Also, note that focusing on instruction for a particular modality, such as reading, may have proven fruitful in the past, but student data might indicate that another modality now needs more attention.

**SAMPLE TEXT C. NEEDS ANALYSIS PROMPT 3**

**Classroom Teacher Challenges**

One challenge that classroom/content teachers face is having classrooms that are composed primarily of language learners. With a limited number of peers proficient in English, it is necessary to proactively teach the skills of classroom conversations and writing. We have had a focus on developing oral language through student use of cooperative routines (think, pair, share; think, write, share; partner practice; etc.) We have noticed, however, that the conversations do not always go as deep as we'd like. Students struggle to maintain the conversations. Teachers provide sentence frames, and students are adept at using them. However, the students rely on them, and are often constrained by them. For these reasons, we are embarking on a school-wide book study of *Academic Conversations* by Jeff Zweirs.

In order to deepen the level of language being used in class, content teachers still need practice in analyzing grade-level text (spoken and written) at the word, sentence, and discourse levels. The discourse level is especially an area we could focus more on. Analyzing the language that is needed to meet content standards and then teaching that language would help raise the rigor of our students' language. A systematic way to attend to this analysis and support is by writing language objectives. This also allows teachers to clearly articulate to students what they are expected to do and how they can do it. Having written language objectives will help teachers provide specific, actionable student feedback to help students advance in English as they meet grade-level standards.

The example in Sample Text C highlights the intentional work that the teachers at Tracy Lake have already done to improve their MLEs' language, and it narrows in on a focus for the coming year. Being specific about what your classroom/content teacher colleagues know and where they need to be in terms of instruction is critical to the success of SWEL peer coaching and helps you to maintain a focus on the topics that you feel are most relevant.

# GOAL SETTING

Central to the success of any initiative is a clear goal to drive the work forward. SWEL coaches are asked to write SMART goals (Doran, 1981). If you can answer "yes" to each of the following questions, you have a SMART goal.

**Specific:** Have you identified a specific area for improvement?

**Measurable:** Have you included a way to measure progress toward meeting the goal?

**Achievable:** Is your goal doable given the time and resources at your school?

**Relevant:** Is your goal relevant to student needs and staff skills?

**Time-bound:** Have you identified a clear end date by which the goal will be met?

The SMART method helps to build boundaries around a goal so that it can serve as a high-level focus for your work. Defining each of the components of your SMART goal—specific, measurable, achievable, relevant, and time-bound—helps to set up a structure that creates accountability for meeting the goal and provides the groundwork for the next goal that is set. Generally, a single SMART goal should suffice for a school year, but it is possible to have two or three SMART goals, depending on the circumstances. Be sure to note that the SMART goal in the SWEL Action Plan is not the same as the goals that coachees set in their one-on-one work with SWEL coaches. Coachee goals focus specifically on their individual instruction while the SWEL Action Plan goal is focused on the school-wide implementation of SWEL coaching. Though the two may be closely related, they are unique and distinct from one another.

In Sample Text D, the team of teachers simultaneously considered the needs analysis as well as individual coaching when writing these sample SMART goals.

### SAMPLE TEXT D. GOAL SETTING

1. By october, all classroom/content teachers participating in the SWEL program will select one area of improvement on one of the SWEL support tools.

2. By the end of the year, 75% of classroom/content teachers participating in the SWEL program will improve in one area of their choice on a SWEL support tool.

3. By the end of the year, 80% of teachers observed will demonstrate proficiency writing language objectives at the sentence or discourse level.

## SWEL IMPLEMENTATION STEPS

Once the goal has been established, it's important to identify the steps you will need to take to set up your action plan for success. Consider what you will need to do to achieve your SMART goal. SWEL implementation asks you to consider the following questions:

- What do you need to get started?
- How will you recruit participants?
- What PD topics will you cover and when will you deliver them?
- How many classroom visits will you make and when will you do them?
- When and how will coaching conversations happen?

In Sample Text E, we share ideas for how to break down these stages into step-by-step plans.

### SAMPLE TEXT E. IMPLEMENTATION STEPS

| Initial Planning | • Meeting with administrators, including principal, assistant principal, and district administrator for ELD programs <br> • Writing Action Plan and sharing with key stakeholders from the administration and ELD teams |
|---|---|
| Recruitment | • Recruiting each coachee during the opening week before students arrive <br> • Following up with teachers who expressed interest <br> • Finalizing list of teachers for one-on-one peer coaching |

| | |
|---|---|
| Professional Development | **6 hours of PD: Whole staff**<br><br>3 hours whole-staff during staff meetings<br><br>3 hours during job-embedded PD rotation<br><br>**Topics**<br><br>- **Scaffolding for ACCESS Scores by Domains:** How to find ACCESS scores (share with specialists), what they mean, our growth, key uses, can dos, reviewing how to scaffold levels in classroom conversations (staff meeting, 1 hr)<br>- **Bricks, Mortar, and Buildings:** Analyzing language at the word, sentence, and discourse level. Language needed to meet content objectives through classroom conversations and writing. Fancy grammar terms not required! (staff meeting, 1 hr)<br>- **Beyond Sentence Frames:** Analyzing and teaching the language needed for classroom conversations (staff meeting, 1 hr)<br>- **Demystifying Language Objectives:** Writing leveled language objectives (add specialists to this rotation using SWEL coach's sub). Teacher practice in writing language standards for upcoming units (job-embedded PD rotation, 1.5 hrs)<br>- **Assessing Students' Language Through Classroom Conversations:** Backward build up and starting with the type of discourse needed in the discipline to develop engaging formative assessments in the content areas. Draws on recent assessment training (specialists will attend; job-embedded PD rotation, 1.5 hrs) |
| Visits | **Classroom Visits**<br><br>- Using sub release time (district fund)<br>- During dedicated peer coaching planning time<br>- During coteaching using the one-teach/one-observe method |
| Coaching | **Teacher Recruitment**<br><br>- One-on-ones with potential recruits<br>- 5-minute presentation at staff meeting (second year)<br><br>**Schedule**<br><br>- 1 day per week for coaching (195 minutes coaching, 160 minutes PD planning)<br>- Coaching day will be Mondays (day of job-embedded PD)<br>- Sub release days as needed for classroom visits (using district budget) |

## SUPPORTS

As discussed in Chapters 1 and 2, it is considerably easier to do the work of SWEL teacher leadership in a distributed or shared leadership model and with support from structures that are put in place to assist the work of ELD teacher leaders. If there are already structures in place for staff meetings or PD, how could you capitalize on those structures to fold SWEL coaching work into existing systems and routines? The more you can leverage existing structures, such as professional learning communities or predetermined PD days, the easier it will be to implement a nonevaluative SWEL peer coaching model. However, if structures need to be put in place to make the work feasible, such as arranging for common planning time for peer coaching conversations, you will need to consider what changes need to be made, who has the authority to make these changes, and how all stakeholders affected by these changes can be included in the decision-making process. Here are some supports that facilitate the model in schools:

- Dedicated time for delivering PD
- Dedicated time for meeting with colleagues as a peer coach
- Common planning time
- Leadership responsibilities written into ELD teacher job descriptions
- Ongoing administrator support (district and building)
- Existing structures for PD delivery, like monthly late arrival or early release days
- Support among colleagues in the building

The support section of the action plan is a place to name the people and structures that already exist and will help to make SWEL teacher leadership work more feasible. The action plan includes the following prompt:

> Identify who you anticipate will be in support of the SWEL project at your school. How might you capitalize on their support? In addition, identify any systems, policies, or norms that will support SWEL implementation at your school over the next year.

These prompts provide an opportunity to reflect on the supportive people and structures that already exist. See Sample Texts F and G for some examples of how action plans have identified existing supports.

### SAMPLE TEXT F: SUPPORTS EXAMPLE 1

1. **Support Staff**
   a. ELD teacher on special assignment and ELD supervisor
   b. Principal and assistant principal
   c. Classroom teachers will allow a SWEL coach to enter and observe in the classroom; they will also participate in staff development and coaching sessions; there are several staff members already involved in equity work and the equity work fits well with SWEL.
2. **Systems, Policies, and Norms That Align With SWEL**
   a. Literacy walkthroughs: Learning target focus
   b. New math curriculum: Learning target and language around word problems
   c. Media directors and coteaching

### SAMPLE TEXT G: SUPPORTS EXAMPLE 2

- District ELD coordinator
- Elementary ELD coach
- District SWEL coach cohort
- Principal

**Initiatives and systems at the school that will support SWEL**

- Professional learning communities & WIN (What I Need)
- National Urban Alliance
- Restorative practices

Like the two examples in Sample Texts F and G, the SWEL coach at Tracy Lake included a list of people who supported their work, including both ELD colleagues and administrators, as well as the structural supports that they leveraged to make SWEL coaching work at the school.

# CONCERNS AND OBSTACLES

It is wise and realistic to plan ahead for obstacles because even the most successful initiatives eventually encounter some sort of resistance or systemic snag as they are being implemented, even if it's just a routine fire alarm practice run. The concerns and obstacles that present themselves at each setting will be unique: While the staff at one school may resist because they suffer from "initiative fatigue" due to too many competing priorities, another school might be enthusiastic about the concept but struggle because they are short staffed and still trying to fill open positions. Still others might find it difficult to prioritize this work because they feel that the focus needs to be squarely on reading or math, or because ELD initiatives are perceived as focusing on some students rather than all students. Whatever the case may be in your setting, naming and reflecting on the potential concerns and obstacles can be helpful in coming up with ways to address or, in some cases, work around them. See Sample Text H for the concerns and obstacles named at Tracy Lake.

### SAMPLE TEXT H. CONCERNS AND OBSTACLES

**Time Management**

Time management will be a challenge. It will be a challenge to balance time between teaching (80%) and coaching (20%). It will also be a challenge to balance coaching time between planning PDs and time spent coaching. In order to overcome this challenge, I will maintain my organizational notebook system, spreadsheet detail schedule/plan overview, and Google calendar. I will have a full day per week to dedicate to coaching, which will help me to focus on SWEL coaching and allow me to be available during educators' preparation periods and time allotted for PD planning.

**Coachee Ownership**

Teachers will have more ownership in the process if the coaching is optional, grassroots, and teacher led. I used one-to-one teacher-to-teacher recruitment conversations to draw upon teachers' self-interest to increase ownership. All identified coachees have expressed excitement to join SWEL.

**My Coaching Skills**

I have received training through SWEL. I will attend additional coaching training through my district and participate in TESOL's SWEL Professional Learning Community. I will continue to read articles about coaching and reflect on my own practice. I will ask my coachees for feedback. I will reflect with other SWEL coaches through district cohort meetings. I will also reflect with other SWEL coaches.

## RESOURCES

Consider the resources that you have gathered in reading this book as well as resources that already exist in your school professional community to facilitate the process of launching a peer coaching model in your school. What resources do you have to support SWEL implementation at your school? What resources do you still need?

As you'll notice in Sample Text I, resources can be gathered from a variety of sources.

### SAMPLE TEXT I. RESOURCES

- SWEL Coaching Cycle
- Coaching articles
- Reflective Practice Tool and training (based on York-Barr, Sommers, William, Ghere, Gail, & Montie's book and trainings)*
- *Academic Conversations: Classroom Talk that Fosters Critical Thinking and Content Understanding*, by Zwiers & Crawford+
- *The K–3 Guide to Academic Conversations: Practices, Scaffolds, and Activities*, by Zwiers & Hamerla^
- Math and science resources
- Language/standards integration (from district website)
- WIDA Assessment Training

\* eric.ed.gov/?id=ED456572
+ www.routledge.com/Academic-Conversations-Classroom-Talk-that-Fosters-Critical-Thinking-a/Crawford-Zwiers/p/book/9781571108845
^ us.corwin.com/books/academic-conv-k-3-251602

# TO-DO TIMELINE

At this point, you are ready to create a to-do list and a timeline to get started. If possible, schedule your precoaching observation(s) before any PD and coaching has taken place. Consider now what you need to do to launch SWEL in your school. Include items like recruitment, administrator approval of your action plan, preparing for PD, allocating space for PD, and scheduling classroom visits and coaching conversations. Identify tentative dates when you will carry out each of the items listed (and remember that this is a dynamic plan, so dates can be changed if necessary). See Sample Text J for an example timeline.

### SAMPLE TEXT J. TO-DO TIMELINE

**May–July**

- Find out where SWEL PD fits into overall school PD plan
- Revise action plan
- Get administrator approval for action plan
- Give recruitment presentation to whole staff with building administration
- Follow up with potential coachees
- Schedule PD dates and put on master calendar for the upcoming school year

**August–September**

- Meet with coachees (educators interested in peer coaching)
- Precoaching observations of coachees
- October–November
- All-staff PD Session #1
- PD small-group session in professional learning community (PLC)
- Resource sharing with coachees

**December–January**

- Resource sharing with coachees
- PD small-group session in PLC
- Additional observations as needed

**February–March**

- All-staff PD Session #2
- PD small-group session in PLC
- Resource sharing with coachees

**April–May**

- Postcoaching observations of coachees
- All-staff PD Session #3 (include highlights and areas of growth from implementation over the past year)
- Based on findings from this year, begin the process of writing an action plan for the next academic year

Sample Text J is only one of many possible variations of how the work of peer coaching and PD delivery might look. You may also want to build out PD plans in the SWEL Action Plan for Professional Development and then link that document into your SWEL Action Plan. Be sure to keep in mind existing structures and schedules when drafting your timeline, taking advantage of existing systems as often as possible and being strategic in how you lobby for new structures.

## ADMINISTRATOR APPROVAL

The final step in drafting the action plan is to get administrator approval. If this is your very first SWEL project and cycle, we recommend sharing with your administrator that you are hoping to enact SWEL in your school and suggesting that they read the first two chapters of this book. With that background, when you present your action plan to your administrator as a *draft*, they will be prepared. Explain that it is a work in progress, and seek input. Administrator buy-in is a critical factor in the success of the SWEL model in any school. By sharing your action plan as a draft, you are not only allowing for input from the school administrator(s), but also ensuring that they are fully informed and on board with the work before it begins. It is also a great way to enlist their support and get a valuable perspective, typically informed by the macro-level factors at play, on making the work of SWEL coaching part of the overall school system rather than a short-term initiative.

---

**Discussion Questions**

1. What resources are available to help you with the needs analysis?
2. What is your experience with SMART goals? Why are they helpful?
3. Administrator approval is critical to the success of SWEL. How can you engage leadership in the action planning process? How can you obtain approval from various levels of leadership?

**Takeaway Task**

Using the SWEL Action Plan template (available on the companion site for this book, www.tesol.org/SWEL-book), draft an action plan. This can be done independently or with other coaches at the same site. What excites you most about this plan? What concerns you?

---

## References

DeFrance Schmidt, S., & Rich, C. (2019). *School action plan*. Unpublished document.

Doran, G. T. (1981). There's a S.M.A.R.T. way to write management's goals and objectives. *Management Review, 70*(11), 35–36.

# CHAPTER 9

# THE CYCLICAL NATURE OF THE SWEL MODEL

At the beginning of this book, we asked you to consider how much time your multilingual learners of English (MLEs) spend with credentialed English language development (ELD) teachers. For most, the amount of time is minimal. Given the existing opportunity gaps for MLEs in our schools and society, as well as the tremendous untapped potential currently represented by MLE populations, it is incumbent upon us to consider how to build classrooms that allow them to thrive. Providing a continuous and consistent learning environment for MLEs in every classroom with every teacher by leveraging ELD teacher expertise is one approach to closing those gaps. The true beauty of this approach lies not in its 1st year of implementation, but in its ability to adapt to the needs of MLEs and their teachers from year to year, across the adoption of new standards, and within the framework of each state's policies.

### District Highlight

A midsized suburban district with a growing MLE population was an early partner in school-wide English learning (SWEL) and stands as an excellent example of incremental change over time. In the beginning, a cohort of approximately 10 ELD teachers trained to become SWEL coaches. Each year, a handful of additional ELD teachers would train to become SWEL coaches—and those who had already trained participated in book studies and bimonthly meetings to share experiences, ideas, and resources as a small group. After a couple of years, the ELD coordinator was able to build willingness to be a teacher leader into the ELD job description for all new hires to the district, as well as secure grant money to continue the training and professional development offered to SWEL coaches. Over the past 2 years, the same ELD coordinator successfully lobbied for dedicated SWEL coaching time in the schedules of the ELD teachers who enacted this work at their schools. It took time and patience, but SWEL is now deeply embedded in their school system, resulting in intentional support of MLEs in all school spaces throughout the school day. Not only that, but the ELD coordinator is now one of our lead SWEL facilitators!

Most industries have some form of quality assurance. From software to healthcare, it is a common practice to collect data on processes that are not working and make improvements based on that data. The SWEL model is a continuous improvement, data-driven model that relies on schools to regularly identify areas for growth in instruction for MLEs and to develop strategies to make improvements. Our students deserve this, and ELD teachers have the expertise to make this happen. When ELD teachers take on the role of teacher leaders, MLEs immediately benefit from a continual source of site-based quality assurance. Additionally, the model is cost effective and capitalizes on expertise that is already present in almost every school. The cyclical nature of the SWEL model serves as a mechanism for schools to do better with resources that already exist.

## TURNING A SHIP: CHANGING SYSTEMS TAKES TIME AND COLLABORATION

Shifting the culture of a school is a slow-moving process. Initiatives that are implemented slowly and strategically tend to have a greater likelihood of lasting than those that are forced or thrown together haphazardly. Remember, change is difficult for many people, especially teachers who are under a tremendous amount of pressure and always strapped for time. If SWEL is slow to roll out in your school, do not worry. We like to say, "Start with the friendlies," meaning start SWEL with colleagues who are interested and already on board. This approach will result in a more trusting dynamic than a forced partnership and will be seen by your peers as collaborative, instead of hierarchical. We can rely on research to tell us why "working with the friendlies" is a great way to get the SWEL ball rolling in your school or district. In Rogers' diffusion of innovation model (1962), he identified five segments of the population based on their responses to new ideas or ways of doing things:

- **Innovators:** They are quick to jump on new changes or technologies even though they may represent a risk of some sort.
- **Early Adopters:** They are excited to try something new and find out if it is effective and worthwhile.
- **Early Majority:** This is a larger segment of the population who aren't quite as eager as the early adopters, but who are willing to change with proof of concept and essential to large-scale adoption of change.
- **Late Majority:** They are later to take up the change but eventually do so following the early majority.
- **Laggards:** They are very late to adopt changes, even with proof of concept, or may simply refuse to change.

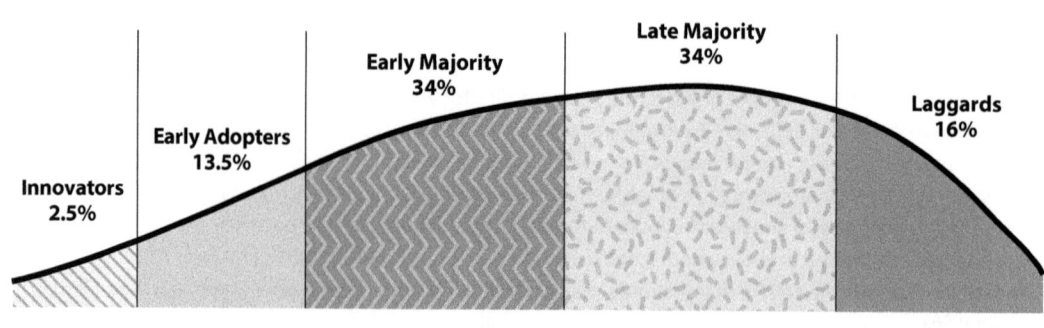

**FIGURE 1.** A visual representation of Rogers' (1962) diffusion of innovation model.

SWEL coaches who aim to start their work with the innovators and early adopters will be able to get their feet wet with colleagues who understand that change requires experimentation, trial and error, and unforeseen circumstances. Although a goal of the SWEL model is to shift the culture of the school to one where the ELD teacher is recognized as a site-based expert in language instruction and a peer coach who has valuable knowledge to share about how to best meet the needs of MLEs, this will not happen overnight. Building relationships and rapport takes time and the innovators, early adopters, and early majority will play a key role in cultural shifts.

---

**VOICES FROM THE FIELD**

There were a lot of small changes for our building [since implementing the SWEL peer coaching model], but I think the biggest thing for me was that there was a transformation of the mindset around MLEs. It got our teachers, our admin, and everyone to realize that it's not an extra thing to serve our MLEs, but it can be integrated into so much that they're already doing. That was a huge eye-opening piece for them . . . They asked, "How can I implement it into what I'm already doing and how do I make it relevant for these kids?" . . .

Seeing that transformation was kind of amazing, because even in the math department, which everyone thought, "Okay, well how much language is there in that!," they were like, "Oh there are all these things that I can be doing that I'm kind of doing but now I just look at it with a more intentional eye and it makes more sense!" It's kind of amazing. I built those relationships. I had the support of the administration. Those are really key components to making that all happen. *(SWEL coach)*

---

Teachers know how to design lessons that are engaging and stimulating for their students. What we often forget is that teachers also need to be engaged and stimulated. A site-based community of practice (Lave & Wenger, 1991) is one way for teachers to experience continual and relevant learning. If we can move beyond the egalitarian culture of teaching that insists that no one knows more than anyone else and consider that we all have *different* knowledge bases and we all benefit when we are willing to learn from each other, students will be the ultimate beneficiaries. We all enjoy knowing that our contributions are helpful to others. When we feel like we have nothing worthwhile to share with others, we become stagnant—and low morale is sure to follow.

There's also something to that old adage, "Many hands make light work." SWEL coaches have reported that, though it may have been initially difficult to convince colleagues that working together in a SWEL peer coaching relationship would be fruitful, it eventually became clear that the SWEL coaches lightened their colleagues' workload because they were no longer guessing at what would be effective for the MLEs in their classrooms. In the coteaching environment, the SWEL model provides added structure that equips classroom/content teachers with purpose and direction. SWEL coaches who model strategies for coachees support both the MLEs' and the coachee's learning. During coplanning, SWEL coaches often suggest relatively quick and easy strategies (e.g., adding visuals) that can be taken up independently by classroom/content teachers. These expressions of SWEL coaching ultimately distribute the collective workload because all teachers are tending to the success of MLEs.

> **VOICES FROM THE FIELD**
>
> The professional development sessions were very well received, and it was great to see teachers working collaboratively (in grade-level teams/grade cluster professional learning communities) to bolster their language supports in lesson and unit plans. *(SWEL coach)*
>
> The reading teacher asked me for help with her language objectives, so one day we sat down together and discussed the language she expected from her small groups of students for each type of lesson she has. (She had a cycle of different skills she worked on with students, rotating the focus of the lesson so that students worked on slightly different learning targets each day of the week.) Our session helped her not only articulate the language objectives she had for the different focuses of the lessons, but it helped her think through how she could help students meet those objectives. *(SWEL coach)*
>
> In my second observations, there were some teachers who had grown immensely. They were the ones who showed up to each professional development session, asked questions, and really made sure to implement these skills in the classroom. *(SWEL coach)*

It is worthwhile to consider teacher growth and job satisfaction, but neither is fully possible without improving MLE achievement. Though the SWEL model is not explicitly designed to collect student data, many coaches have chosen to do so and anecdotal evidence tells us that they are seeing more accessible instruction and gains in learning for MLEs.

## GETTING STARTED: KEY CONSIDERATIONS FOR IMPLEMENTATION

Before you launch the SWEL model in your school, it is helpful to learn from other SWEL coaches' challenges and successes. We recommend treating this section like a checklist to ensure that you are off to a strong start.

- **Garner Administrator Buy-In:** This one is #1 on the list for a reason. Without building-level support, a building-wide initiative cannot succeed.

- **Plan Ahead:** A great time to plan for the SWEL model in your school is the year *before* implementation. Last-minute initiatives run the risk of contributing to teacher initiative fatigue and can get lost in the flurry of other priorities.

- **Recruit! Recruit! Recruit!:** In the year prior to implementation, give a brief presentation to your staff about what you are planning to achieve (a sample template for this presentation can be found on the companion site for this book, www.tesol.org/SWEL-book) so that teachers can plan ahead.

- **Start With the Friendlies:** It's better to start small with enthusiastic partners than to start big with teachers who are not on board with the initiative. Also, be sure to only bite off as much as you can chew. We have found that it's much better to coach just one or two colleagues if it means that you are able to do so without too much stress.

- **Make Sure That Your Goal is SMART:** Is it specific, measurable, achievable, relevant, and time-bound? A solid SMART goal is critical to the direction and success of the initiative.

- **Fold Into Existing Structures:** Do you already have a professional learning community model at your school? Professional development Tuesdays? Cognitive coaching training offered by the district? If so, fold SWEL *into* these structures, rather than *on top of* them. Convince your colleagues that this is not just one more thing. How about your school improvement plan? Is there a place for SWEL coaching in one of the goals? In one example of this concept, SWEL coaches collaborated with their math department colleagues to ensure that MLE needs were met as they launched a new math curriculum at the middle school.

- **Advocate for Coaching Time:** Discuss with your administrator when coaching will happen. Coaches who allocate clear blocks of time report more success in the initiative. In some schools, this is a simple scheduling issue. In others, this may necessitate advocating for release time. Some successful SWEL coaches work with no release time, while others have up to 50% release time to support their classroom/content teacher colleagues. There is no magic formula. Just be sure to plan ahead.

- **Commit to Continued Learning:** Accept that you will not be an expert at adult learning theory from the onset. Andragogy is different from pedagogy. Give yourself some slack and seek out opportunities for professional development in coaching, professional development delivery, public speaking, and/or teacher leadership. The SWEL Teacher Leader Professional Learning Community is one way to continue your learning and growing as a SWEL coach.

If you can check off all of the items on this list, you will be well positioned for a strong implementation of the SWEL model in your school.

---

### VOICES FROM THE FIELD

I can see my MLEs are having an easier time of transferring knowledge from one space to another and they have made significant gains in that. If their classroom teachers are incorporating these pieces into their content learning, when they get separate language instruction whether or not it's on the same topic, they're able to see that there is a connection as opposed to what has typically happened. Typically, they are siloed and they do language development, but it doesn't really relate to what they're doing in their classrooms and content areas or vice versa. *(SWEL coach)*

Watching classroom/content teachers utilize the information which I provided through the SWEL program was very rewarding. The curricula that classroom/content teachers were presenting to students was made more accessible as well as adding a language focus [to go with every] content focus. *(SWEL coach)*

---

## MEASURING PROGRESS AND ADJUSTING AS NEEDED

During the 1st year and all subsequent years of implementation, it will be critical to have a plan in place to measure progress toward your SMART goal. Many SWEL coaches connect with other SWEL coaches for support and to share progress. Taking an inventory of progress toward meeting your goal can also be an important touchpoint in the event that adjustments need to be made.

> Remember: The SWEL Action Plan is considered a dynamic document and can be revised and revisited over time as needed.

Maybe you still have not been able to do precoaching observations (though you'd planned to do so months ago) or you gave an all-staff training that was poorly attended. Keeping tabs on your progress and sharing this information with your school administrator can be an important strategy for success. We also recommend planning to present progress toward the goal to the whole staff at the end of the school year. This is a good time to give a recruitment presentation for the following academic year as well.

Toward the end of your 1st year of implementation, consider the following questions:

- What are some "glows" in SWEL implementation this year? (What is going well?)
- What are some "grows" in SWEL implementation this year? (What needs work?)
- What could I do differently to set up our school for success prior to the start of the next school year?
- What are some areas in which our school's MLEs still need more support?

Use these questions to guide drafting an action plan for each subsequent year. Continuation action plan writing is not as laborious as initial action plan writing because many of the components remain constant. The primary area for consideration is the SMART goal. Your response to the final question ("What are some areas in which our school's MLEs still need more support?") should point you in a helpful direction. Remember: You will not solve *all* issues with one action plan, in one year. Focus your attention on one area that is particularly critical to the well-being and success of your MLEs. You can also shift your focus in subsequent years. Narrow, clear, and achievable goals are more likely to succeed than broad, generalized goals.

## MOVING FROM INITIATIVE TO SYSTEMIC STRUCTURE: MAKING SWEL PART OF "HOW THINGS ARE DONE"

All students, including MLEs, deserve schools that continually seek to serve them better. MLEs bring linguistic and cultural assets to our school communities that would not exist otherwise. Starting with a foundation of a site-based ELD teacher leader or SWEL coach, the SWEL model provides schools with an opportunity to ensure that MLEs experience continuous instruction with explicit attention to English language learning throughout the school day. Though initially, ELD teachers and school administrators may hesitate to take a portion of time out of the ELD teachers' day and reallocate it to indirect support through peer coaching, experienced SWEL coaches report that this time is well spent and results in a greater benefit to MLEs.

A fellow education professor and colleague shared, "If you want to work in school improvement, you'll need to travel. No one will acknowledge your expertise unless you are at least 90 miles away." Unfortunately, this rings true all too often in the field of education. ELD teachers are applied linguists—experts in second language acquisition and content-based instruction. However, ELD teacher knowledge is frequently an untapped resource. By disrupting the egalitarian culture of teaching and promoting a distributed leadership model in which *all* teachers acknowledge and share their respective areas of expertise, our learners can be better served. Denying teacher expertise is not an act of humility, but a disadvantage to our students' learning.

Let's own our professionalism. Our students deserve it.

**Discussion Questions**

1. What role can your administration play in helping to ensure a successful start to SWEL coaching?

2. Are there specific classroom/content teachers you look forward to working with as a SWEL coach? How might you go about asking them to participate?

3. Who are your go-to supports in your setting? How can they be helpful as you plan for SWEL coaching?

**Takeaway Task**

Explain SWEL coaching to a few trusted colleagues and ask them to define it back for you. Use these discussions to refine your description of the role of a SWEL coach until you feel confident sharing it more broadly.

## References

Lave, J., & Wenger, E. (1991). *Situated learning: Legitimate peripheral participation.* Cambridge University Press.

Rogers, E. M. (1962). *Diffusion of innovations.* Free Press of Glencoe.

# APPENDIXES

All appendixes are editable and available for download on the companion site for this book: www.tesol.org/SWEL-book

# APPENDIX A
## SWEL SUPPORT TOOL 1
Multimodal Instruction Observation Form

School: _____ Date: _____

Coach: _____ Teacher/Coachee Initials: _____

☐ Precoaching/support data collection in this classroom
☐ Postcoaching/support data collection in this classroom
☐ Additional data collection (between or beyond pre- and post-) in this classroom

### A. STUDENTS

Total # of students in the classroom: _____

Multilingual learners of English in the classroom:

| MLE (name or pseudonym) | Receptive Language Levels | | Productive Language Levels | |
|---|---|---|---|---|
| | Listening | Reading | Speaking | Writing |
| | | | | |
| | | | | |
| | | | | |
| | | | | |
| | | | | |
| | | | | |
| | | | | |
| | | | | |

If you would like additional space for writing notes, please download this document from the companion website for this book (www.tesol.org/SWEL-book). You should be able to then add more writing space using your return key in each of the note-taking boxes.

## B. MULTIMODAL INSTRUCTION

All students have the opportunity to:

- ☐ write
- ☐ listen
- ☐ read
- ☐ speak: student to teacher
- ☐ speak: student to student *(check one)*
    - ☐ No opportunities provided for student-to-student interaction
    - ☐ 1–2 opportunities for student-to-student interaction
    - ☐ 3–4 opportunities for student-to-student interaction
    - ☐ 5 or more opportunities for student-to-student interaction

The teacher: *(check all that apply)*

- ☐ presents information/instructions orally and in writing
- ☐ reinforces oral language with written cues and/or written material on the board
- ☐ presents visual representations of academic concepts (e.g., pictures, charts, graphs, maps, diagrams, props, realia)
- ☐ uses gestures, facial expressions, and/or actions to demonstrate meaning
- ☐ models and/or guides instructional concepts
- ☐ provides dictionaries and/or other word resources available in home language(s) and in English

**Observation Notes:**

## C. COACHING CONVERSATIONS

The following are a number of optional topics for coaching conversations.

- Is the work hands on?
- Is the work meaningful?
- Is the work culturally relevant to students?
- Are students engaged throughout the lesson?
- Are all students engaged when the teacher provides opportunities to speak?

- Does the classroom offer a print-rich environment with words relevant to the current topic of instruction?
- Is the room organized so that students know what to focus on during instruction?
- What are some additional communication techniques you can incorporate (e.g., inflection of voice, facial expressions, gestures, facing the students when speaking)?
- How can we activate prior knowledge for multilingual learners of English?
- How can we evaluate and build background knowledge for students?

**Coaching Conversation Notes:**

*Note:* This tool is based on "Collaborative Program Evaluation That Leads to Program Change" [Conference session], by A. S. Mabbott, D. Kramer, & C. Lundgren, 2009, May 28–30, International Conference on Language Teacher Education, Washington, DC.

# APPENDIX B
## SWEL SUPPORT TOOL 2
English Language Development Observation Form

School: _____ Date: _____

Coach: _____ Teacher/Coachee Initials: _____

- ☐ Precoaching/support data collection in this classroom
- ☐ Postcoaching/support data collection in this classroom
- ☐ Additional data collection (between or beyond pre- and post-) in this classroom

### A. STUDENTS

Total # of students in the classroom: _____

Multilingual learners of English in the classroom:

| MLE (name or pseudonym) | Receptive Language Levels | | Productive Language Levels | |
|---|---|---|---|---|
| | Listening | Reading | Speaking | Writing |
| | | | | |
| | | | | |
| | | | | |
| | | | | |
| | | | | |
| | | | | |
| | | | | |
| | | | | |

*If you would like additional space for writing notes, please download this document from the companion website for this book (www.tesol.org/SWEL-book). You should be able to then add more writing space using your return key in each of the note-taking boxes.*

## B. LESSON PLAN OBJECTIVES

**Learning Target or Content Objective**

## C. LANGUAGE OBJECTIVES

*Directions: Choose the appropriate language level below and fill out the box accordingly. You only need to fill out one of the three boxes: word level, sentence level, OR discourse level. See the Building Leveled Language Objectives document (Appendix D, available at www.tesol.org/SWEL-book) for language objective sentence frames and examples.*

**Word-Level Language Objective:** *(check all that apply)*

- ☐ Language Objective: Word level (vocabulary, morphology, and/or phonology)
  - ☐ Includes a function
  - ☐ Includes vocabulary or phonological/morphological topic
  - ☐ Includes examples of the language
  - ☐ Includes supports

Please write the word-level language objective here:

OR

**Sentence-Level Language Objective:** *(check all that apply)*

- ☐ Language Objective: Sentence level (grammar and/or syntax)
  - ☐ Includes a function
  - ☐ Includes language structure/syntax
  - ☐ Includes examples of the language structure
  - ☐ Includes supports

Please write the sentence-level language objective here:

OR

**Discourse-Level Language Objective:** *(check all that apply)*

☐ Language Structure: Discourse level (text type)
  ☐ Includes a function
  ☐ Includes a text type
  ☐ Includes supports

**Please write the discourse-level language objective here:**

## D. STUDENT AWARENESS OF LANGUAGE LEARNING (METALINGUISTIC AWARENESS)
*Check all that apply.*

☐ Language objective is derived from the content objective/learning target.
☐ Language objective is written for students to see.
☐ Language objective is read out loud for students to hear.

**Observation Notes:**

## E. COACHING CONVERSATIONS

*The following are a number of optional topics for coaching conversations.*

- Are all students engaged when the teacher provides opportunities to speak?
- Does the classroom offer a print-rich environment with words relevant to the current topic of instruction?

- How can we ensure that the students understand the language that the teacher uses while also challenging their language learning?
- How can we activate prior knowledge for multilingual learners of English?
- How can we develop classroom-based assessments that measure mastery of language objectives?
- What should be understood about the various language levels represented in the classroom?
- How can we develop classroom-based assessments that measure the intended content knowledge rather than language knowledge?

**Coaching Conversation Notes:**

*Note:* This tool is based on "Collaborative Program Evaluation That Leads to Program Change" [Conference session], by A. S. Mabbott, D. Kramer, & C. Lundgren, 2009, May 28–30, International Conference on Language Teacher Education, Washington, DC.

# APPENDIX C
## SWEL SUPPORT TOOL 3
Supporting the Language of Identity Observation Form

School: _____  Date: _____

Coach: _____  Teacher/Coachee Initials: _____

- ☐ Precoaching/support data collection in this classroom
- ☐ Postcoaching/support data collection in this classroom
- ☐ Additional data collection (between or beyond pre- and post-) in this classroom

## A. STUDENTS

Total # of students in the classroom: _____

Multilingual learners of English in the classroom:

| MLE (name or pseudonym) | Receptive Language Levels | | Productive Language Levels | |
|---|---|---|---|---|
| | Listening | Reading | Speaking | Writing |
| | | | | |
| | | | | |
| | | | | |
| | | | | |
| | | | | |
| | | | | |
| | | | | |
| | | | | |

*If you would like additional space for writing notes, please download this document from the companion website for this book (www.tesol.org/SWEL-book). You should be able to then add more writing space using your return key in each of the note-taking boxes.*

## B. OPPORTUNITIES FOR USE AND EXPOSURE IN THE LANGUAGE OF IDENTITY

MLEs have the opportunity to do the following in their home language(s):

- ☐ write
- ☐ listen
- ☐ read
- ☐ speak

The teacher: (check all that apply)

- ☐ presents information/instructions orally and in writing
- ☐ reinforces oral language with written cues and/or written material on the board
- ☐ presents visual representations of classroom concepts (e.g., pictures, charts, graphs, maps, diagrams, props, realia)
- ☐ uses gestures, facial expressions, and/or actions to demonstrate meaning
- ☐ models and/or guides instructional concepts
- ☐ provides dictionaries and/or other word resources available in home language(s) and in English

**Observation Notes:**

## C. COACHING CONVERSATIONS

The following are a number of optional topics for coaching conversations.

- Is the home language text authentic?
- Are all students engaged when the teacher provides opportunities to use their home language?
- How can we ensure that the students maintain home language skills while also developing their language of access?
- How can we activate prior linguistic knowledge for multilingual learners of English?
- How can we develop classroom-based assessments that integrate the home language?
- What should be understood about the various home languages, varieties, and literacy backgrounds represented in the classroom?

**Coaching Conversation Notes:**

*Note:* This tool is based on "Collaborative Program Evaluation That Leads to Program Change" [Conference session], by A. S. Mabbott, D. Kramer, & C. Lundgren, 2009, May 28–30, International Conference on Language Teacher Education, Washington, DC.

# APPENDIX D
## Building Leveled Language Objectives

Language objectives are used to guide the language instruction required for students to master the content objective and, ultimately, the standard that guides the lesson or unit plan. *A language objective does not need to be written for each of the three levels of language in a single lesson.* Rather, use the following steps to figure out what language your students will need to learn and/or to demonstrate their mastery of the lesson through reading, speaking, writing, and/or listening activities. The language objective video lecture that accompanies this document can be found on the companion website for *Teacher Leadership for School-Wide English Learning* (www.tesol-org/SWEL-book).

**Before writing a language objective, it's important that you think through the following: What language do you notice in your lesson materials and what language do your students need to be taught?**

| |
|---|
| A. Identify your **content objective(s)**: |
| B. **Language function(s):** What are you asking students to do with language? (e.g., analyze, compare/contrast, explain, interpret, argue, persuade, categorize, describe, predict, question, retell, summarize, justify with evidence; see Language Objective chart) |
| C. **Content vocabulary:** What key vocabulary (word level—"the bricks") do you need to introduce/review with students? How will you engage students with that vocabulary in the lesson? How is this vocabulary being introduced, developed, or reviewed in this lesson? |
| D. **Syntax:** What syntax (sentence level—"the mortar") is present in the materials that you are going to teach? |

> E. **Discourse:** What text type or genre (discourse level—"the building") will students need to produce?

**Language Objective Levels: Choose one of the three sentence frames to write your language objective.**

**Word Level**

I can _____ [function] using _____ [vocabulary, or phonological/morphological topic], such as _____ [examples of language], with the support of _____ [support(s)].

> *Word level phonological (sounds) and morphological (parts of words) examples:* fifteen vs. fifty (stress), affixes and word roots

**Sentence/Syntax Level**

I can _____ [function] using _____ [language structure/syntax], such as _____ [examples of language structure], with the support of _____ [support(s)].

> *Sentence level examples:* ordinal numbers, adjectives, past tense *–ed*, connecting words, language of comparison

**Discourse Level**

I can _____ [function] in _____ [language genres], with the support of _____ [support(s)].

> *Discourse level examples of genres:* science lab report, five-paragraph essay, iambic pentameter poetry, business letter, mathematical proof, formal debate, persuasive essay structure.

*The following Language Objectives chart shows each of the language functions, along with examples of language, supports, and sample language objectives at each of the three levels of language. Language function words in bold are used by the edTPA teacher assessment system (www.edtpa.com).*

| Language Function | Examples of Language | Examples of Supports | Language Objective Examples |
|---|---|---|---|
| **Classify**<br><br>Related functions: Arrange, organize, **categorize**, **construct**, create, generate, **summarize**, arrange, group | *Word level:*<br>Content vocabulary ("bricks," or words in bold) | Tree Map<br>Hierarchical Organizer<br>Pictograph<br>Word bank | *Elementary/Secondary Math [word level]*<br>I can classify different types of shapes using content vocabulary, such as <u>circle</u>, <u>square</u>, <u>rectangle</u>, and <u>oval</u>, with the support of a word bank and pictures. |
| | *Sentence/syntax level:*<br>Descriptors<br>Adjectives | | *Elementary/Secondary Math [sentence level]*<br>I can classify different types of shapes using descriptive adjectives, such as <u>three-sided</u>, <u>symmetrical</u>, <u>equal</u>, and <u>parallel</u>, with the support of a categorizing graphic organizer. |
| | *Discourse level:*<br>Three-sentence paragraph,<br>Math talks | | *Elementary/Secondary Math [discourse level]*<br>I can classify different types of shapes in math talks with the support of manipulatives and home language knowledge. |
| **Compare/Contrast**<br><br>Related functions: **Describe** (similarities and differences), distinguish, **identify**, recognize, separate, differentiate | *Word level:*<br>Content vocabulary ("bricks," or words in bold) | Double Bubble Map<br>Bridge Map<br>Venn Diagram<br>Semantic Structures Analysis<br>T-Chart<br>Fact-Opinion Charts | *Secondary Social Studies [word level]*<br>I can compare the experiences of immigrants and refugees using past tense verbs with the *–ed* ending, such as <u>lived</u>, <u>traveled</u>, and <u>walked</u>, with the support of a regular past tense verb list and a T-chart. |
| | *Sentence/syntax level:*<br>However, but, as well as, on the other hand, not only . . . but also, either . . . or, while, although, unless, similarly, yet, compared to, similar to, different from, and yet, as opposed to, alternatively, apart from, by contrast, contrary to that, conversely, in spite of this, nevertheless, nonetheless, notwithstanding, regardless, some . . . , but others, still, then again, by the same token, correspondingly, likewise, too | | *Secondary Social Studies [sentence level]*<br>I can compare the experiences of immigrants and refugees using the language of comparison, such as <u>different from</u>, <u>similar to</u>, and <u>similarly</u>, with the support of a Venn diagram and a T-chart. |
| | *Discourse level:*<br>Reports, explanations (essays), academic discussions | | *Secondary Social Studies [discourse level]*<br>I can compare the experiences of immigrants and refugees in a report on the Somali diaspora with the support of a Venn diagram, an essay outline, and a T-chart. |

*(continued)*

| Language Function | Examples of Language | Examples of Supports | Language Objective Examples |
|---|---|---|---|
| **Order**<br><br>Related functions: **Categorize**, organize, develop, discover, complete, process, outline, **retell**, order | *Word level:*<br>Content vocabulary ("bricks," or words in bold) | Flow Map<br>Cycle Graph<br>Flow Chart<br>Timeline<br>Outlines | *Elementary Science [word level]*<br>I can order the steps of the butterfly lifecycle using the numbering suffixes *–st* and *–th*, such as *fir/st/*, *four/th/*, *fif/th/*, and *six/th/*, with the support of a timeline and a number line. |
| | *Sentence/syntax level:*<br>First, second, third . . . ; next; before; after; afterwards; later on; time; not long after; now; as; when; immediately; preceding; initially; meanwhile; following; until; soon; today; as | | *Elementary Science [sentence level]*<br>I can order the steps of the butterfly lifecycle using sequencing words, such as *initially*, *later on*, *following*, and *finally*, with the support of an outline. |
| | *Discourse level:*<br>Procedural paragraph or essay, written or oral directions, explanations, recipes | | *Elementary Science [discourse level]*<br>I can order the steps of the butterfly life cycle in a procedural three-paragraph essay with the support of a graphic organizer. |
| **Infer**<br><br>Related functions: **Predict**, extrapolate, restate, represent, **summarize**, reconstruct, **synthesize**, derive, deduce, **explain**, create, **construct** | *Word level:*<br>Content vocabulary ("bricks," or words in bold) | Multiflow Map<br>T-Chart | *Elementary/Secondary Social Studies [word level]*<br>I can infer from the evidence presented in multiple texts using academic vocabulary, such as *conclusion*, *synthesis*, *analysis*, and *interpretation*, with the support of a word bank and an anchor chart. |
| | *Sentence/syntax level:*<br>Future tense (use of will), if . . . not, if . . . then (conditional connectors), descriptive verbs adjectives | | *Elementary/Secondary Social Studies [sentence level]*<br>I can infer from the evidence presented in multiple texts using connectives, such as *is caused by*, *so that*, and *additionally*, with the support of the connective anchor chart and a bubble map. |
| | *Discourse level:*<br>Explanations (written and oral), persuasive arguments (written and oral), advocacy letter, speech or debate | | *Elementary/Secondary Social Studies [discourse level]*<br>I can infer from the evidence presented in multiple texts in a formal debate structure with the support of note cards and a debate partner. |

*(continued)*

| Language Function | Examples of Language | Examples of Supports | Language Objective Examples |
|---|---|---|---|
| **Locate**<br><br>Related functions: Define, seek information, count, **identify**, indicate, match, name, point, recall, recite, reproduce, repeat, state, select, record | *Word level:*<br>Content vocabulary ("bricks," or words in bold) | Circle Map<br>Attribute Diagram<br>Web<br>SQ3R<br>Concept Definition Map<br>Outlines<br>Cornell Note-Taking | *Secondary English Language Arts [word level]*<br>I can <u>locate</u> supporting details in *The House on Mango Street* using <u>the correct final sound</u> in words, such as <u>cracked, needed, decided, worked,</u> and <u>closed</u>, with the support of <u>word charts</u> and <u>sound symbol notations</u>. |
| | *Sentence/syntax level:*<br>To be, action verbs, prepositions | | *Secondary English Language Arts [sentence level]*<br>I can <u>locate</u> supporting details in *The House on Mango Street* using <u>dialogue verbs</u>, such as <u>said, replied,</u> and <u>remarked</u>, with the support of <u>Post-it notes</u> and <u>Cornell notes</u>. |
| | *Discourse level:*<br>Informational articles, scientific reports, newspaper articles, textbooks | | *Secondary English Language Arts [discourse level]*<br>I can <u>locate</u> supporting details in *The House on Mango Street* with my understanding of the <u>narrative structure</u> with the support of <u>Post-it notes</u> and <u>an outline</u>. |
| **Describe**<br><br>Related functions: Inform, **explain**, **identify**, report, **retell**, recount, reorder, represent, depict, paraphrase, **summarize**, conclude, convert, prepare, transform, translate, prepare, generalize, extrapolate | *Word level:*<br>Content vocabulary ("bricks," or words in bold) | Circle Map<br>Bubble Map<br>Web<br>SQ3R<br>Concept Definition Map<br>Outlines<br>Cornell Note-Taking | *Secondary Science [word level]*<br>I can <u>describe</u> density using <u>suffixes that change adjectives into nouns</u>, such as <u>–ity (density, applicability)</u> and <u>–ness (thickness)</u>, with the support of my <u>lab partner</u> and an <u>anchor chart</u>. |
| | *Sentence/syntax level:*<br>Adjective use; descriptive language; superlatives/comparatives; ____ said; the book says; first, second, next, . . . ; according to | | *Secondary Science [sentence level]*<br>I can <u>describe</u> the density of H2O in different stages of the water cycle using <u>comparative and superlative structures</u>, such as <u>dense, denser,</u> and *the densest* with the support of my <u>Cornell notes</u>. |
| | *Discourse level:*<br>Lab report, academic presentation, slideshow presentation, narrative essay, biography, autobiography, journal entry | | *Secondary Science [sentence level]*<br>I can <u>describe</u> density in a <u>science lab report</u> with the support of my <u>Cornell notes</u> and an <u>outline</u>. |

*(continued)*

| Language Function | Examples of Language | Examples of Supports | Language Objective Examples |
|---|---|---|---|
| **Analyze**<br><br>Related functions: Calculate, **interpret**, classify, **categorize**, classify, **predict**, deduce, differentiate, **examine**, discriminate, distinguish, group, illustrate, **infer**, order, recognize, relate, transform | *Word level:*<br>Content vocabulary ("bricks," or words in bold) | Brace Map<br>Multiflow Map<br>Flow Map<br>Tree Map<br>Circle Map<br>Fishbone<br>Organizers for Main Idea/<br>Supporting Details | *Secondary English Language Arts [word level]*<br>I can <u>analyze</u> the motivations of two or more characters in *Of Mice and Men* using <u>suffixes that change verbs into nouns</u>, such as <u>*–tion* (intention, discrimination), *–ment* (disagreement), and *–sion* (decision, discussion)</u> with the support of <u>word building cards</u>. |
| | *Sentence/syntax level:*<br>Is a part of, is related to, to be, same, different, similarities, differences, the common traits, to, so that, nevertheless, thus, accordingly, if . . . then (conditional connectors), makes, causes, because, creates, results in, due to, on account of, therefore | | *Secondary English Language Arts [sentence level]*<br>I can <u>analyze</u> the motivations of two or more characters in *Of Mice and Men* using <u>contrasting words</u>, such as <u>*either/or, neither/nor, yet, and however*</u>, with the support of a <u>fishbone organizer</u>. |
| | *Discourse level:*<br>Academic essay, speech, classroom discussion, written explanation, descriptive essay, science article | | *Secondary English Language Arts [discourse level]*<br>I can <u>analyze</u> the motivations of two or more characters in *Of Mice and Men* in a <u>personal letter to a book character</u> with the support of an <u>informal letter format graphic organizer</u>. |
| **Justify**<br><br>Related functions: **Argue**, persuade, discriminate, **prove**, deduce, document, support, **question**, validate, verify, debate, **construct**, **persuade** | *Word level:*<br>Content vocabulary ("bricks," or words in bold) | Circle Map<br>Tree Map<br>Opposing Forces Chart<br>Prediction Tree | *Elementary Social Studies [word level]*<br>I can <u>justify</u> my position on how to create more jobs using <u>stress on the correct syllable in key content vocabulary</u>, such as <u>*employment, economy,* and *benefits*</u>, with the support of a <u>key vocabulary word bank with symbols to mark stress</u>. |
| | *Sentence/syntax level:*<br>I think, according to, for example, in fact, most important, if . . . not, if. . . . then, I believe, because, since, based upon, one should (must, will), understand, on the contrary, need to, therefore, from my point of view | | *Elementary Social Studies [sentence level]*<br>I can <u>justify</u> my position on how to create more jobs using <u>opinion statements</u>, such as <u>*I think . . . , I believe . . . ,* and *My point of view is that . . .*</u>, with the support of an <u>opposing forces chart</u>. |
| | *Discourse level:*<br>Editorials/opinions letters, debates (oral and written), scientific articles and lab reports | | *Elementary Social Studies [discourse level]*<br>I can <u>justify</u> my position on how to create more jobs in an <u>editorial submission to the local newspaper</u> with the support of <u>a small group</u> and <u>a graphic organizer</u>. |

*(continued)*

| Language Function | Examples of Language | Examples of Supports | Language Objective Examples |
|---|---|---|---|
| **Synthesize**<br><br>Related functions: Arrange, **categorize**, combine, compile, compose, **construct**, create, deduce, **explain**, formulate, generalize, generate, integrate, modify, organize, prepare, plan, produce, propose, rearrange, reconstruct, relate, reorganize, revise, **summarize** | *Word level:*<br>Content vocabulary ("bricks," or words in bold) | Circle Map<br>Webs<br>Thinking Stems | *Elementary English Language Arts [word level]*<br>I can synthesize information from a *Time for Kids* article using academic content vocabulary, such as *analysis, study, and overview*, with the support of a partner and a highlighted text. |
| | *Sentence/syntax level:*<br>Conjunctions, in other words, that is to say, to put it differently | | *Elementary English Language Arts [sentence level]*<br>I can synthesize information from a *Time for Kids* article using connecting phrases, such as *in other words, to put it differently*, and *that is to say*, with the support of a bubble map. |
| | *Discourse level:*<br>Scientific article, informative paragraph, biographical essay, structured classroom discussion | | *Elementary English Language Arts [discourse level]*<br>I can synthesize information from a *Time for Kids* article in a five-sentence paragraph with the support of a graphic organizer and an academic content vocabulary word list. |
| **Evaluate**<br><br>Related functions: Appraise, **argue**, assess, **compare**, conclude, consider, **contrast**, criticize, critique, decide, **describe**, determine, discriminate, distinguish, grade, judge, **justify**, recommend, validate, verify, test, support, rate, rank, measure, **interpret**, relate, **identify**, **explain**, indicate, confirm | *Word level:*<br>Content vocabulary ("bricks," or words in bold) | Double Bubble Map<br>Multiflow Map<br>Cause-Effect Chain<br>Opposing Forces Chart | *Elementary Social Studies [word level]*<br>I can evaluate why cities are located where they are using the *–tion* suffix in content vocabulary, such as in *position, elevation, and location*, with the support of a word part cards and a partner. |
| | *Sentence/syntax level:*<br>I think, according to, for example, in fact, most important, for instance, for example, specifically | | *Elementary Social Studies [sentence level]*<br>I can evaluate why cities are located where they are using location words (prepositions), such as *next to, near, toward*, and *to the north/south*, with the support of an anchor chart and a map. |
| | *Discourse level:*<br>Descriptive narrative, reports, classroom discussions, writing about or discussing philosophical questions | | *Elementary Social Studies [discourse level]*<br>I can evaluate why cities are located where they are in a structured academic discussion with the support of sentence starters and a partner. |

This document was inspired by S. Clyne, 2006 (www.colorincolorado.org/sites/default/files/Academic-Language-Function.pdf).

# APPENDIX E
## Planning for Word-Level Language Guide

Most word-level language objectives focus on semantics (word meaning), but others focus on morphology (word parts) and phonology (word sounds). Use this guide and the language objectives video lecture (available on the *Teacher Leadership for School-Wide English Learning* companion website, www.tesol.org/SWEL-book) to guide your colleague through the process of writing a language objective at the word level.

---

**Step 1: Name the Content Objective/Learning Target**

---

**Step 2: Decide Which Language to Teach**

**Noticing:** What do I notice about my students' language that needs attention? Choose one area:

*Phonology:*

*Morphology:*

*Semantics:*

**Forecasting:** What word-level language do students need to have to successfully engage with the content?

*Text:*

*Task:*

*Test:*

**Step 3: Choose a Function**

The function drives the language objective. A function is how language is used to carry out cognitive processes (such as those described in Bloom's Taxonomy, 1956). This language needs to be explicitly taught (e.g., *describe, explain, retell*).

**Step 4: Identify Language Supports**

Identify a tool that will assist in developing language use and understanding.

*Sample Language Supports*

- Word wall
- Labeling pictures, graphics, or items in the classroom
- Working with a partner/in a small group

- Internet
- Picture or word dictionary
- Anchor charts
- Sentence frames
- Think alouds

- Teacher modeling
- Venn diagram
- Sample text
- Modeling tasks
- Guided notes

**Step 5: Decide on the Level of Language**

**Word Level (Bricks):** Check the area that you will focus on at the word level and provide content-based examples of that area.

Phonology (word sounds)  ☐ ex:_____

Semantics (word meaning)  ☐ ex:_____

Morphology (word parts)  ☐ ex:_____

**Step 6: Write a Language Objective**

**Word-Level Sentence Frame:** Fill in all sections based on the preceding information.

I can _____ [function] using _____ [vocabulary, or phonological/morphological topic], such as _____ [examples of language structure], with the support of _____ [support(s)].

*Appendixes*

> **Sample Word-Level Language Objectives**
>
> Semantics: I can explain how bats are different from other mammals using vocabulary such as *herbivore*, *frugivore*, and *insectivore* with the support of sentence frames.
>
> Phonology: I can explain how bats are different from other mammals using correct stress for words, like *herbivore*, *frugivore*, and *insectivore*, with the support of an audio recording.
>
> Morphology: I can explain how bats are different from other mammals using the suffix *–ivore* for words like *herbivore*, *frugivore*, and *insectivore* with the support of flashcards.

## Reference

Bloom, B. S. (1956). *Taxonomy of educational objectives, Handbook I: The cognitive domain.* David McKay.

# APPENDIX F
## Planning for Sentence-Level Language Guide

Sentence-level language objectives focus on syntax (also called grammar, structure, or form). Use this guide and the language objectives video lecture (available on the *Teacher Leadership for School-Wide English Learning* companion website, www.tesol.org/SWEL-book) to guide your colleague through the process of writing a language objective at the sentence level.

---

**Step 1: Name the Content Objective/Learning Target**

---

**Step 2: Decide Which Language to Teach**

**Noticing:** What do I notice about my students' language structure that needs attention?

**Forecasting:** What sentence-level language do students need to have to successfully engage with the content?

*Text*:

*Task*:

*Test*:

---

**Step 3: Choose a Function**

The function drives the language objective. A function is how language is used to carry out cognitive processes (such as those described in Bloom's Taxonomy, 1956). This language needs to be explicitly taught.

### Step 4: Identify Language Supports

Identify a tool that will assist in developing language use and understanding.

*Sample Language Supports*

- Word wall
- Labeling pictures, graphics, or items in the classroom
- Working with a partner/in a small group

- Internet
- Picture or word dictionary
- Anchor charts
- Sentence frames
- Think alouds

- Teacher modeling
- Venn diagram
- Sample text
- Modeling tasks
- Guided notes

### Step 5: Decide on the Level of Language

**Sentence Level (Mortar):** Provide the area of syntax that you will focus on in this lesson. Include examples of this type of language from the context.

Syntax:

Examples:

### Step 6: Write a Language Objective

**Sentence-Level Sentence Frame:** Fill in all sections based on the preceding information.

I can _____ [function] using _____ [language structure/syntax],

such as _____ [examples of language structure], with the support of

_____ [support(s)].

---

**Sample Sentence-Level Language Objectives**

I can summarize how bats contribute to pollination using ordinal numbers, such as *first*, *second*, and *third*, with the support of a word wall.

I can compare per capita consumption of India and Canada using comparative language, such as *greater than*, *less than*, and *as _____ as*, with the support of sample sentences.

I can compare the experiences of immigrants and refugees using past tense verbs with the *–ed* ending, such as *lived*, *traveled*, and *walked*, with the support of a regular past tense verb list and a T-chart.

## Reference

Bloom, B. S. (1956). *Taxonomy of educational objectives, Handbook I: The cognitive domain*. David McKay.

# APPENDIX G
## Planning for Discourse-Level Language Guide

Discourse-level language objectives focus on text type and pragmatics. Use this guide in tandem with Chapter 3 from *Teacher Leadership for School-Wide English Learning* and the language objectives video lecture (available on the book's companion website, www.tesol.org/SWEL-book) to guide your colleague through the process of writing a language objective at the discourse level.

---

**Step 1: Name the Content Objective**

---

**Step 2: Decide Which Language to Teach**

**Noticing:** What do I notice about my students' language that needs attention, given this text type?

**Forecasting:** What discourse-level language do students need to have to successfully engage with the content?

*Text:*

*Task:*

*Test:*

---

**Step 3: Choose a Function**

The function drives the language objective. A function is how language is used to carry out cognitive processes (such as those described in Bloom's Taxonomy, 1956). This language needs to be explicitly taught.

### Step 4: Identify Supports

Identify a tool that will assist in developing language use and understanding.

*Sample Language Supports*

- Word wall
- Labeling pictures, graphics, or items in the classroom
- Working with a partner/in a small group

- Internet
- Picture or word dictionary
- Anchor charts
- Sentence frames
- Think alouds

- Teacher modeling
- Venn diagram
- Sample text
- Modeling tasks
- Guided notes

### Step 5: Decide on the Level of Language

**Discourse Level (Building):** Provide the text type that you will focus on in this lesson (e.g., lab report, persuasive essay, opinion editorial, debate, interview).

**Discourse:**

### Step 6: Write a Language Objective

**Discourse-Level Sentence Frame:** Fill in all sections based on the preceding information.

I can _____ [function] in _____ [text type] structure, with the support of _____ [support(s)].

---

### Sample Discourse-Level Language Objectives

I can <u>describe</u> density in a <u>science lab report</u> with the support of my <u>Cornell notes</u>.

I can <u>describe</u> how bats disperse seeds in <u>an organized oral presentation</u> with the support of <u>a cycle diagram</u>.

I can <u>compare</u> per capita consumption patterns with classmates in <u>a group discussion with the support of a bank of sentence starters</u>.

---

## Reference

Bloom, B. S. (1956). *Taxonomy of educational objectives, Handbook I: The cognitive domain.* David McKay.

# APPENDIX H
## The SWEL Lesson Plan Inventory

**Is your lesson linguistically appropriate for your student population?**

Use this inventory to strengthen your lesson plan so that all learners improve their English language skills while mastering critical content knowledge. Check the boxes that are true for your lesson plan.

*Note*: This inventory is for planning purposes only, does not take the place of a lesson plan, and is not an evaluative tool for instruction. This inventory is focused on language and assumes that cultural relevance is already attended to.

- ☐ Lesson plan has a clear content objective (learning target).
- ☐ The lesson has an area of content-area language to focus on in this lesson through
  - ☐ a) noticing students' areas of language needs and/or
  - ☐ b) forecasting areas of language need in lesson text, tasks, or tests.
- ☐ The lesson plan has a clear language objective.
- ☐ The language objective begins with a function (what students will be doing with language) that supports the content objective.
- ☐ The language objective ends with a support (a tool to support students with the language that you are teaching).
- ☐ Language objective focal area:
  - ☐ a) If the language objective is at the word level, there is a focal area of phonology (how words sound), morphology (parts of words), or semantics (vocabulary). At least three examples are included.
  - ☐ b) If the language objective is at the sentence level, there is a focal area of syntax (grammar, how words fit together). At least three examples are included.
  - ☐ c) If the language objective is at the discourse level, there is a named text type. At least three examples are included.
- ☐ The lesson plan includes multimodal instructional strategies and activities aimed at learning the language of the language objective.
- ☐ The lesson plan includes an assessment (formative or summative) of the language of the language objective.

# APPENDIX I
## SWEL Planning for Professional Development

*Note: When completing this action plan, omit any identifiers (e.g., student or staff names, subject areas, grade levels).*

| School: | |
|---|---|
| School Year: | |

| Professional Development Needs Analysis |  |
|---|---|
| **Dispositions:** Describe the learning needs of the staff at your school in each of the following essential dispositions for effectively and respectfully serving language learners in the content-area classroom. ||
| **Essential Disposition:** | **Learning Needs of My Staff in This Area:** |
| Educators empathize with circumstances related to immigration. | |
| Educators are culturally sensitive and sustaining. | |
| Educators believe that marginalization and oppression affect the educational experiences of multilingual learners of English. | |
| Educators support their students' home language development. | |
| Educators recognize the challenges of learning English and content simultaneously. | |
| Educators are committed to ongoing professional development. | |
| **Knowledge:** Describe the learning needs of the staff at your school in each of the following essential knowledge frames for effectively and respectfully serving language learners in the content-area classroom. ||

| Essential Knowledge: | Learning Needs of My Staff in This Area: |
|---|---|
| Educators know about second language acquisition and approaches to teaching language through content. | |
| Educators know about approaches to supporting home language literacy. | |
| Educators know about the theories of cultural relevance and sustainability. | |
| Educators know who immigrants are and how immigration happens. | |
| Educators know systems of oppression and how they affect the educational experiences of multilingual learners of English. | |
| Educators know approaches to advocacy and the legal requirements for adequately serving multilingual learners of English. | |

**Skills:** Describe the learning needs of the staff at your school in each of the following skill areas for effectively and respectfully serving language learners in the content-area classroom.

| Essential Skills: | Learning Needs of My Staff in This Area: |
|---|---|
| Educators can plan for language instruction. | |
| Educators can teach and assess language. | |
| Educators can differentiate for multilingual learners of English. | |
| Educators can support home language literacy. | |

*Appendixes*

| | |
|---|---|
| Educators can enact culturally relevant practices. | |
| Educators can advocate for immigrant families. | |

**SMART Goals:** State SMART (Specific, measurable, achievable, relevant, time-bound) goals. What would you like to accomplish through professional development facilitation over the academic year?

**Resources:** Consider the professional development content and coaching tools presented in *Teacher Leadership for School-Wide English Learning*. What resources do you have to support SWEL professional development at your school? What resources do you still need?

**Timeline:** Provide a detailed timeline for the implementation of your professional development.

**To-Do:** What do you need to do to launch SWEL professional development in your school? Include items like recruitment of participants, administrator approval of your plan, materials preparation, allocating space, modification of SWEL professional development session plans for your specific site needs, etc. Be sure to identify tentative dates when you will carry out each of the items listed.

**Administrator Approval**

Signature: _____ Date: _____

# APPENDIX J
## School-Wide English Learning (SWEL) Action Plan

| Name: | |
|---|---|
| School email address: | |
| School: | |
| District (if applicable): | |

**Needs Analysis**

Explain (1) a description of the MLE language backgrounds, language levels, and types of MLEs (i.e., highly literate newcomers, long-term English learners, and/or students with limited or interrupted formal education); (2) the unique needs of your MLE populations; and (3) the challenges that your classroom/content teacher colleagues encounter.

**Goal Setting**

State SMART (specific, measurable, achievable, relevant, time-bound) goals. What would you like to see happen or change in classroom/content teacher practices over the academic year?

**SWEL Implementation Steps**

What do you need to get started? How will you recruit participants? What professional development topics will you cover, and when will you deliver them? How many classroom visits will you make, and when will you do them? When and how will coaching conversations happen?

## Supports

Identify who you anticipate will be in support of SWEL at your school. How might you capitalize on their support? In addition, identify any systems, policies, or norms that will support SWEL implementation at your school over the next year.

## Concerns and Obstacles

Identify any concerns or obstacles that you anticipate might present themselves over the coming year. How might you overcome and/or work around them?

## Resources

Consider the professional development content and coaching tools presented in the book, *Teacher Leadership for School-Wide English Learning*. What resources do you have to support SWEL implementation at your school? What resources do you still need?

## To-Do Timeline

What do you need to do to launch SWEL in your school? Include items like recruitment, administrator approval of your action plan, preparing for professional development, allocating space for professional development, and scheduling classroom visits and coaching conversations. Identify tentative dates when you will carry out each of the items on your to-do list.

## Administrator Approval

Signature: _____ Date: _____

# RESOURCES INDEX

This index sorts the various articles, videos, handouts, web pages, and other resources referred to in this book. Because these resources are most often linked to specific professional development plans, page numbers are included so that you may easily find activities related to the topic you need. All of these resources are available on the companion website for this book, www.tesol.org/SWEL-book.

| Resource | Page | Resource Type |
|---|---|---|

## English Language Development
*Instruction and Assessment*

| Resource | Page | Resource Type |
|---|---|---|
| Bricks, Mortar, and Buildings: A Metaphor for Understanding Academic Language | 115 | Video |
| Language Demands Inventory | 43 | Coaching Materials/ Handout |
| Mulberry Street, New York City | 114 | Image |
| Plargs Amplified Text | 119 | Digital Handout |
| Plargs Engineered Assessment | 124 | Handout |
| Plargs Quiz | 120 | Handout |
| Plargs Quiz Answer Key | 125 | Coaching Materials |
| Plargs Vocabulary Cards | 121-123 | Printout |
| Profession Cards | 113 | Printout |
| Said Salah Ahmed: The Lion's Share in Somali | 117 | Video |
| Venn Diagram Listening Activity | 117 | Handout |
| Writing Academic Language Objectives (ALOs) Objectives | 115 | Video |
| Appendix D: Building Leveled Language Objectives | 195-201 | Coaching Materials/ Handout |
| Appendix E: Planning for Word-Level Language Guide | 202-204 | Coaching Materials/ Handout |
| Appendix F: Planning for Sentence-Level Language Guide | 205-206 | Coaching Materials/ Handout |
| Appendix G: Planning for Discourse-Level Language Guide | 207-208 | Coaching Materials/ Handout |

## Advocacy

| Resource | Page | Resource Type |
|---|---|---|
| "ABCs of Family Engagement: Key Considerations for Building Relationships With Families and Strengthening Family Engagement Practices" | 105 | Article |
| Influential Court Cases: Summaries | 107 | Handout |
| Issues That Impact MLEs | 141 | Handout |

## Content and Language

| Resource | Page | Resource Type |
|---|---|---|
| Content Area Language Challenge Sheet | 89 | Handout |
| ELD Matrix of Grammatical Forms | 89 | Article |
| Five Stages of SLA Activity Sheet | 87 | Handout |
| My Morning Routine | 77 | Image |
| Stages of Second Language Acquisition: ELD, ELL, LEP & Bilingual | 87 | Video |
| Vitamin D Passage | 89 | Handout |
| Vowel Sort Cards | 75 | Printout |
| Vowel Sort Cards Answer Key | 75 | Coaching Materials |

| Resource | Page | Resource Type |
|---|---|---|

## Culture

| Resource | Page | Resource Type |
|---|---|---|
| "Curriculum as Window and Mirror" | 96 | Article |
| EDTalks: Kao Kalia Yang | 66 | Video |
| Multilingual Learner of English Profile Template | 136 | Handout |
| Funds of Knowledge | 95 | Video |
| Funds of Knowledge Activity Sheet | 95 | Handout |
| Funds of Knowledge Plan | 95 | Handout |
| "I didn't know" Think Pair Share | 66 | Handout |
| Making Sure Each Child Is Known | 67 | Video |
| Sample Multilingual Learner of English Profile | 136 | Handout |
| Windows and Mirrors Activity Sheet | 96 | Handout |

## Differentiation

| Resource | Page | Resource Type |
|---|---|---|
| Modality Audit | 127 | Handout |
| WIDA Can Do Descriptors | 127, 130 | Webpage |
| WIDA Can Do Name Charts | 130 | Webpage |
| WIDA Can Do Philosophy | 127, 130 | Video |

## Home Language

### Development

| Resource | Page | Resource Type |
|---|---|---|
| "It's Not Uncommon for Schools to Have Dozens of Home Languages—And Our Classrooms Need to Reflect That" | 74 | Article |
| Crafting School Language Policies | 74 | Handout |
| Getting to Know the MLEs in Your Classroom | 72, 73 | Handout |
| "Getting to Know Your ELLs: Six Steps for Success" | 72 | Article |
| I CAN'T SPEAK MY MOTHER TONGUE (Music Video) – Fung Bros ft. Dough-Boy | 72 | Video |
| Importance of Students' Home Languages (First Languages) | 74 | Video |
| What to Do First in the ELL Classroom | 72 | Video |

### Literacy

| Resource | Page | Resource Type |
|---|---|---|
| 04 Andy Brown Translanguaging A Multilingual Learning | 131 | Video |
| 10 Amazing Benefits of Being Bilingual | 93 | Infographic |
| "Bilingualism: What Happens in the Brain?" | 93 | Article |
| "Dispelling the Myth of 'English Only': Understanding the Importance of the First Language in Second Language Learning" | 134 | Article |
| "MIT Scientists Prove Adults Learn Language to Fluency Nearly as Well as Children" | 93 | Article |
| Session 5: Classroom Examples | 131 | Video |
| To Translate or Not To Translate, That Is the Question! Worksheet | 91 | Handout |
| Translanguaging: A CUNY-NYSIEB Guide for Educators | 131 | Handout |
| "When Is It OK to Use Google Translate in the English-Learner Classroom?" | 91 | Article |

| Resource | Page | Resource Type |
|---|---|---|
| "Why Bilinguals Are Smarter" | 93 | Article |

## Immigration

| Resource | Page | Resource Type |
|---|---|---|
| Animated Map Shows History of Immigration to the US | 100 | Video |
| Hand Model of the Brain | 98, 99 | Video |
| "Immigration Facts: The Positive Economic Impact of Immigration" | 63 | Article |
| Immigration Myth Cards | 63 | Printout |
| Immigration Trauma Simulation Guide | 64 | Handout |

## Marginalization/Oppression

| Resource | Page | Resource Type |
|---|---|---|
| Critical Incidents in Immigrant Education Activity | 69 | Handout |
| Critical Incidents in Immigrant Education Activity Teacher Trainer Guide | 69 | Coaching Materials |
| Standing Up: What Is Calling in vs. Calling Out? | 102 | Video |
| Students Learn a Powerful Lesson About Privilege | 103 | Video |
| Understanding Privilege: Reflection | 103 | Handout |
| What I Should Have Said | 102 | Handout |
| What Is Privilege? | 103 | Video |
| Why Does Privilege Make People So Angry? \| Decoded \| MTV News | 103 | Video |

## Professional Development, Ongoing

| Resource | Page | Resource Type |
|---|---|---|
| Appendix A: SWEL Support Tool 1: Multimodal Instruction Observation Form | 186-188 | Coaching Materials/Handout |
| Appendix B: SWEL Support Tool 2: English Language Development Observation Form | 189-192 | Coaching Materials/Handout |
| Appendix C: SWEL Support Tool 3: Supporting the Language of Identity Observation Form | 193-194 | Coaching Materials/ Handout |
| Appendix H: The SWEL Lesson Plan Inventory | 209 | Coaching Materials/ Handout |
| Appendix I: SWEL Planning for Professional Development | 210-212 | Coaching Materials/ Handout |
| Appendix J: School-Wide English Learning (SWEL) Action Plan | 213-214 | Coaching Materials/ Handout |
| Know Better, Do Better Conversation Cards | 80 | Printout |
| Uncovering Education Myths | 79 | Handout |

# See what else TESOL Press has to offer!

## bookstore.tesol.org

www.ingramcontent.com/pod-product-compliance
Ingram Content Group UK Ltd.
Pitfield, Milton Keynes, MK11 3LW, UK
UKHW051653180426
11947UKWH00021B/1925